CRIMINAL JUSTICE ORGANIZATIONS

Structure, Relationships, Control, and Planning

ROBERTO H. POTTER
UNIVERSITY OF CENTRAL FLORIDA

GAIL SEARS HUMISTON
UNIVERSITY OF CENTRAL FLORIDA

The publisher is not engaged in rendering legal or other professional advice, and this publication is not a substitute for the advice of an attorney. If you require legal or other expert advice, you should seek the services of a competent attorney or other professional.

© 2017 LEG, Inc. d/b/a West Academic
444 Cedar Street, Suite 700
St. Paul, MN 55101
1-877-888-1330

Printed in the United States of America

ISBN: 978-1-63460-485-7

Preface

Developing an "Organizational Sense"

Welcome to our text focusing on the organizations that make up the United States criminal justice system (CJS). In this text, we will focus on the organizations within the CJS, and also the organizations with which they interact in the total social environment. One of the major challenges students (and others) face in a course on criminal justice organizations (CJOs) is thinking at the organizational level. Mostly we tend to think in terms of the individuals who commit or are alleged to have committed crimes. With regard to the CJS, we tend to focus on the individuals who arrest, prosecute, defend, judge, detain, rehabilitate, and monitor those who commit or are alleged to have committed crimes. Making a shift to thinking about the organizational entities in which CJO actors operate is sometimes a difficult transition. Yet, in our minds, we know officers, attorneys, and other such actors represent the organizations in the CJS, not themselves, when they are enforcing the law. Well, we hope that is the case.

Even though we live in a society that is increasingly dominated by organizations, not individuals (a case we will make shortly), we still tend to think about the individuals who work in the organizations—not the organizations for which they work. This is true whether we talk about universities, churches, government agencies, non-profit organizations or for-profit corporations and small businesses. Those who have worn glasses and had a change in prescription will understand that shifting prescriptions can cause a little discomfort, until one becomes accustomed to the new prescription. Shifting from a focus on the individuals within an organizational setting to the organization alone, as a single entity, is like getting that new prescription. You are using a different set of lenses. Thinking then about the relationships among and across different organizations, and the lens changes again. That is exactly what we are hoping to help you do by reading this text—develop a new set of lenses to examine the CJS and its impact, as well as the impact of other organizations on the CJS—an "organizational sense." We will suggest to you that having this different set of lenses available to you will provide a great set of tools for those who want to lead the CJS, as well as those who want to study the CJS. Of course, we better deliver on a statement like that, right?

For the Applied World

Increasingly, Criminal Justice (CJ) leaders need to develop an "organizational sense." From the smallest jurisdiction to the federal government, CJ leaders are involved with, affected by, and affect multiple organizations within their own jurisdiction, as well as beyond those boundaries. While there is a tendency to think of such involvements as between individuals, those individuals are really representatives of other organizations. In professional relationships, it is the interests of the organizations they represent that matter; not their individual interests (ideally, at least). For that reason, at a minimum, it is important that CJ leaders learn to think in organizational (intra- and inter-) terms. We hope this text will assist current and future leaders to do this.

In 1959 C. Wright Mills noted that in order to fully grasp what is going on around us in society we needed to understand our own biography within the historical phase of society in which we are living (p. 5). We will develop the idea that we live in an age of society dominated by organizations more fully in this text. For now, we want to channel Mills by saying that in order to more fully grasp what is going on in the world of American criminal justice we must understand the organizations that comprise the criminal justice system (CJS), as well as those organizations with which our organization of membership interacts in the wider social world. Other Western democracies are experiencing similar issues at this point in history.

We can no longer view the world of the CJS simply from our individual standpoint, job or interest. We work in organizations with persons from other organizations. Sometimes those working relationships are collaborative and cooperative; sometimes they are competitive; sometimes they are both at the same time. And, we cannot forget that sometimes organizational relationships are oppositional. It is nothing personal—it is organizational! It is no longer enough for leaders in criminal justice (including legislatures) to focus on the internal workings of their home agency. It certainly is no longer sufficient to continue to do things as they have always been done because "that's how they've always been done."

Mills (1959) wrote of developing a "sociological imagination." We are stating that CJS leaders need to develop an "organizational sense" or "organizational consciousness" that allows them to view the social world(s) in which they operate as greater than the sum of the individuals with whom they interact. It is the cumulative effect of organizational forces at play within the CJS, across the nation, and increasingly around the world to which we must pay attention. Mills wrote that developing a sociological imagination was simultaneously "a terrible lesson; in many ways a magnificent one" (p. 5). Developing such a world view may be a bit like the old saying about what lawyers learn in law school: You spend the first year learning to think like a lawyer, and the rest of your life regretting you did.

Once you learn to think at the organizational level, you will find that events in the CJS and social world make a different type of sense and have a different realm of logic and reason. We believe future leaders will find this a beneficial skill set for negotiating the world of the CJS. We also believe those currently in leadership positions will find value in re-thinking some of their decision-making from this perspective. Unlike the lawyers, then, developing an organizational sense is not something you will wish you hadn't done. It is something that will benefit you and those you serve. It may on occasion make you wish you didn't see something clearly from an organizational level, but mostly you will be glad you can.

Why Now?

This text is being written at what we believe can arguably be called the most important point in time for the legitimacy of the American (United States) criminal justice system in the early Twenty-first Century. The criminal justice system as a whole (institution) and constituent parts (organizations/agencies) has not been the subject of such scrutiny since the 1960s. Whether it is the relationships between police and the communities they are supposed to serve; or, jails, prisons and probation (corrections) and the outcomes they are supposed to produce; or the courts and the processes by which charging, pleading, and judicial decisions are made; no part of the criminal justice system seems to be pleasing anyone. This dissatisfaction may also be turned inward on organizations themselves and affect morale, as well as the difficulties associated with recruiting and workforce development. We should add that the legislative process by which criminal laws, penalties, and processes are enacted is also being scrutinized, though possibly less directly than the more operational components of the "system."

We would argue that there is a tendency to move from the official actor-community member interaction level to the "system as oppressor" level without much attention paid to the incredible diversity of organizational entities that comprise the "system" and the individuals who work within those organizations. One thing that distinguishes the American criminal justice system from those of our Commonwealth and European cousins, as well as the other nations in the Americas, is our emphasis on local control—at least at the state level—and the diversity of size across our official agencies of social control. Very few other nations allow criminal justice agencies to exist separately at the state/province/territory level. In most other nations CJOs are mostly controlled at the central State level (exclusions include Australia and Canada). We are unaware of any nations that allow such agencies to exist officially at a county/parish and/or city level of control. Yet, these are key features of the United States criminal justice system—a level of state, county and local government operational control without equal.

Understanding the organizational structures, dynamics, and interactions among criminal justice organizations (CJOs), as well as with other non-CJ organizations, is an absolutely essential knowledge set for CJ professionals—and, we would argue—for other citizens who want to be full participants in our democracy/republic. Yet, we would argue that even among official agents of social control (i.e., police, corrections, prosecutors, defense counsel, judges and court staff), there is little knowledge of criminal justice organizations and dynamics beyond the county or circuit/district in which they happen to operate. This lack of cross-organizational knowledge has changed for police and prosecutors since the events of September 11, 2001 to be certain. For other actors in the system "business as usual" often means focusing only on a specific county or judicial district. For academics, we would argue this is replicated by a focus on specific organizational sectors as "specialties" of research and teaching.

Authors' Experiences

Let us use the biographies of the authors (Potter, the elder; Humiston, the younger) to demonstrate how our consciousness of (or imagination) of criminal justice has changed over the course of society in the past 40 years. When Potter began his first job in the criminal justice system (CJS) as a therapist in a psychiatric prison back in 1977, the organizational environment in which the CJS operated seemed remarkably "closed" by comparison with 2016. That is, there appeared to be little involvement of any other organizations beyond the police, prosecutors and defense, courts, and corrections in the operations and process of justice. Perhaps that first job was a glimpse of things to come, since Potter was employed by what was, at that time, the Florida Department of Health and Rehabilitative Services (HRS) to work inside a Department of Corrections facility. Think of this as an early "contracting for services" within formal government agencies. However, there were few non-governmental organizations involved in the CJS at that time.

Two years later (1979) Potter was employed on the federally-funded Florida juvenile justice (JJS) diversion project. We, a state university

(University of Florida), were employed by HRS to operate a multi-judicial circuit diversion to services demonstration program. As the service delivery organization, we contracted one of the first non-governmental organizations (NGOs) that would deliver services to juveniles. Within only a few years, whole service segments for juveniles would be "contracted-out" to non-profit organizations.

In his first job after completing graduate school, Potter evaluated a series of programs that involved private contractors, such as the TASC program, providing services to justice agencies and their clients. This came at the end of the Law Enforcement Assistance Act (LEAA) funding flood, which took a great deal of money out of the justice system. State and local governments had to start looking at ways to run justice organizations with less money. During his work with the Florida Juvenile Justice Institute, the focus was still on the core government agencies that processed juveniles through the JJS (still part of HRS). When Potter returned to Florida in 2008 from 23 years in exile, a Florida Department of Juvenile Justice (FDJJ—no longer HRS) presenter at a conference noted that 90 percent of the work sponsored by FDJJ was carried out by contractors—many of which were county government agencies—but nearly as many were not-for- and for-profit organizations. Before leaving Florida in 1985, Potter was part of the team that re-built the Florida Network of Youth and Family Services. At that time, the organization represented the runaway shelters in Florida—all non-profit organizations. Within 15 years of being re-established, and with the breakup of HRS, the Network became one of the primary providers of services previously provided by one of the divisions of HRS, with a budget and scope of services we would not have even dreamed about in the mid-1980s.

During his period of federal government employment at the Centers for Disease Control and Prevention (CDC; 1998-2008), Potter also coordinated an effort to produce a "Surgeon General's Call to Action" (CTA) on corrections and community health. As part of that effort (2004-2006), the CTA team assembled an informal working group comprised of personnel from the Departments of Health and Human Services (the CDC's home Department), Justice (particularly the Office of Justice Programs and Bureau of Prisons agencies), the federal Courts (Federal Probation), and the Department of Veteran's Affairs. A broader group was brought together that included representatives of a variety of criminal justice associations and advocacy groups (e.g., American Correctional Association, National Commission on Correctional Health Care, American Public Health Association, etc.), government associations (e.g., National Association of County Organizations,

Center for State Governments, etc.), practitioner groups (e.g., Association of State Correctional Administrators, American College of Correctional Physicians, etc.), inmate/prisoner advocates, and academic researchers. While we had no direct representation from private correctional contractors, their interests were represented by those from association groups. The Call to Action was never published, supposedly because of a conflict of interest—a so-called unfunded mandate contained in the document—by the federal organization that housed CDC and the Surgeon General. At a 2016 meeting to discuss the next Bureau of Justice Statistics' inmate survey, almost all of these same organizations were represented.

Compared to Potter's experiences, Humiston's viewpoint of the CJS were shaped by the perspective of one outside the system. Being raised in a middle-class, rural setting in the 1970s left her unprepared for the consequences of a violent marriage while raising three children. The no-arrest policies of the 1980s meant that her experiences with CJOs was limited to police officers who merely referred her to a local domestic violence shelter. Information and services were (and still are) fragmented and primarily provided by non-profit organizations. These outside, appendage organizations typically included shelters, public housing, food stamps, Medicaid, and advocates for protection orders. Legal issues such as bankruptcy, divorce, and child support which accompany separation from an abuser requires the hiring of specialized attorneys and navigation of federal and local civil courts. Today, domestic violence victims are more likely to encounter police with mandatory arrest policies, prosecutors that may or may not have "no-drop" policies, criminal court processes, and controls by the state's children and family services.

As a result of navigating the government and non-government agencies that control and serve domestic violence victims, Humiston spent many years strategizing her own path to becoming a domestic violence "survivor." A large part of this process required her to learn the civil and criminal justice statutory and court processes. She learned why criminal justice officials and privately hired attorneys remained detached, unhelpful, and sometimes malicious in their attitudes toward her and other victims. The journey from victim to survivor included education and experiences in the law and criminal justice social sciences, both of which woefully address the networks between public officials, private attorneys, government agencies, and non-profits that claim to serve victims. As a victim and survivor, legal assistant, advocate, and social researcher, Humiston recognizes the disconnections between services and shortfalls in using terms such as "referral," "service provision," and "outcomes of safety" as though they are synonymous. A referral to a service agency most certainly does not result in providing a service. And even more so, a referral does not result in the safety of an individual. Decades of research in criminal justice has yet to scratch the surface of networked governance in criminal justice, as traditional academics fail to recognize the roles and relationships of organizations appended to criminal justice.

Humiston's dissertation eventually merged with Potter's work with offender reentry partnerships at University of Central Florida. Our involvement with local inmate and prisoner re-entry programs allowed us to observe the broadening of organizations involved in the local level CJS. We began to "map" the variety of government agencies, non- and for-profit, community- and faith-based organizations, as well as educational organizations that expressed interest in "partnering" to create re-entry opportunities for returning individuals.

In many ways Florida has provided an outstanding environment in which to observe the need to understand how organizations interact to produce juvenile and criminal justice. In the area of adult corrections, we have seen a significant shift toward non-governmental organizational actors involved in the delivery of the operations and services of the CJS. Our governors and legislators here in Florida seem to want to continue the privatization of many CJS functions, rather than diminish them. A significant proportion of county-level probation services (misdemeanor) are carried out by private agencies, including community- and faith-based organizations. And, of course, Florida is one of the majority of states (44) that allow private bail bonds; the United States and the Philippines being the only two nations that allow this practice (where bail exists, of course).

At the beginning of the Twenty-first Century, Richard Harding (2001) predicted that the era of wholesale privatization of prisons had run its course, but that the piecemeal privatization of discrete correctional services would increase. That is, while states and local governments might not be as keen to let a private corporation run their entire jail or prison operation, they might be happy to contract food, laundry, education, and health services, for example. Managers and leaders in every organizational component of the CJS must now deal with a network of suppliers, none can function without such inter-organizational relations across CJOs and organizations in the wider community.

We offer this stroll through the past 40 or so years to illustrate how understanding one's own experiences with different periods of the CJS can affect the need to understand how organizations interact to produce this thing we call "justice." When Potter began his work life, there were few organizations outside the government with much involvement in the system(s).

As Potter approaches potential retirement age, the complexity of organizations involved across all aspects of the JJS/CJS has increased exponentially. It is no longer possible for an effective CJS manager/leader to focus exclusively on the internal operations of her/his home agency. We will return to this theme throughout this text.

Why This Is Important

Understanding how organizations operate—not just the people inside them—is an increasingly important skill set for effective CJS leaders. This will involve all of the factors that influence organizational decision-making, from what data systems to operate for decision-making purposes, to strategies for regulating costs within an agency, perhaps by contracting out certain functions. Potter sometimes half-jokingly suggests to those interested in becoming jail or prison executives that they major in hospitality management, and minor in criminal justice. The point is that one's focus has to be as much on managing relations with other organizational entities as on the internal operations of a CJO to be an effective leader in our current intersection of biography and societal history. That is what we want to impart in this text.

At the broader level, developing this organizational sense will open one's eyes to a range of understandings for other events in the social world. This is also what makes such awareness intimately personal. We locate our notion of organizational sense very firmly in the ideas offered by Mills (1959) and Peter Berger (1963) about understanding society and how it develops. Criminal justice organizations play a major role in achieving and/or impeding social change. For this reason alone, understanding these agencies and institutions at the organizational-societal level is necessary for those who would lead in this important social institution.

For The Academics

As we have prepared to deliver a graduate course titled "Criminal Justice Organizations" over the past decade, we have found a curious lack of text books that focus on the organizational-level analysis of the formal CJS. Moving beyond the formal CJS organizations, there is even less attention paid to other organizational sectors that influence and are influenced by the CJS. Even the best (we won't reveal our favorites) text books pay little attention to inter-organizational issues. This usually consists of a short section or maybe one chapter on some definitions of rational, natural, and open systems theories of organization. Rather, they tend to focus primarily on management and administration within organizations (intra-organizational). They do a really great job on issues of management and administration, however; this is not our focus here.

Likewise, much of the peer-reviewed journal material on CJS organizations tends to be intra-organization-focused (we would argue "natural systems" oriented). Many of these articles are aimed at fairly standard human resource issues within the CJS setting. Some provide descriptions of organizational characteristics, which is closer to a true organizational-level analysis as we will present in this text. Yet, there are very few articles that examine cross-organizational relationships, and even fewer that focus on relationships among CJOs and non-governmental organizations.

This is especially interesting given that among those attempting to develop a "theory of criminal justice," they "focus on the variation in the responses of criminal justice to crime as the outcome. Responses include decisions, attitudes, and styles of behavior by criminal justice officials; structural and procedural changes of criminal justice institutions, and the development of and changes in the substantive criminal law by the legislature" (Duffee and Allen, 2007, p. 16). Other than the "structural and procedural changes of criminal justice institutions," and "behavior by criminal justice officials," (we assume acting in their organizational roles), there is relatively little attention paid to what we will present later as elements of organizational analysis at the organizational and comparative levels. Even the utilization of components of "Institutional Theory" by most CJ theorists focuses on a limited area of Institutional Theory that leaves out most inter-organizational and inter-sectoral (disciplinary) behaviors. The application of organizational approaches mostly to policing and corrections personnel is another example of how limited we believe the application of organizational theory has been to the CJS.

We are hopeful that we can provide a "nudge" to the emerging theory of criminal justice to re-focus on the organizational and comparative levels of organizational theory. We believe this will strengthen claims to separate Criminal Justice theory from Criminology, at least for analytic purposes. The text will argue that CJOs are, indeed, unique from most other organs of government, and certainly from non-governmental organizations. We believe it is at the organizational and comparative levels where these distinctions really lie. To that extent, we believe we can more accurately address the issue raised by Duffee and Allen (2007) asking why society chooses "the criminal sanction over other forms of social control" in the United States (p. 21).

Likewise, we hope to explain why criminal sanctions are "de-selected" by society and replaced by other institutional/organizational sectors.

Conclusion

We have tried to provide a text that will present organizational theory, types of organizational analysis, and the application of organizational development and evidence-based practice implementation for students, practitioners, and academics. We know it will fail some of those audiences at various times, of course. We welcome feedback from readers as to how we can improve the text for specific audiences where the reader believes it fails. In the end, we hope you find the text useful and even enjoyable to read. Thank you for taking time to read it.

Acknowledgements and Dedications

This text is a product of several years of course development and writing. Over that time there are many people who have played a role in our thinking and in our motivations to complete the text. First among those are our students in the Criminal Justice Organizations course at the University of Central Florida. They have allowed us to "pick their brains" about what did and what didn't work in the classroom and on-line. Our students have also helped us focus in on what the vast majority of students at the undergraduate and Master's level need to know about organizational relationships and planning in the Criminal Justice and allied fields.

Next, we want to thank our former department chair, colleague, and supportive critic, Robert H. Langworthy. Bob did not want to teach this course when he hired Potter, so he turfed it off to Potter. It was Bob who modeled the utilization of organizational theory and chaired Humiston's dissertation, and Potter who entrusted her to teach another section of the course. The rest is, as they say, history.

We also want to thank John Fuller (West Georgia) and Cindy Rickards (Drexel) for their comments and suggestions on the draft text. Likewise, James Cahoy, Elizabeth Eisenhart, Greg Olson, and Laura Holle at West Academic for all their guidance and assistance in preparing the text. Any omissions, errors, etc., are those of the authors alone, even with such help!

Most importantly, we appreciate the love and support of our spouses, Lyndy Potter and Paul Humiston. Shortly after we began writing this text, Lyndy was diagnosed with lung cancer. So far, so good.... As we were in the process of preparing the final draft for review, Humiston's husband, Paul, was diagnosed and lost his battle with colon cancer. We want to thank the members of our families and friends, as well as medical service providers, for their support during these times to keep us on track. We also want to thank each other for assuming heavier teaching or writing roles when the other of us was occupied with health care issues.

Roberto H. Potter

This book is dedicated to my wife Lyndy Potter, whose bravery in the face of life's myriad problems has motivated her to continue to serve others in spite of overwhelming odds against her. I have been blessed to have you with me for the past 22 years. Thank you for the inspiration and patience you provide.

Gail Sears Humiston

I wish to dedicate this book to my late husband, Paul Humiston, who put himself in harm's way to love and support me and my children for 22 years. Your unwavering morality and honesty continue to light my way still through dark days. I must also thank the rest of my family. To my parents, Richard and Jacqueline Sears, I owe everything. Dad, I wish you were here. Thank you Melissa Schaefer, Brittany Stage, and Thomas Sauder for being my motivation and strength for moving forward in all things. Finally, two mentors are directly responsible for my contributions to this book. The first, for obvious reasons, is Hugh Potter. Hugh—thank you for patiently answering all my questions through the last five years. Finally, I am indebted to James F. Kane, Esq. Jim taught me everything I know about civil law. More importantly, I am inspired to achieve his level of professionalism and citizenship, regardless of the actions of others.

About the Authors

Roberto Hugh Potter is a sociologist who specializes in issues related to social control and criminal justice. Over the past 40 years he has had the great fortune to work in multiple organizational settings. These include a State of Florida criminal justice research agency and the Office of the State Courts Administrator at the Florida Supreme Court. He has worked also in the non-profit field as a researcher, trainer, and administrator with the Florida Network of Youth and Family Services and Families First (Atlanta). His federal tenure was with the Centers for Disease Control and Prevention, where he focused on violence prevention, correctional health and substance abuse, and served for a period as the "Goal Team Leader for Healthy Institutions" during an abortive attempt to restructure the CDC. Sprinkled in amongst these non-academic jobs were periods of academic employment at the University of New England (Australia), Morehead State University (Kentucky), and back in his home state as a Professor at the University of Central Florida.

Across these positions, and especially with his focus on the behavioral health issues facing the criminal justice system, Potter has had the opportunity to observe and be involved with a range of organizations that seek both to effect and affect criminal justice while being directly affected by the system. From these experiences the emphasis on interorganizational relationships, and the ways in which various organizations seek to exert control over the formal criminal justice control agencies, have contributed to his interest in producing this text with Dr. Humiston. This is his third text, following *Pornography: Group Pressures and Individual Rights* (1996, Federation Press, Sydney), and with Timothy Akers and Carl Hill, *Epidemiological Criminology* (2013, Jossey-Bass, San Francisco). A native Floridian and graduate of the University of South Florida (BA, 75) and the University of Florida (MA, 77; Ph.D., 82), he is happy to be back in his home state where he hopes to continue translating the knowledge gained from social science research to the justice sector.

Gail Sears Humiston is an Associate Lecturer in the Department of Criminal Justice at the University of Central Florida. Her relevant "real" world work experience includes six years of working for an Illinois law firm, an internship with a public defender, and assistantship as a victim advocate in a states attorney's office. After experiencing and working in the Illinois court systems and graduating from Illinois Central College (paralegal AAS, 2001), University of Illinois at Springfield (Criminal Justice BA, 2005), Illinois State University (Criminal Justice MS, 2008), she moved to Florida to obtain her doctoral degree from the University of Central Florida (Public Affairs Ph.D., 2014). Her doctoral education culminated in the *Offender Reentry: A Mixed Model Study of Interorganizational Commitment to Partnership* dissertation which led to the writing of this text.

Humiston's personal observations of the complexities of victim services and court processes allowed her to understand the parallel issues of offender reentry and connecting services. To perform research at the organizational level, she found it necessary to reach outside the discipline and literature of criminal justice to find the theories that explained the contingencies and constraints of linking CJOs to CBOs. She was fortunate to be influenced by pioneer Robert Langworthy and "old-school" Sociologist, Roberto H. Potter, who were able and willing to direct her in the completion of her dissertation and specialty of criminal justice IORs. She is a self-proclaimed "typical criminal justice student" who simultaneously worked full time and raised three children while progressing through her college education. One difference may be, however, that her legal experience taught her to find her own answers. Today, her experiences and role as a full-time Lecturer influence her philosophy of translational teaching by bridging the gap between academics and practitioners. Her research interests include criminal justice organizations and interorganizational relationships, offender reentry, gender, comparative justice, and criminal justice education.

Table of Contents

Preface iii

Acknowledgements and Dedications xiii

About the Authors xv

Introduction 1

Section 1   Structure

Chapter 1   Types of Organizations and Origins of Modern Criminal Justice Institutions 13

Chapter 2   Government: Policing Powers and Constraints 29

Chapter 3   Organizational Basics: Systems 41

Chapter 4   Organizational Basics: Structure and Strategy 57

Section 2   Relationships

Chapter 5   Interorganizational Relationships (IORs): Motivations for IORs 81

Chapter 6   Assessing Organizations 103

Chapter 7   The Organizational Core of Criminal Justice and Other Government Organizations 113

Section 3   Control

Chapter 8   Applying Criminal Justice/Criminological Theory to Organizations in the Environment 135

Chapter 9   Professional Associations: Assistance and Enforcement 147

Chapter 10   Research Organizations: Types, Targets, and Ownership 169

Chapter 11   Social Movement Organizations—Friend or Foe? 189

Chapter 12   Criminal Organizations 207

Section 4 Planning

Chapter 13 Organizational Change: The Logic of Planning, Implementing, Outcomes, and Feedback 221

Chapter 14 Criminal Justice Informatics, Data, and Decision-Making 241

Chapter 15 Returning to the Key Questions about Criminal Justice Organizations 263

References 275

Websites 291

Index 297

CRIMINAL JUSTICE ORGANIZATIONS

Structure, Relationships, Control, and Planning

Introduction

This text is about the organizations that comprise the criminal justice process, as well as the ways in which those organizations are organized to produce something called justice. It is about the organizations that are officially part of the criminal justice system (government organizations), as well as a range of other organizations that interact increasingly with those organizations in the formal parts of the system. These include for-profit contractors/providers, non-profit contractors/providers, volunteer organizations, advocacy organizations, professional associations, and criminal organizations. We treat these organizations as entities in themselves. That means we are interested in how organizations interact, not necessarily what goes on within the organizations themselves. That is why we wrote of developing an "organizational sense" in the Preface.

We begin with the idea that organizations involved in the delivery of justice are constructed around a series of decision-points. That is, each agency has responsibility and/or authority over certain decisions made in the process that leads to the outcome we call justice. This applies to those formal (i.e., Constitutional or statutory) organizations in the justice process and the non-formal (i.e., for- and non-profit and non-governmental) organizations that process individuals at various points in the system/process.

Decision-making requires **information**. Organizations that make decisions at various points in the justice process use information to make the decisions over which they have responsibility. The source of information, how that information is utilized, and how the information is stored and/or evaluated for future decision-making purposes is an important, and we argue often overlooked, component of criminal justice information.

The complexity of the information utilized by justice-associated organizations will vary widely. For example, police officers will have to depend sometimes on the information presented to them by complainants, the situation, and the alleged offender. Sometimes they will have access to broader information on a suspect's prior record, "wants and warrants," etc. Prosecutors, on the other hand, will have the benefit of more and perhaps systematic information when making case processing decisions. In some jurisdictions, judges still may have pre-sentence investigation reports to assist in sentencing decisions. Correctional authorities may have access to a wider range of assessments, educational information, and so forth to base program decisions on. Yet, community-based providers may be legally prohibited from access to certain information that may actually assist in their decision-making. Information and the sources from which it is obtained is increasingly important to the justice system. Yet, we know little about how it interacts with organizational design or process in this system.

Over the course of the lead author's (Potter) professional life, since around the mid-1970s, the importance of scientifically-based information has increased in developing justice strategies and interventions. The 1970s saw the first real efforts to scientifically evaluate programs in justice systems. The overreactions to Martinson's "nothing works" statement by legislators and others seemed to slow the development of evaluated programs in favor of continued use of professional/clinical judgment and "cause I like it" sorts of programs. In the 1990s, came the increasing use of "meta-analysis," "systematic analysis," and other forms of statistical study of prior research. From these, notions of "best practices" and "evidence-based practices" began to take hold. One cannot underestimate the prestige factor of the medical profession employing these techniques, many developed by social scientists, and their adoption by legislative decision-makers. Today, almost every funding announcement for programs carries some phrase akin to "must employ evidence-based practices" to qualify for funding. (See Figure Intro. 1.)

What we hope is unique about this text is the explicit linking of organizational theory with information systems and the nature of evidence

FIGURE INTRO. 1 DISTINGUISHING ORGANIZATIONAL PRACTICES

BEST PRACTICES—Based on the collective experiences and wisdom of the field rather than scientifically tested knowledge.

WHAT WORKS—Implies general outcomes, but does not specify the kind of out comes desired.

EVIDENCE BASED PRACTICE—Implies that:
1. there is a definable outcome(s);
2. it is measurable; and
3. it is defined according to practical realities

Source: Crime-Justice Institute http://nicic.gov/pubs/2004/019342.pdf

employed for decision-making in the criminal (including juvenile) justice system. We will explore the organizations involved at each decision point in the process, the types of information they utilize to make decisions about actions to take, and how the evidence-base for guiding those decisions is achieved and utilized. We will also pay attention to the primary data sources employed to retrieve that information. All of this will be done in the context of organizational theory, with special emphasis on the internal and external environments in which justice system organizations operate.

Another unique feature of this text is the application of these same features to other "conventional" organizations and criminal enterprises as organizations. We will examine organized criminal enterprises from the same perspective as formal justice system agencies. After all, they are part of the external (and sometimes internal) environment of formal justice system agencies. An intriguing question arises as to whether the same organizational theories applied to criminal justice agencies and allied organizations can be applied to criminal enterprises. Or, are criminal enterprises significantly different from justice organizations to require a different frame of analysis?

While this text will touch on some issues of management, professionalism, leadership—what we would characterize as "natural systems" concerns—it is not essentially about those topics. There are far too many great texts on management, supervision, leadership, administration, and professionalism to replicate them. Many of those who have written those texts have helped frame our thinking over the years. Their influence on our ideas will be sometimes obvious and acknowledged, and at other times underlying without explicit recognition. In short, they do too good a job for us to try to overcome; we want to go in a different, yet related, direction.

In the end, this is a text about organizations, organizing, decisions, decision-making, information, information systems, evidence, generating evidence, employing/implementing evidence, and environments. The task is to make this seemingly complex web of concepts open, understandable, and useful.

Why Study Organizations in a Criminal Justice Program?

> An organization is a system for mobilizing and coordinating the efforts of various, typically specialized, groups in the pursuit of joint objectives (Blau, 1965, p. 324).

> Most analysts have conceived of organizations as *social structures created by individuals to support the collaborative pursuit of specified goals* (Scott & Davis, 2007, p. 11).

We are going to begin this book with the proposition that social order is a desired state of being for most members of society. Social order can be achieved in smaller groups through informal means of social control, such as gossip and social disapproval. As social groupings get larger ("collectives"), however, the impact of informal social control methods becomes less effective.

Argyris and Schon (1978) wrote that when members of a collective begin to make decisions in the name of the group, delegate authority to some members to act on behalf of the other members, and set boundaries between collective members and the rest of the world, we have organization. This is especially true as rules begin to emerge to govern the behavior of the individuals associated with the organization. How members of the collective, especially a politically-organized collective, choose to enforce those rules begins to move us in the direction of criminal justice organizations.

As Duffee and Allen (2007) note, the selection of criminal law and organizations to enforce rules, as opposed to some other social institution (such as public health or education) is a core topic for criminal justice sciences:

> Instead of focusing on crime as a dependent variable, a criminal justice theory would focus on the variation in the responses of criminal justice to crime as the outcome. Responses include decisions, attitudes, and styles of behavior by criminal justice officials; structural and procedural changes of criminal justice institutions, and the development of and changes in the substantive criminal law by the legislature. (p. 16)

From the organizations that comprise the federal government(s), to state/provincial governments, to local governments and any other entities authorized to create criminal laws, we see that societies have developed an array of organizations to enforce the rules of the political state.

The organizations that comprise the juvenile/criminal justice systems ("CJS") represent the organizational sector granted the authority to enforce organizationally-developed rules through the enforcement of the criminal law. They do so by utilizing persuasion, physical force (violence) and deprivation of liberty and treasure. The impact of this organizational sector cannot be underestimated when it comes to the domestic control of citizens and residents. In the not so humble opinion of these writers, to ignore the organizational behavior of these official agencies of formal social control leaves a large gap in our understanding of the juvenile/criminal justice systems. This includes both the behavior of organizations as entities in the broader social environment as well as the behavior of individuals and groups within those organizations.

> Criminal justice theory seeks to explain and examine the variations in, and the causes of, aspects of government social control systems, which select the criminal sanction over other forms of social control and shape the nature of the criminal sanction to be employed. Criminal justice theory may seek to explain whole systems, typically by comparing cultures, nations, or states. It may also be concerned with the sanction selection and implementation behavior of an agency or of single individuals, such as official decision makers (Duffe & Allen, 2007, pp. 21–22).

Understanding organizational development, processes, operations, and outcomes is, then, a key requirement in studying or leading the criminal justice system.

It is not enough simply to know the organizational structure and functions associated with each component of the juvenile/criminal justice system. These organizations exist in a broader social context, or environment, that places demands on the CJS. Likewise, the CJS exerts demands back on the broader social environment. We call this idea of acting on and being acted on simultaneously "**reflexivity**." Over the past 40 years of studying and working in and with the CJS, we have seen the social environment in which the CJS operates change dramatically. One of the themes to be developed here is the increasing role of the external social environment on the CJS and the impact of the CJS on the outside environment, especially in terms of the association with non-governmental organizations and criminal organizations.

Why study organizational theory in Criminal Justice? Because we need to understand the forces that control those to whom we transfer the power to control ourselves and those we perceive as threats to us. Whether we take the position that the criminal law represents a consensus on the part of all citizens, or that it represents the interests of some elite group, understanding how CJ organizations operate to implement and execute the criminal law is a key to controlling them. Understanding how the organizations that comprise the CJS deal with the environmental forces affecting them is core to determining how effective the CJS organizations are. The organizational theories we will discuss here provide the framework for understanding, researching, and changing the organizations to which we transfer this awesome power to control ourselves. And, if you are not already one of those to whom we transfer this power, perhaps someday you will be. We hope this text gives you a wider lens through which to view criminal justice.

Decision-Making Theme

One of the main themes of this text is the idea that justice is constructed around a series of decision-points. Officers, attorneys, judges, and other agents entrusted with the power of the government use information to decide whether to divert citizens toward or away from traditional processes, such as arrest, prosecution, sentencing, and punishment. Important decisions, such as plea bargains negotiated in court hallways, are often made informally in settings with low visibility (Walker, 2011, p. 36). The series of organizational decision-making points vested with police, courts, and corrections is characterized as the **criminal justice system**.

Over the years, social scientists have developed several **models** of the criminal justice system, including Herbert Packer's (1964) due process and crime control model, the wedding cake model of decision-making (Gottfredson & Gottfredson 1988) and Silberman's (1978) criminal case funnel. One of the original and most popular conceptualizations of criminal justice as a "system" was introduced by the President's Commission on Law Enforcement and Administration of Justice in 1967 (Walker, 2011, p. 39). (See Figure Intro. 2 in this text, or pp. 58–59 at https://www.ncjrs.gov/pdffiles1/Digitization/174NCJRS.pdf).

Generally, a **system** can be defined as a set of connected elements or parts which form a more complex whole. It may also be described as a set of procedures or organized method of accomplishing a goal or task. The Crime Commission's model of criminal justice as a system identified the connections between police, courts, and corrections through the flow of cases. It served to identify patterns and problems associated with discretionary decision-making throughout the system. Over the last five decades, the pervasiveness of discretionary decision-making has since been researched to better understand the factors that influence those decisions and the dynamics between the system components. It is beyond the scope and purpose of this text to thoroughly review criminal justice agencies as a system. Nor do

INTRODUCTION 7

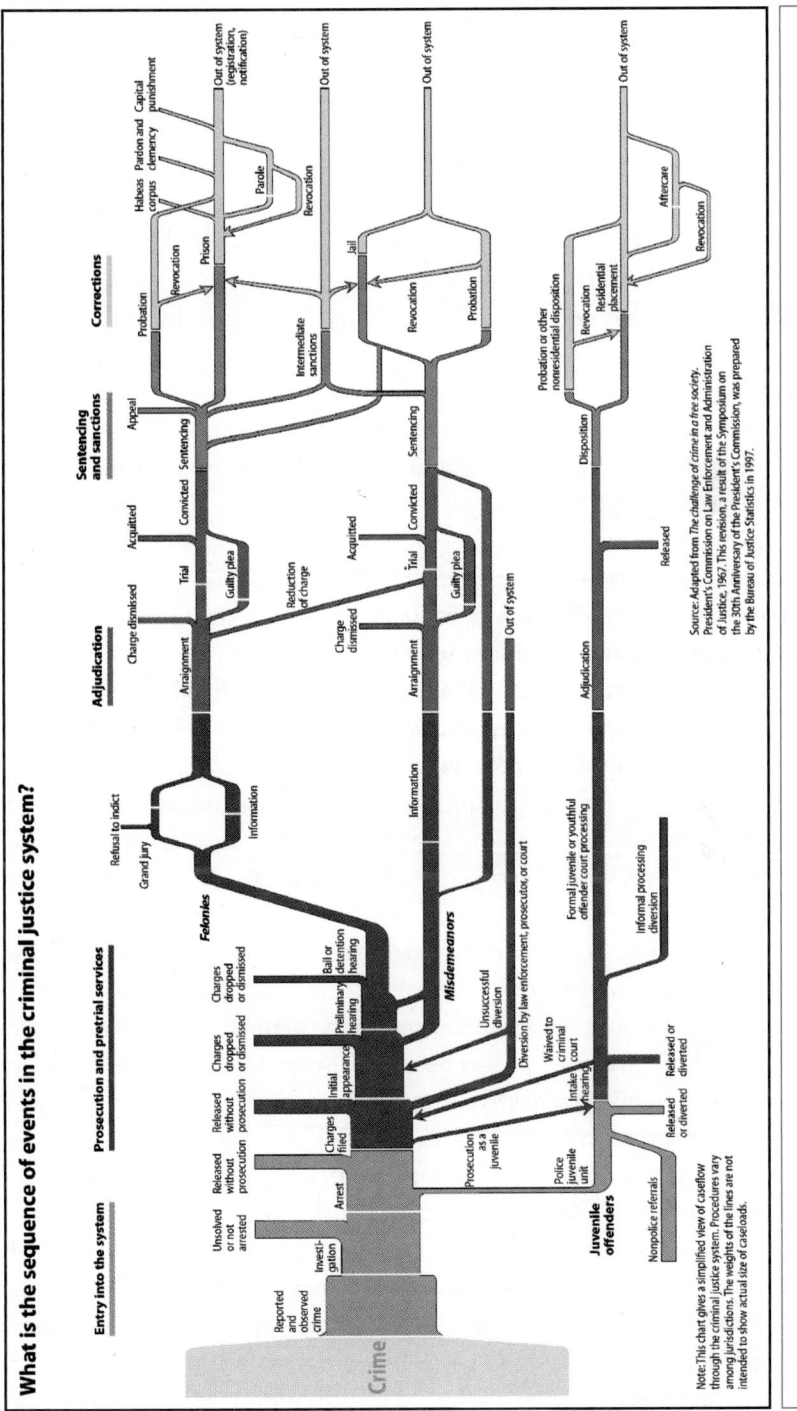

Figure Intro. 2

we seek to provide a thorough review of factors that influence of types of individual decision-makers.

Although we step away from the focus on criminal justice as a system, we will, review and acknowledge the system perspective of examining organizations in general. The system perspective views organizations from one ecological vantage point (Aldrich & Pfeffer, 1976, p. 80). This perspective borrows from biology by examining the relations of organisms to one another and their physical surroundings. That is, the environment is made up of various organizations which may interact and influence each other. As organizations interact within their environments (i.e., other organizations), they coordinate activities and create a system that links organizational elements, such as information, products, and services. To survive in their environment, organizations seek out resources from other organizations. They subsequently change in response to pressures from the environment.

Taking an ecological or system level view of organizations is limited, however. The researcher is restricted to examining the population as a whole (Aldrich & Pfeffer, 1976, p. 80). We would be limited to studying organizations as they fit within their environment. It would not necessarily allow us to study strategic decisions which affect organizational complexity. Nor does it allow us to examine an agency's process of evolving to "higher forms of social organization or to better organizations" (p. 80). We will expand the ecological approach in later chapters to examine CJO interactions with organizations not normally included in the CJS environment.

The purpose of this text is to describe and analyze criminal justice agencies from the organizational level, rather than system or individual levels. The noun form of **organization** can be defined as a body of people with a particular purpose, such as business, association, charitable giving, or government administration. Organizations, as we know of them today, began to emerge in the 17th century during the Enlightenment period (Scott & Davis, 2007). Organizations became prolific during the European and American Industrial Revolutions which transformed rural, agrarian-based societies to ones of urban industry. Those entrusted with administering and dispensing justice were also transformed. Police became professionalized, attorneys became licensed, and corporal punishment was abandoned for incarceration.

To better explain criminal justice organizations, we focus our review of the literature at the organizational level of analysis and incorporate the theme of decision-making. Decisions made at the organization level allow for the examination of variations *among* organizations, as well as variations *within* organizations (Thompson, 2008, p. xix). By examining differences *among* organizations, researchers have studied the various "levels of complexity and uncertainty [which] give rise to different types of organizations" (p. xix). Variations *within* organizations refers to the various levels inside an organization. According to Thompson, three major **organizational levels** exist:

- technological,
- managerial, and
- institutional or administrative.

It is at the *institutional level* that administrators make decisions that influence the entire organization. Administrators make decisions that affect an agency's missions, goals, operating procedures, strategic planning, interorganizational relationships, resource allocations, training, services, and the like. Therefore, the organizational level of analysis permits us to examine variations in administrative decision-making.

According to Thompson (2008, p. 134), **decisions** made by administrators on behalf of organizations involve two primary variables:

1. preferences regarding *possible outcomes* and,
2. beliefs about *cause-effect relationships*.

These two basic variables may not always be consciously considered, but are operating at some level of decision-making. Organizational **preferences** typically align with expressed missions and goals. In the case of criminal justice agencies, two primary goals typically include increasing public safety and reducing crime. The beliefs about **cause-effect relationships** in obtaining those goals, however, are more varied. For example, some support philosophies and policies of deterrence or incapacitation to reduce crime, while others prefer rehabilitation.

According to Thompson (2008, p. 134), organizations in general vary in their decision-making strategies depending on how certain they are about cause and effect relationships and outcomes. For example, if decision-makers can specify both cause and effect relations and identify relevant outcomes, they will employ what Thompson calls a "computational strategy." *Computational strategy* is characterized as a situation in which data is complete on both outcome preferences and cause-effect relationships. On the other end of the spectrum, if the outcomes and cause-effect relationships are uncertain, authorities will resort to an "inspirational strategy" in making decisions. *Inspirational strategies* are used in situations of incomplete data on outcomes and cause-effect relationships. Finally, if an organization is conflicted by opposing outcome preferences, such as having both therapeutic and custody goals in prisons, administrators employ a *"compromise strategy."* If a prison's primary goal is custody, it may compromise that goal by adding the goal of therapy. Likewise, the strategy of decision-making may also be one of compromise if an organization is unable to obtain necessary inputs, such as clients, materials, or legitimacy (Thompson, 2008, p. 138).

All this is to say that organizations are not merely components of a system floating aimlessly within their environment, waiting to react. Administrators work at the institutional level making decisions based on preferred outcomes and beliefs of cause-effect relationships. Knowledge and data concerning outcomes and cause-effect relationships vary in certainty. Oftentimes, criminal justice administrators lack the theoretical knowledge or empirical data upon which to base their decisions. The result is decision-making based on inspiration and compromises, as opposed to theoretically and empirically based computations.

Numerous texts review the general literature of the criminal justice system and the individuals within the organizations. Our purpose is not to repeat the traditional review of the criminal system models mentioned above. Nor do we seek to repeat the many individual level descriptions of criminal justice job functions. We do not address related issues, such as excessive use of force, violations of civil and Constitutional rights, job stress and burnout, misconduct, promotional aspirations, or racial and gender inequities. Nor do we review interpersonal relationships or victim or citizens perceptions aggregated to higher levels of analysis on topics such as collective efficacy, procedural justice, or police legitimacy.

This text operates at the administrative level and focuses more on the formal organizational structure, particularly as it relates to planning and administering change. In particular, we focus on organizational structures and strategies which must be taken into consideration by administrative decision-makers. Rather than taking the approach of briefly mentioning the fundamentals of organizational research and summarizing the existing literature in criminal justice, we delve more deeply into identifying and defining the general organizational theories and concepts from which the criminal justice literature presumably sprang.

Plan of the Text

This text seeks to fill the gap of examining criminal justice agencies at the organizational level – the administrative or institutional level at which decisions are made. It is divided into four main sections. In the first section, we review the basics of organizational structure as they can be applied to the CJS and allied organizations. Issues of authority and legitimacy, along with the legal foundations of CJOs and affiliated organizations are of core importance here. This section takes the reader through the basics of understanding theories of organizational structures by defining terms; describing organizational types; analyzing systems, structures and strategies; and so much more!

In the second section of this text, we extend our understanding of structures by delving further into relationships between organizations and the various theories that explain them. Students learn that interorganizational relationships (IORs) and organizational structure are actually one and the same! Administrators make decisions about organizational structures which vary according to the relationships they form with other organizations! Many readers may consider the first few chapters among the most difficult in the text. Let us assure you, paying close attention to these chapters will make the remainder of the text much more meaningful to you. We try to put the hard work up front, and then let you begin to apply it more freely as we move forward.

The third section of the text elaborates on the ideas presented in the first two sections to address issues of organizational control between CJOs and non-CJOs. Chapters are grouped around Merton's (1967) ideas on adaptation to goals and means at the organizational level. We do this to "frame" our discussion of other organizational actors in the broader social environment and how they are influenced by and influence CJOs. We argue that many of these organizations get little attention in the criminal justice literature—at least the academic criminal justice literature—while they have enormous influence on criminal justice legislation, policy, and practice.

In the fourth section we return to the decision-making theme to introduce some ideas on how CJOs plan and implement evidence-based policies. In our collective experience, this is especially important as CJOs reach out, either by choice or necessity, to other organizations in the broader social environment in order to address problems that have been "assigned" to the CJOs. This brings us back neatly to the core questions of "criminal justice theory"—why are some social activities the responsibility of CJOs rather than other organizational sectors? Finally, we offer what we believe is a very brief overview of the role of "informatics" in the CJ decision-making process for organizations. This is another area we would argue receives too little attention in academic criminal justice. This is especially true in the era of "joint" task forces, specialty courts, and re-entry programs and questions of "effectiveness"—how do we know what we do has the desired impact (and no unintended impacts)?

We have tried to develop learning objectives for each chapter that will assist you to focus on what we believe to be the important "take-aways" from each chapter. We welcome feedback from readers on how helpful they are, as noted in the Preface. Switching to the organizational view is not something most people do easily, so we hope we have made the transition a bit easier as a result of reading this text. Enjoy!

Key Words

Best practices
Cause-effect relationships
Criminal justice system
Criminal Justice Theory
Decisions
Decision-making
Ecology
Environment
Evidence-based practices

Information
Institutional (Administrative) level
Model
Organization
Organizational levels
Preferences
Reflexivity
System
What works

CHAPTER 1

Types of Organizations and Origins of Modern Criminal Justice Institutions

Learning Objectives:

1. Describe the issue of "interest" in distinguishing organizations and its relationship to consensus and conflict approaches in criminology and criminal justice.
2. Define organizations and formal organizations.
3. Identify, describe, and analyze the different types of formal organizations.
4. Describe educational organizations and how they may work with criminal justice organizations.
5. Describe the methods of investigating non-government organizations and government organizations.

Introduction

You may be asking yourself "why do we need to learn about criminal justice organizations?" If you think about it, organizations are everywhere! Organizations have become the dominant feature of a modern society (Scott & Davis, 2007). They mark the transition from a traditional society with an agrarian based economy to a modern society dominated by industries. The industrial revolution ushered in an age of surplus production, specialized divisions of labor, and specialized non-production roles. As a result, organizations are in the business of "organizing." Decisions must be made about the organization's mission, goals, tasks to be performed, coordination of tasks, and hierarchy of authority.

You may have other questions, such as—Aren't all organizations the same? Why won't studying an organization text from the Business School or Sociology do the trick? Why bother to study organizational theory in a criminal justice degree at all? We deal with the last question in our chapters on organizational theory (i.e., structure and interorganizational relationships), so let us start with the first two here.

The differences between the various organizations that comprise the criminal justice system and other governmental and non-governmental organizations will be a key theme of this text. For example, how is a police organization similar to or different from a religious organization (e.g., church, synagogue, mosque, temple)? How is a jail or prison distinct from or similar to a for-profit corporation? After all, aren't some jails and prisons run by either for-profit or non-profit organizations? Why do we have formal courts when private attorneys can mediate a range of issues for government? Finally, criminal organizations (such as gangs) are organizations, so how are they different from or similar to criminal justice organizations (CJOs)?

Differences

One of the first ways in which CJOs differ from other organization types is the issue of "**interest**." Morgan (2006) describes interests as "predispositions embracing goals, values, desires, expectations, and other orientations and inclinations that lead a person to act in one way rather than another" (p. 156). In Morgan's terms, then, interests operate at the individual level to lean toward a particular area of pursuit, such as law enforcement work. While this may help explain why someone might chose a particular organization for which to work, it does not explain the segment of society for which the organization "works."

It is customary to divide criminal justice/criminological theories into "consensus" versus "conflict" approaches according to whose interests are served by the criminal justice system (CJS). Some writers treat "interactionist" approaches separately, but for our purposes, we will fold them into the broad "conflict" approach. The key difference between consensus and conflict approaches when it comes to "interest" is "whose interests?" Those associated with the consensus approach argue that the interests of the whole society are represented by CJOs. Those associated with conflict approaches see the interests of a range of groups and classes being represented by CJOs. The "pluralist" conflict theories see protected interests represented from multiple and shifting groups over time, not simply one group or class. The more extreme conflict theorists, especially "Marxist" and "critical" theorists, focus squarely on the interests of the "capitalist class." Quinney (1977) provided a

Marxist conflict-oriented discussion of "interest" in the operation of the CJS: "Although justice is to be applied to individual cases, the general objective is the promotion of social order ... And in capitalist society the healthy order is the one that benefits the capitalist class, the class that owns and controls the productive process" (p. 3). Although the extreme critical theory position has mellowed a bit in the past 40 years or so, the role of those who control the primary organs of finance and commerce are still singled out—think the One Percent (1%)—as those whose interests are protected by the criminal law.

Our point here is that the interests of a for-profit corporation are clear. They represent the owners of the corporation and/or its shareholders. They do not represent the broad interests of the nation or world. Non-profit organizations represent something of a middle-range of interests. However, the interests represented and protected by CJOs will remain a matter of debate, at least as long as there are criminal justice and criminology faculty. This confusion about whose interests are protected by CJOs ties into other themes of this text—authority and legitimacy.

What Is a Formal Organization?

The remainder of this chapter will describe and distinguish the major types of organizations, followed by a discussion of the origins of modern criminal justice institutions. Generally, **organizations** can be defined as "social structures created by individuals to support the collaborative pursuit of specified goals" (Scott & Davis, 2007, p. 11). They may be described as collective actors, either human or juristic, that may "take actions, use resources, enter into contracts, and own property" (p. 6). Organizations are comprised of various components, "each of which affects and is affected by the others" (p. 24). These six major components form the structures and systems of a complex organization, into which we will delve further in our chapters on Structures and Strategies.

Our typology addresses formal organizations, rather than informal. **Formal organizations** are the juristic or "artificial structure[s] created to coordinate either people or groups and resources to achieve a mission or goal" (Peak, 2012, p. 58). Formal organizations may be grouped into three broad categories: for-profits, non-profits, and government. Before we start learning more about criminal justice organizations, it would be beneficial to learn what they are not. Organizations are created and governed in different ways, which distinguishes criminal justice agencies from all others. Let us begin with for-profits.

For-Profits: Sole Proprietorships, Partnerships, Corporations, and Limited Liability Companies

Generally, a **for-profit** is a business created to generate profits for owners (Beatty & Samuelson, 1996). The simplest for-profit is a **sole proprietorship** which is owned by a single person. In a sole proprietorship, the owner and business are one and the same; they may sign documents or checks with "d/b/a" which designates "doing business as." Essentially, the owner pays all the bills (e.g., rent, salaries, benefits, equipment, technology, malpractice insurance, etc.) and keeps the money that is left, if any, as income. Taxes are paid out of the owner's income, while the business does not pay taxes. This model of business could be used by a single, independent attorney. Because the owner and business are essentially the same entity, the owner's assets are vulnerable to liability law suits. In order to protect those personal assets, s/he would purchase malpractice insurance.

All other for-profits have more than one owner, which requires the creation and regulation of relationships (Shade, 2010). According to Shade (2010), these relationships are called business associations. A **business association** "is a device through which individuals or entities conduct business" (Shade, 2010, p. 1). Business associations are about relationships and the specific rules and regulations of those relationships.

Generally, the three main categories of people involved inside a business association are: owners/investors, managers, and employees (Shade, 2010). Owners are given more specific names, depending on the type of business association. For example, in corporations, owners are called "shareholders" (whereas managers are called "directors" and "officers"). In limited partnerships, owners are called "general partners" or "limited partners," and in a limited liability company, they are called "members." State statutes are the primary mechanism for regulating relationships within business associations. However, common law may apply to some types of businesses and federal statutes may apply in certain situations.

In addition to relationships within an organization, a business association can develop relationships with external "third parties," such as suppliers, attorneys, and accountants. These external relationships are governed through areas of the law, such as contracts, torts, and property (Shade, 2010). The regulation of relationships with external third-parties is not the same as rules governing the relationships between the owners, managers, and employees within an organization. The distinctions between internal and external organizational relationships are a topic we will address further in our chapters on Structure and Interorganizational Relationships.

For-profit business associations come in many forms. The three general types are partnerships, corporations, and limited liability companies (Shade, 2010). Let's describe these business organizations and how they are created.

Partnerships

Partnerships vary in type according to whether the partnership is an independent legal entity (separate from its owners) and the degree of owner liability. The three major types of partnerships include: general partnerships, limited partnerships, and limited liability partnerships (Shade, 2010). The first of these, the **general partnership** ("GP"), is defined as "an association of two or more persons to carry on as co-owners of a business for profit" (p. 40). It is similar to a sole proprietorship in that a GP is "unincorporated." That is, a GP may be created without the filing of any documents with a government authority. Moreover, it is the only type of business association that does not require such filings due to its historic roots in common law. Like a sole proprietorship, a GP is not an entity separate from its owners. Each partner has unlimited joint and separate personal liability for the expenses and obligations of the business. Therefore, owners must protect their personal assets by purchasing insurance, such as malpractice insurance. And, like a sole proprietorship, the GP business does not file a tax return. Rather, taxes are only paid at the personal level, as the partners are taxed through their incomes returns (i.e., pass-through taxation). General partnerships are regulated primarily by state statutes, but partners can modify the statutory requirements through a written partnership agreement.

It is not uncommon for attorneys to use a GP structure for their law firms. Partners of a law firm take distributions from the business. That is, excess business income is distributed between partners. The distributions may not be equal in amounts, however. A senior partner is likely to take a larger portion than a junior partner. This is one of the reasons why you hear that it is so important for attorneys to work their way up to becoming a "partner" in a law firm. Partners are considered "owners" and get to reap financial benefits from the excess income brought in by the salaried associate attorneys who are "employees." Employees may earn bonuses, should the partners decide to share the financial success of the business with non-partners.

The second common type of partnership is a **limited partnership** ("LP") which contains two classes of partners. "There are one or more *general partners* who manage the business and one or more *limited partners* who are essentially passive investors and have virtually no management authority" (Shade, 2010, p. 42). This form of partnership is in limited use today, but allows limited partners to invest capital to a business without exposing their personal finances to liabilities beyond their original investment. General partners, however, have unlimited liability for debts and obligations. The partnership business does not pay taxes, as both general and limited partners pay taxes on their personal incomes. Unlike GPs, LPs are not based on common law and are strictly created according to statutory law. To create an LP, the general partners must execute and file a Certificate of Limited Partnership with the appropriate state official, most likely the Secretary of State. LPs are similar to GPs in that they may be governed by a contractual partner agreement.

The third type of partnership is the **limited liability partnership** ("LLP") which is "a subset of a general partnership that permits general partners to limit their personal liability" (Shade, 2010, p. 44). LLPs are grounded in statutory laws, with Texas being the first to pass such laws in 1991. Because general persons are permitted to protect their personal assets from the partnership's liabilities and obligations, LLPs have supplanted LPs. The creation of an LLP is relatively easy. Owners file a certificate with the state authority and adopt a name that includes "LLP" or similar designation. Like the other partnerships, the partners pay income taxes, while the LLP does not. Today, all 50 states have statutes that allow for the creation of LLPs, and they are typically used for professional partnerships such as law and accounting firms.

Corporations

Corporations are the second major category of for-profits. They are different from partnerships in that **corporations** are considered to be legally separate from their owners (Shade, 2010). They are treated by legislatures and courts as real persons or entities, and are required to identify themselves in their name by incorporating labels such as "Inc." or "Corporation." An example of separate entity status is Microsoft, as the company is capable of owning property, making contracts, and being sued independently from Bill Gates, and vice versa. Because the shareholder owners and the business are separate entities, they each pay taxes. After the corporation pays all the business-related expenses and its taxes, profits may be distributed to shareholders in the form of dividends. Shareholders subsequently claim the dividends as income when filing their tax returns. A corporation is also characterized by its use of a board of directors (elected by the shareholders) which appoints the organization's officers, such as a chief executive officer (CEO) and chief financial officer (CFO), to manage the day-to-day operations. Because shareholders can buy and sell their shares freely, the corporation's existence or "life" continues beyond those of its owners.

Corporations are regulated by state statutes, and creating one is relatively easy in comparison to most government bureaucratic processes. To create a corporation, the initial owners file a document called *Articles of Incorporation* (i.e., Articles) along with a filing fee (Shade, 2010). The Articles are filed with the appropriate state authority, which is usually the Secretary of State. The initial "organizing" of a new corporation is completed through the preparation and adoption of the corporate *By-laws* which "provide the basic rules for governance of the corporation and define the duties and authority of various corporate officers. The bylaws are not filed with any governmental authority" (p. 71). The Articles typically identify the board of directors and is drafted in unison with the Bylaws. This allows the directors to hold their first annual meeting and vote for the adoption of the Bylaws, as well as appointing officers, designating the number of stock shares in the company, and any other acts deemed necessary for governance. Upon appointment by the directors, the officers are empowered to legitimately manage the business such as opening a corporate bank account, issuing stock certificates or shares, and filing for a tax identification number. As noted by Shade, these last steps enacted by the officers are typical for management purposes, but "they are not conditions to the creation of the corporation" (p. 72).

Limited Liability Companies

A final type of for-profit organization is the **limited liability company** or LLC. An LLC is a hybrid business association which combines the characteristics of a partnership and corporation (Shade, 2010). LLCs are regulated by state statutes and contract laws, and they became widely used in the 1990s. An LLC "combines the tax treatment of a partnership with the limited liability of a corporation and allows more flexibility of management than either a corporation of partnership" (p. 49). LLCs are created by filing the appropriate documents with the state, wherein owner are called "members" rather than shareholders or partners. Most LLCs are "closely held" which means the stock is privately held and company stock is not publicly traded on the stock exchange. Members enjoy the limited liability of corporations, single pass-through taxation of partnerships, and management flexibility beyond that of partnerships and corporations, making LLCs a more popular choice than other forms of partnerships.

Non-Profits: Faith-based, Non-Faith-Based, and Non-Governmental Organizations

Partnerships, corporations, and limited liability corporations exist for the purpose of generating profits for owners. They are distinctively different from numerous types of **tax-exempt organizations** which are allowed to generate funds without paying taxes (Taylor, 2011). Although government entities are technically tax-exempt, the types of organizations to which most refer are called "non-profits." **Non-profits** are organizations formed for the common good or to further a social cause; therefore income is used to keep the organization operating. They are typically created to operate for "religious, charitable, scientific, or educational purposes, or for the prevention of cruelty to children or animals" (p. 11). Their tax exempt status is primarily regulated by the Internal Revenue Service (IRS), and obtaining tax-exempt status requires the filing of an application. They would also be incorporated through the filing of Articles of Incorporation with the proper state authority, like corporations and most partnerships. To maintain their status, most would file federal tax returns annually.

The majority of these organizations are referred to as "501(c)(3)s" which refers to the section (§) of the tax code that permits their exempt status (Taylor, 2011). *Section 501(c)(3) organizations* include: big money foundations (e.g., Bill & Melinda Gates Foundation and MacArthur Foundation), community foundations (e.g., Silicon Valley Community Foundation (California)), big public charities (e.g., United Way and Salvation Army), healthcare organizations, colleges and universities, and groups for amateur athletics groups or prevention of cruelty to animals. Other tax-exempt sections include § 501(c)(6) for business groups such as the American Bar Association, § 501(c)(19) for veterans' organizations like the American Legion, § 501(c)(5) for labor organizations such as the AFL-CIO, and § 501(c)(4) for social welfare or advocacy groups such as the National Rifle Association and AARP.

Interestingly, non-profit organizations "spin off" or create sister-organizations to qualify for particular tax code exemptions (Taylor, 2011). Organizations that qualify under § 501(c)(4) are politically active and are affiliated with the more common 501(c)(3)s that serve non-political functions.

"For example, the AARP Foundation, exempt under § 501(c)(3), is affiliated with AARP, the § 501(c)(4) organization that is politically active" (p. 29).

There is great diversity in the purposes and sizes of these organizations. Accordingly, researchers and criminal justice officials tend to distinguish them into various non-legal categories which may include the following: faith-based, non-faith-based, and non-government. **Faith-based organizations** (FBOs) are non-profits organized for religious purposes. **Non-faith-based organizations** (non-FBOs) are secular non-profit organizations created for purposes that may be charitable, scientific, educational, or political. **Non-governmental organizations** (NGOs) is a term commonly applied to service, professional, and occupational associations that may not fall under one of the § 501(c) categories. A note of caution to CJOs looking to partner with non-profits—not all who claim to be a "non-profit" are properly incorporated by filing the appropriate documents with the state.

We will return to the subject of how the range of non-governmental organizations described here interact with CJOs in our section on professional associations, research organizations, and social movement organizations. Again, we believe the impact of these organizations and the need for CJOs to interact with them is vastly under-examined in the academic criminal justice literature. The same may well be true of the professional literature in criminal justice.

Government: Criminal Justice Agencies and Non-Criminal Justice Agencies

The "tax exempt" status applies to the broad non-profit organizations described above. However, it also applies to government entities that enjoy immunity from the federal income under the general doctrine of intergovernmental tax immunity (Taylor, 2011). The **government** is a federal, state, or local agency or office, elected or appointed, with the authority to administer government functions. At the federal level, the U.S. Constitution expressly creates the legislative, executive, and judicial branches of government. Congress is empowered to delegate authority via statutes, which has resulted in the creation of numerous regulating agencies, such as the Internal Revenue Service and Environmental Protection Agency. Likewise, state governments are structured according to the three branches of government, and they too have legislative powers to form regulatory agencies. States also delegate certain functions to local governments, however. The term "local" government typically refers to circuit, county, or municipal jurisdictions. The types of powers and services conferred to them by the state include fire protection and education, as well as police, judicial, and jail services (McCarthy & Reynolds, 2003). All told, nearly 90,000 local government units exist in the United States.

Regular citizens may view government as one large, bureaucratic apparatus. However, those who work in criminal justice tend to distinguish themselves from other government agencies. Accordingly, **criminal justice organizations** (CJOs) are entities possessing the government's authority to use force against citizens in the primary areas of police, courts, and corrections. This authority is typically vested in an agency that provides direct government services, but it may be contracted out to non-government organizations. For example, G4S is an internationally known private contractor that provides various policing and correctional services. Other examples include CoreCivic (formerly Corrections Corporation of America) and Judicial Correction Services, Inc. Although government workers may consider private contractors to be interlopers, they may be included in the CJO reference.

In comparison to CJOs, **non-criminal justice organizations** (non-CJOs) are government entities tasked with administering government functions that are not included in the criminal justice system of police, courts, or corrections. The non-CJO term applies to the public fire protection and educational organizations mentioned earlier. However, some may use the non-CJO term to refer to other organizations, including for-profits and non-profits. Another term for any and all non-CJOs, for-profits, and non-profits is **community-based organizations** (CBOs).

Potential Partners: Educational Organizations and Sources of Information on Non-CJOs

Before we delve further into the description and historical background of CJOs, you may be asking why so much space and time has been dedicated to describing for-profits, non-profits, and non-CJOs. One reason is that many outsiders are surprised to find that state and local criminal justice agencies frequently seek out and apply for federal grants to plan, implement, and assess innovative programs to control and prevent crime. The Department of Justice provides numerous grants, many of which require some form of partnerships between CJOs and non-CJOs (see http://ojp.gov/funding/index.htm). Accordingly, we felt it necessary to introduce the broader categorizations and distinctions of various non-CJOs. And, we're not done quite yet. Our lead author's experience in community-based planning and evaluation, from a variety of organizational perspectives, dictates that we elaborate on understanding potential CJO partners. First, we address educational organizations. Then, we provide methods of gathering information on organizations that may want to partner with CJOs.

We take a closer look at educational organizations for two reasons. First, educational organizations defy general descriptive categories. Second, the evaluations of federally funded programs often facilitate the need for CJOs to form partnerships with researchers. In general, **education organizations** are created for the purposes of education, and they are diverse in that they fall under all three broad categories of for-profit, non-profit, and government. They may also be described as public or private. There are three levels of education: primary, secondary, and tertiary. The first two levels, also known as elementary education and high school, are compulsory in the U.S. Local governments typically provide public education for these two levels. Non-profit organizations, such as those associated with religious institutions, may also provide education through private institutions. Some municipalities may contract with for-profits to provide services, as well. CJOs may find themselves working with schools at the primary and secondary levels in connection with issues of juvenile delinquency.

It is more likely, however, for CJOs to work with a variety of researchers employed in higher education. This third, tertiary level of education includes colleges, technical training institutes, nursing schools, and distance learning centers. Each state in the U.S. has established its own state university system that enjoys a government tax-exempt status (Taylor, 2011). These universities and colleges are public, and are financially supported by state budgets. However, state appropriations for higher education have been declining (or not kept pace with educational spending), making public universities increasingly reliant on federal funding through federal student loans, Pell grants, research grants, and veterans' educational benefits (Pew Charitable Trusts, 2015). State universities are even more complex due to their formation of § 501(c)(3) organizations to solicit endowments, hold investments, and produce income (Taylor, 2011). In comparison to state universities, private colleges and universities are also tax-exempt; however, it is due to their § 501(c)(3) status. Finally, although it is less common, a four-year or graduate college or university may be a for-profit. One nationally known for-profit example is the University of Phoenix. If this university is teaching in your state, they would have to file the appropriate documentation with the state to conduct business.

The complexity of state university systems, with their mixture of direct funding from states, indirect federal funding through students and research, and incorporation of non-profit structures for other revenue sources, illustrates the need for CJOs to understand and investigate potential partners. It is common for criminal justice officials to partner with researchers at universities or research institutes, such as The Urban Institute or Rand Corporation, for program planning and evaluation. It is also likely that CJOs need to partner with other types of organizations to exchange information or provide various services, such as treating offenders or training officers. According to Taylor (2011), non-profits, in particular, may make good partners as they "control vast amounts of capital, exercise influence, and engage in substantial political activity" (p. 30). Of course, there's the other side of the coin. Many organizations may have objectives too distantly related from those of CJOs or may not have the capacity to contribute to a partnership. Yet, they want to partner as a means of obtaining federal funding.

TABLE 1.1: TYPES OF FORMAL ORGANIZATIONS

- **For-profits**—businesses created to generate profits for owners
  - **Sole proprietorship**—an unincorporated business owned by a single person. Only the owner pays income tax.
  - **General partnership**—an unincorporated association of two or more co-owners who carry on a business for profit. Only the partners pay income taxes.
  - **Limited partnership**—a partnership that consists of two types of partners—general and limited. Only general partners are personally liable for losses incurred by the partnership. Partners pay taxes on incomes. The LP does not pay taxes.
  - **Limited liability partnership**—a partnership that permits general partners to limit their liability and are typically used for professional partnerships such as law and accounting firms. The partners pay income taxes, while the LLP does not.
  - **Corporations**—an incorporated business association of shareholders whose liabilities are limited to the cost of their shares. Corporations are separate legal entities that are taxed separately from their owners and exist perpetually beyond any individual's position within the company. The business and shareholders each pay income taxes.
  - **Limited Liability Company**—offers the limited liability of a corporation and the tax status of a partnership.
  - **Other forms of organization**—includes business trusts, cooperatives, joint stock companies, and franchises.

- **Non-profits**—organizations formed for the common good or to further a social cause; income is used to keep the organization operating; may be incorporated as a "501(c)" which exempts them from some federal income taxes.
  - **Faith-based organization (FBO)**—a non-profit organized for religious purposes; may or may not be incorporated; FBO is not a legal term.
  - **Non-FBO**—a secular non-profit organization created for purposes that may be charitable, scientific, educational, or political.
  - **Non-governmental organization (NGO)**—another common term applied to service, professional, and occupational associations that may not fall under the 501(c) category.
- **Government**—a federal, state, or local agency or office, elected or appointed, with the authority to administer government functions.
  - **Criminal Justice agency (CJ)**—a government agency possessing the authority to use force against citizens in the primary areas of police, courts, and corrections.
  - **Non-CJ agency**—a government agency tasked with administering government functions that are not included in the criminal justice system of police, courts, or corrections.
- **Education**—organizations created for the purposes of education which may be for-profit or non-profit, and may also be described as public or private.
  - **Primary education**—compulsory education during early childhood; a/k/a elementary education.
  - **Secondary education**—the second stage of compulsory education in the U.S.; a/k/a high school.
  - **Tertiary education**—the third level of education which includes higher education at colleges, technical training institutes, nursing schools, and distance learning centers.

Not all organizations make good partners. CJO administrators will find most organizations faithfully believe in community partnerships (Humiston, 2014). However, not all organizations have the capacity (e.g., knowledge, personnel, other resources) to meaningfully contribute to criminal justice goals. Inviting everyone into a partnership initiative all at once may not be a constructive endeavor, for reasons we discuss later in our chapter on

Interorganizational Relationships. For now, we'll discuss ways to investigate potential organizational partners. A search of public documents allows CJOs to identify organizational leaders, their positions within an organization, and, in some instances, the organization's resources.

Investigating non-government organizations (e.g., corporations, limited liability companies, and non-profits) typically involves a search for incorporation documents and may involve a search of tax return information. As discussed earlier, most organizations initially file documents, such as Articles of Incorporation, with the proper state authority. The exceptions are sole proprietorships and common law partnerships. Organizations that file Articles would also file Annual Reports or similar documents to disclose updated information. If a business was created in a different state, then the organization is identified as being "foreign." If an incorporated entity fails to file their annual reports, the state will automatically dissolve it.

The state authority which maintains public documentation of non-government organizations is usually the Secretary of State. In the case of Florida, the search of public documents can be performed through the Florida Department of State's Division of Corporations at http://www.sunbiz.org/search.html. The information garnered from these public documents may include the following: age of the business; name and address of the registered agent; names and addresses of directors, members, and partners; organization's current mailing address; federal employer identification (FEI) number; and names and addresses of officers or managing members.

Another source of information for some non-profits may be tax returns. According to Taylor (2011), the public can examine IRS Forms 990 and 990-EZ for exempt organizations at the Foundation Center using its online tool at http://foundationcenter.org/find-funding/990-finder. However, it does not include religious organizations because they do not file such IRS forms.

CJOs may also partner with other government entities. Investigating government organizations may involve searching annual reports, directories, budgets, local charters, and state or federal statutes. Like many non-government organizations, government organizations file public information. The best information may be found in an Annual Report. Government annual reports, directories, and budgets provide detailed information as to budgets, Constitutional officers (elected), and appointed administrators (not elected). It should also provide a clear organizational chart as to the government's structure, hierarchy, and functions. One example of a comprehensive description of a local government is Orange County Government, Florida, at http://www.orangecountyfl.net/OpenGovernment/Budgets.aspx#.

V9WkNfkrJpg where the public can find this type of information in the yearly adopted and proposed budgets.

Information on the powers of a government may be found in local charters, various statutes, and other various public websites. For example, investigating county powers may be done by reviewing their charters. In Florida, county charters have been compiled by the Florida Association of Counties, and may be found at http://www.fl-counties.com/charter-county-information. Of course, state and local county information can be found at other websites, such as Florida's Department of State: Division of Library and Information Services at http://dos.myflorida.com/library-archives/research/florida-information/government/. Florida statutes are found at http://www.leg.state.fl.us/statutes/. Finally, an examination of federal Title 26 tax codes and other statutes can be found in the United States Code at https://www.gpo.gov/fdsys/browse/collectionUScode.action?collectionCode=USCODE (Taylor, 2011).

Conclusion

This chapter has provided a basic introduction to some of the differences among the types of organizations that are involved in the current criminal justice system. Leaders in the CJS are increasingly required to work across a range of other government and non-governmental organizations, yet we see relatively little mention of this in much of the academic criminal justice literature. This will serve as a foundation for the variety of organizational types that we will discuss in Section 3 of the text.

The current chapter also offered an introduction to the more legal- and administrative-based ways of researching organizations, as well as some of the key data sources for information on organizations. You will find this information can be used for a variety of courses in school, as well as in the CJ workplace. If you wind up working cases that involve any aspect of racketeering and/or organized crime, knowing to look in these areas will be a great help. We will return to those topics in Section 3. Next, we turn back to a more detailed discussion of government organizations in the criminal justice system.

Key Words

501(c)(3) organization
Annual Report
Articles of Incorporation

Business association
By-Laws
Community-based organization

Conflict
Consensus
Corporation
Criminal justice organizations
Educational organization
Faith-based organization
Formal organization
For-profit corporation
General partnerships
Government
Interest
IRS form 990
Limited liability corporation/ company
Limited liability partnerships
Limited partnerships
Marxist
Non-criminal justice organizations
Non-faith-based organization
Non-profit organizations
Non-governmental organizations
Organization
Partnerships
Pluralist
Sole proprietorship
Tax-exempt organizations

Government: Policing Powers and Constraints

Learning Objectives:

1. Define and describe police powers, particularly as they relate to the Tenth and Fifth Amendments.
2. Define and describe due process, particularly as it relates to its constraints on police powers.
3. Define and describe equal protection, particularly as it related to its constraints on police powers.
4. Distinguish criminal justice organizations (CJOs) from non-criminal justice organizations (non-CJOs).
5. Describe and provide examples of external challenges to CJOs.
6. Identify and describe the three general types of government employees.
7. Describe and provide examples of internal challenges to CJOs.
8. Describe the societal changes of the "great transformation" and its impact on criminal justice institutions.
9. Define and differentiate authority and legitimacy.

Introduction

Earlier, we defined **government** as a federal, state, or local agency or office, elected or appointed, with the authority to administer government functions. Government is often indirectly involved in providing services, such as building and maintaining public roads, clean drinking water facilities, and affordable low-income housing. In situations such as these, the government does not typically provide the services directly. Rather, it works with other organizations, through contracts or otherwise, that provide the services. This "third-party" approach of "new governance" (Salamon, 2002) requires two basic democratic questions (McCarthy & Reynolds, 2003). *Can* government get involved? And, *should* government get involved? Defining the boundaries of "government function" in such situations may become blurred, indeed. These issues are explored in greater detail in this chapter.

Police Powers—Reserved for the State

There is one public function that sits squarely in the realm of the government's power—policing. **Police powers** refer to the government's ability to "limit, regulate or prohibit personal and business activity and property uses without government compensation to protect public health, safety, morality and general welfare" (McCarthy & Reynolds, 2003, p. 167). This power is rooted in English common law tradition and broadly applied to the passing of criminal and civil laws for purposes of protecting public health and safety. Pursuant to the **Tenth Amendment**, states have the primary power and duty to police, which is recognized by the federal government. In turn, states delegate much of this power to local circuits, counties, and municipalities (McCarthy & Reynolds, 2003).

The government's policing powers are felt in both criminal and civil matters, and is expressed in the **Fifth Amendment** which states, in part, "No person shall be … deprived of life, liberty, or property, without due process of law; nor shall private property be taken for public use, without just compensation" (Congress, n.d., p. 1473). (See https://www.congress.gov/content/conan/pdf/GPO-CONAN-REV-2016-10-6.pdf). Under civil law, the government may use "eminent domain" to take private property, with compensation, for the public interest. Criminal law, on the other hand, is regulatory in nature. Under its police powers, the government may deprive a person of life, liberty, or property without compensation. "What distinguishes eminent domain from the police power is that the former involves the *taking* of property because of its need for the public use while the latter involves the *regulation* of property to prevent the use thereof in a manner that is detrimental to the public interest" (Congress, n.d., p. 1596). (See https://www.congress.gov/content/conan/pdf/GPO-CONAN-REV-2016-10-6.pdf).

The power of the government to take a person's life, liberty, or property is awesome and expansive, but not exhaustive. Police powers are limited by due process. **Due process** of law is specifically expressed in the Fifth and

Fourteenth Amendments, with the former applying to the federal government and latter applying to the states. It is further implied by the Fourth, Sixth, and Eighth Amendments, as well as other laws.

> Due process does not have a fixed meaning but expands with jurisprudential attitudes of fundamental fairness.... Unlike some legal rules, [due process] is not a technical conception with a fixed content.... [It has] evolved through centuries of Anglo-American constitutional history and civilization, [and] cannot be imprisoned within the treacherous limits of any formula.... Due process is compounded of history, reason, the past course of decision, and stout confidence in which strength of the democratic faith which we profess. Due process is not a mechanical instrument. It is not a yardstick...It is a delicate process of adjustment inescapably involving the exercise of judgment by those whom the Constitution entrusted with the unfolding of the process. (Gifis, 1996, p. 159)

The constitutional safeguard of due process applies both substantively and procedurally (Gifis, 1996). **Substantive due process** requires that statutes and regulations be enacted for legitimate government objectives. **Procedural due process** protections guarantee "procedural fairness where the government would deprive one of his property or liberty" (p. 158). The courts are entrusted with reviewing the constitutionality of due process procedures, such as warranted and unwarranted search and seizure, self-incrimination, rights to counsel, specificity of charges, jury, and confrontation of witnesses (McCarthy & Reynolds, 2003).

In addition to due process, the powers of the government are also constrained by Constitutional guarantees of equal protection (Branham, 2013; McCarthy & Reynolds, 2003). **Equal protection** is the Fourteenth Amendment constitutional guarantee that "No *State* [emphasis added] shall... deny to any person within its jurisdiction the equal protection of the laws" (Congress, n.d.). The post-Civil War passage of the amendment did not take away the police powers of the states (Gifis, 1996). Rather, it requires that laws and discretion be based on reason, rather than being applied arbitrarily based on race, gender, or other extra-legal factors. According to McCarthy and Reynolds (2003), equal protections are violated in cases of intentional discrimination in the administration or enforcement of laws. Charges may arise when one group is charged and prosecuted, whereas others are not due to political or arbitrary considerations.

Earlier, we defined **criminal justice organizations (CJOs)** as entities possessing the government's authority to use force against citizens in the primary areas of police, courts, and corrections. Now, we can further describe CJOs as institutions created by governments for the purpose of exercising their police powers. Police powers in criminal cases may include the taking of an individual's life, liberty, or property without compensation for regulatory purposes to protect public safety. However, the powers of the government, and by extension CJOs, are limited by constitutional protections of due process and equal protection. Due process requires the "delicate" exercise of judgment bestowed on those who are constitutionally entrusted. Equal protection requires that laws and discretion be reasonable and not arbitrary.

CJOs are distinctive in that they are authorized to use force against persons in the taking of their freedom, property, and even their lives. However, with unique powers come unique administrative challenges which further differentiate CJOs from other types of organization. CJOs are challenged by individuals and groups both inside and outside the organization, often on the bases of due process and equal protection considerations (McCarthy & Reynolds, 2003).

External challenges to CJOs come in various forms, such as law suits, political demonstrations, and independent investigations. Law suits are a common method of challenging police powers by defining due process procedures. For example, if police violate due process during the collection of evidence, courts may exclude the evidence from trial by granting a defense attorney's motion to suppress. In corrections, inmates may bring suits alleging infringement on their rights such as freedom of speech, association, and religion (First Amendment), protection of property and persons from unwarranted search and seizure (Fourth Amendment), privacy (Fifth and Fourteenth Amendments), and conditions of confinement (Eighth Amendment) (Branham, 2013).

In addition to due process, CJOs are subject to external criticisms of violating equal protection laws. Political rallies and demonstrations of today echo many of the same condemnations of previous generations. The Black Lives Matter movement parallels the Civil Rights Movement of the 1960s wherein minority groups question the use of discretion by police in their use of deadly force (more on this in later chapters). Independent investigations by external authorities may be used in more egregious situations, as in the federal investigation of local misconducted and corruption in Ferguson,

Missouri, following the killing of an unarmed African American male (Department of Justice, 2015).

CJOs may also be **internally challenged**, oftentimes by employees. Employment practices and positions vary between jurisdictions (McCarthy & Reynolds, 2003). Generally, however, the positions of officers and employees inside a government agency include the following: elected officials, appointed officials, and career service employees. **Elected officials** are not classified service employees because they are elected and their reappointment is contingent upon being re-elected. Sheriffs and State/District Attorneys are examples of officials that are typically elected at the local level. An example of an elected official at the state level is the State Attorney General. **Appointed officials** are hired by the elected officials. Appointees have a professional or confidential relationship, such as federal U.S. Attorneys who are appointed by the President and confirmed by the Senate. It is not uncommon for appointments to follow political affiliations. In the case of civil service appointees, they may be hired because they have certain qualifications and skills that make them the best candidate for the position. Civil service appointees are found throughout various federal and state agencies. The **career service employees** go through processes that include standardized testing, interviews, and the like. They are in a competitive system where they compete for promotions based on merit.

Individual employees and employee unions are likely sources of internal challenges in the area of employment practices (McCarthy & Reynolds, 2003). Equal treatment underlies questions related to hiring, job assignment, and promotion policies. Generally, challenges of government employment practices have included "entrance examinations, educational requirements, height and weight minimums, physical skills, strength and endurance tests, job assignments, and non-rotation policies harmful to promotion possibilities, merit promotion examinations, pay classifications, and maternity leave policies" (p. 116). Unions are often concerned with issues of drug and disease testing, comparable pay across positions based on education and training (rather than gender), and privatization of government functions. Accordingly, administrators must be able to defend their policies or negotiate remedies in court-ordered consent decrees, collective bargaining agreements, and arbitrated or mediated dispute resolutions.

Our description of CJO administrative constraints is not exhaustive. Other sources of limitations on CJOs would include a discussion of legislative budget restrictions, non-elected government agencies, and contracted third-parties. However, we have set the stage for these discussions in later chapters.

From "The Great Transformation" to Continuous Transformation—An Historical Background to Criminal Justice Organization

Now that we have distinguished CJOs from other organizations in terms of legal foundations, powers, and constraints, we can describe their history. Just about all criminal justice overview textbooks will trace the roots of the current Criminal Justice System (CJS) back to Assyrians and other ancient peoples. Yet, the organizations that comprise the contemporary CJS are quite young in social terms. "Modern" policing is traced back to the establishment of the London Metropolitan Police by Sir Robert Peel in 1829 (Gaines & Kappeler, 2011), with Boston beginning the first formal police agency in 1828. The roots of our current corrections system are traced to the same time period, with the US Bureau of Prisons coming into being in 1930. The beginnings of a separate Juvenile Justice System was in Illinois (Chicago) in 1899. Public prosecutors in the US can be traced back to the early Nineteenth Century, before police organizations. Public defenders, while implicit in the US Constitution, were first recognized as necessary in the mid-1800s, but not institutionalized until well into the Twentieth Century. In short, we are dealing with a relatively young set of social organizations and institutions.

Many of these organizational innovations are the product of what Polanyi (1944) termed the "great transformation." This period covers roughly the period of the Enlightenment, the rise of capitalism as a major economic system, the industrial revolution, and the rise of the modern nation-state. The key point of the great transformation for criminal justice is that it represented one of the first major upheavals in relations of authority, at least in Western civilization. The traditional authorities and power of the Church and monarchies/aristocracies began to rapidly fail against the emerging power and authority of the State, industry and science.

Since the great transformation, the entire world has experienced a series of transformations. Some of these were experienced in non-Western regions via colonization by Western powers. Others were the result of emerging economic situations. Some have been the result of changing technologies. All have resulted in some form of alteration in the collective consciousness of groups and entire nations. All modern human rights movements trace their existence and accomplishments back to these original breakdowns in the dominant social order. While social change may not change as rapidly as technological change, the two are increasingly intertwined.

We have taken a brief historical tour of major changes in the social, economic, and technological world to demonstrate that the CJS is a relatively new social institution, or relatively enduring pattern of social behavior. Many perceive the CJS to be an inherently "conservative" institutional form, as its charge is often to protect the status quo. There is a seeming paradox in studying these formal organizations of social control (see below); they are simultaneously charged with defending the status quo, until it changes, and then they must defend the new order. The evolving social challenge to existing authority structures and those who enforce the rules of the authority structure will be with us throughout this text. A key question for us is how CJS organizations adapt to changing social and technological environments effectively while constrained by a range of legal and social factors. Among the latter is the special case of perceived legitimacy and fairness when seeking to enforce the law on a neutral basis.

The Authority and Legitimacy of Criminal Justice Organizations

We begin this section with observations by the German Sociologist Max Weber nearly 100 years ago: "[A] state is a human community that (successfully) claims the *monopoly of the legitimate use of physical force* within a given territory... The state is considered the sole source of the 'right' to use violence... Like the political institutions historically preceding it, the state is a relation of men dominating men, a relation supported by means of legitimate (i.e., considered to be legitimate) violence" (emphasis in original) (Gerth & Mills, 1973 [1946], p. 78).

This is, and should be, a sobering set of statements for students of criminal justice. The criminal justice system is the only set of state institutions, beyond the government military institutions, authorized to use physical force to enforce "legitimate" state orders. In some instances, this includes deadly force. Of course, we have other forms of coercion beyond brute physical force. Ultimately, all "police powers" rest on the assumption that criminal justice authorities will carry out the lawful orders of a court or entity that can legitimately order them to do so, including the use of physical force and/or deprivation of liberty (Akers, Potter, & Hill, 2013). We will leave it to the reader to decide whether all of the "tricks of the trade" we use to get people to comply with the law are fundamentally coercive. If they are, we are at least authorized to use them—within the bounds of the law.

These observations are important in the study of criminal justice organizations because, as Weber noted, these powers are grounded in *organizations*, not *individuals* (Gerth & Mills, 1973[1946]). Such powers are conferred by a "constitution" based in some broadly accepted rational norm. Without legitimacy bestowed by constitution, authority quickly fades. In Weber's terms, we are now dominated by "virtue of legality… belief in the validity of legal statute and functional 'competence' based on rationally created *rules*" (Gerth & Mills, 1973[1946], p. 79).

Authority is provided by the State to its institutions. Legitimacy, however, is a bit less clear-cut. We want to begin with the knowledge that while some members of a society may recognize that authority flows from the State, they do not necessarily recognize the legitimacy of the State or the laws that flow from it. We note this here because so much recent attention to legitimacy by criminal justice and psychologically-oriented researchers has focused on the interpersonal interactions between citizens and police or other agents of formal social control (Gau, 2014; Terrill, Paoline, & Gau, 2016; Tyler, 2003). The Institutional dimension of perceived legitimacy is of equal importance in the study of criminal justice organizations.

Bottoms and Tankebe (2013) provided an overview of structural and procedurally-oriented approaches to issues of legitimacy in relation to criminal justice. They argue that:

> "… legitimacy needs to be perceived as always *dialogic* and *relational* in character. That is to say, those in power (or seeking power) in a given context make a claim to be the legitimate ruler(s); then members of the audience respond to this claim; the power-holder might adjust the nature of the claim in light of the audience's response; and this process repeats itself. It follows that legitimacy should not be viewed as a single transaction; it is more like a perpetual discussion, in which the content of power-holders' later claims will be affected by the nature of the audience response" (p. 129; emphasis in original).

If a group or organized segment of society does not recognize the legitimacy of a particular government, it is unlikely that they will recognize procedural encounters with criminal justice agents as valid, regardless of how procedurally honest those encounters might be.

This should not be read to mean that interpersonal encounters between citizens and criminal justice officials from police through courts and corrections are irrelevant. Rather, and especially for those who begin encounters believing in the basic legitimacy of the system, each encounter provides an opportunity for criminal justice professionals to reinforce the legitimacy of the institution and the organizations that comprise it. Likewise, failure on the part of criminal justice professionals to reinforce the procedural justice expectations of citizens can weaken support for the legitimacy of individual officials, organizations and the institution. To utilize another term, each encounter is "reflexive," in that it is created by the assumption of legitimacy and also creates the conditions under which legitimacy is perceived and reinforced.

An entire text could be written on the importance of authority and legitimacy for the institution of criminal justice and the organizations that comprise that domain. We will leave that to others. For our purposes here, we want to stress that while authority may be claimed by the State, legitimacy is always a matter of negotiation between the State and its representatives in interaction with members of a variety of groups and organizations, as well as all individuals under the jurisdiction of the State. In sum, legitimacy of criminal justice organizations is something that exists beyond interactions and during each and every interaction agents of the CJS have with those under their jurisdiction.

The issues of legitimacy and authority will be with us throughout this text. Unlike other organizational forms, criminal justice organizations—especially those "authorized" by the state—have powers not provided any other legal organizational forms. As we will see, some of the organizations in the criminal justice environment utilize physical force and other forms of coercion, but without the legitimacy of a government to authorize such use.

Another area of importance is how outside groups and organizations respond to perceptions of legitimacy and authority. Later in the text we will examine how social movements, such as "Black Lives Matter," use political processes to challenge the legitimacy and authority of the CJS to achieve changes in the system. Other groups and organizations, such as criminal cartels or some supremacist movements, may work outside the accepted political processes to attempt to challenge the status quo.

One should never allow this "awesome power" of state-authorized criminal justice organizations to be far from mind. As we explore ways of analyzing criminal justice and associated organizational forms and relationships, keep our role in the "relation of men dominating men" close. Even when we as system actors believe we are doing righteous things, not everyone else will. Understanding how organizational and group affiliations can impact perceptions of legitimacy and authority will be another theme we develop in the text.

TABLE 2.1: DEFINITIONS OF "LEGITIMACY" AND "AUTHORITY" ACROSS ORGANIZATIONAL THEORIES BY LEVEL OF ORGANIZATIONAL ANALYSIS—A SAMPLING

Author(s)	Year	Definition
Max Weber	1946 (in Gerth & Mills, p. 299)	Authority—"Submission under legal authority is based upon an *impersonal* bond to the generally defined and functional 'duty of office.' The official duty... is fixed by *rationally established* norms... in such a manner that the legitimacy of the authority becomes the legality of the general rule,... enacted and announced with formal correctness" (italics in original). Legitimacy—as "the probability that to a relevant degree the appropriate attitudes [i.e., acceptance of the validity of the power-holder's claim to be a valid authority] will exist, and the corresponding practical conduct [i.e., obedience] ensue." [Economy & Society, 1978]
March & Simon	1958 (1993, p. 110)	"In joining the organization, he [the employee] accepts an authority relation, that is, he agrees that within some limits... he will accept as the premises of his behavior orders and instructions supplied to him by the organization. Associated with this acceptance are commonly understood procedures for 'legitimating' communications and clothing them with authority for employees. Acceptance of authority by the employee gives the organization a powerful means for influencing him..."
Hodge, Anthony & Gales	2003 (p. 34)	"The essence of authority is rights. These rights are determined (ideally, at least) by obligations. The obligation (responsibility) should determine the nature of the right (authority), and these should be equal or in balance... Two points emerge from this discussion. First, authority is a right determined by an obligation, and second, authority is solely associated with the formal organization that has formal sanction or approval from society... we can define authority as the rationally based formal right to make decisions and influence behavior to implement decisions based on formal organizational relationships."

Conclusion

This chapter may be among the most challenging in the text. It is also among one of the most important! It provides two key elements of why CJOs are worth studying in comparison to other types of organizations in the social environment. First, the chapter provides the legal foundations for the operations of CJOs in comparison with the other types of organizations CJOs encounter and may work with. By understanding how CJOs compare in legal authority and liability does become important for CJO leadership.

The second key element is the vesting of authority in CJOs by the State; with the consent of the governed, of course. The State alone holds the ability to convey the power to deprive one of liberty, treasure, and perhaps even life. That power is transferred to organizations, not individuals. The individuals who exercise the power to arrest, detain, prosecute, sentence, and/or punish do so under the authority of those organizations and the State. They do not do these things on their own. Whether that authority is perceived as legitimate depends not only on individual interactions with law enforcement officials, but also on whether or not the organizations themselves are perceived to be worthy (legitimacy) of exercising the authority vested in them by the state.

We continue to move toward ways of analyzing organizations using various social science theories. As in the current chapter, you are likely to be exposed to ways of analyzing organizations from various theoretical perspectives as we move forward, inching closer to the science!

Key Words

Appointed officials
Authority
Career service employees
Constitution
Criminal justice organizations
Due process
Elected officials
Eminent domain
Employee unions
Equal protection
External challenges
Fifth (5th) Amendment
Fourteenth (14th) Amendment
Government
Great transformation
Institutional
Internal challenges
Legitimacy
Police powers
Procedural due process
Regulation
Substantive due process
Taking (appropriation)
Tenth (10th) Amendment

CHAPTER 3

Organizational Basics: Systems

Learning Objectives:
1. Identify and describe the three levels of organizational analysis.
2. Describe and compare the sociological perspective to the psychological perspective of theory and research.
3. Discuss the relationship between the disciplines of sociology and psychology with criminology and criminal justice.
4. Identify, describe, and analyze the three major paradigms or system levels of examining organizations and criminal justice agencies.
5. Describe and analyze open and closed system approaches to observing organizations.
6. Identify, describe, and analyze the six major categories of an organization.
7. Describe and analyze the external and internal elements of organizations.

Introduction

This chapter can be described as being presented in multiples of three. We will present and discuss three levels of organizational analysis, three major theoretical paradigms for analyzing organizations, and six (a multiple of three) categories of organizational elements. Like so much in this text, while they may be presented separately, they will all interact with each other. By the end of the chapter you will begin to see how we build to our concentration on the inter-organizational level of analysis.

The Three Levels of Organizational Analysis

Theoretical and empirical analyses of organizations operate at different levels. The **level of analysis** of organizations refers to the size of scale of a research target. There are three levels of analysis which include: 1) **macro** which refers to structural and policy analyses, 2) **meso** which refers to organization, community, family, and group analyses, and 3) **micro** which refers to the analyses of individuals. At the micro or social psychological level, the focus is on the behavior of individuals or their interpersonal relations (Scott & Davis, 2007). In organizational research, micro-level analyses view the organization as context or an environment which impacts the attitudes or behaviors of individuals. At the meso or organizational level, the emphasis of a theory or research is on explaining the structures or social processes as characteristics of the organization. Researchers may focus on the various subunits within a single type of organization (e.g., departments, work groups, or authority ranks), structural components or routine operations across a variety of organizations (e.g., hierarchy, specializations, or communication networks), or the behavior of the organization itself as a whole. Finally, the macro or ecological level takes a societal or system view of the world. At the macro level, organizations are perceived as existing within a larger system made up primarily of other organizations upon whom they are dependent.

The level of analysis used in research is heavily influenced by core disciplines, such as psychology and sociology (Akers, Potter, & Hill, 2013). The **sociological perspective** examines how society influences people, and vice versa. Operating at the macro or societal level of analysis, sociological pioneers such as Robert K. Merton and Max Weber laid the foundation of theories and processes in research on organizations. **Psychology**, on the other hand, is the study of human thoughts, feelings, and behaviors. Accordingly, theories and research developed by organizational psychologists favor the study of individuals and operate at the micro level (Akers, Potter, & Hill, 2013).

Sociology and psychology, as well as other fields, have heavily influenced the interdisciplinary nature of criminology and criminal justice. Accordingly, researchers are "strongly influenced by the core discipline from which she or he approaches criminology" (Akers, Potter, & Hill, 2013, p. xxxiv). In the context of deviant behaviors, criminologists and criminal justice researchers grounded in sociology tend to see the environment being problematic and requiring change, whereas those drawing from psychology perceive the individual as needing rehabilitation.

Because our topic is organizations in criminal justice, we will be focusing on the meso or organizational level of analysis. This approach differs substantially from existing literature and research. Well-established theories exist at the organizational level for the examination of the structures, strategies, administrations, and motivations of criminal justice agencies and partnering organizations. The literature in criminal justice, however, has been limited. At the macro or system level, the rational or normative paradigm has prevailed (Crank, 2003). At the meso or organizational level, institutional theory has dominated (See our chapter on IORs). Finally, the majority of research exists at the micro level seeking to explain the individual behaviors of criminal justice agents, such as police and correctional officers, or deviant behaviors of criminals.

The Three Major Paradigms or System Levels of Examining Organizations and Criminal Justice Agencies

Scholarship on modern-age organizations emerged in the mid-1950s, and originated as a specialized field within the discipline of sociology (Scott & Davis, 2007; Thompson, 2008). Building on the work of earlier pioneers, such as economic sociologist Max Weber, American sociologist Robert K. Merton, and engineer Frederick W. Taylor, social scientists developed theories of organization. Earlier research on criminal justice organizations exists, such as Clemmer's research on prison life in 1940, but the focus was on a single type of organization or subject, rather than attempting to generalize across varieties of organizations (Scott & Davis, 2007, p. 8).

As social scientists explored the general patterns of organizational structures, they adopted a "systems approach" of observation. Generally, a **system** can be defined as a set of connected elements or parts (e.g. data, clients, resources) which form a more complex whole. A system may also be described as a set of procedures or organized method of accomplishing a goal or task. Parsons' (1956a, 1956b) sociological analysis of organizations, for example, attempted to explain formal organizations within a 'general theory of social systems.' He asserted that organizations are part of a larger social system. As such, organizations must be supported and legitimized by society. The systems view was also applied to the internal examination of organizations. Thus, organizations are characterized as being composed of internal sub-systems.

During this same time period, the concept of criminal justice as a system was popularized in the 1967 report to The President's Commission on Law Enforcement and Administration of Justice (see https://www.ncjrs.gov/pdffiles1/Digitization/174NCJRS.pdf). The Task Force used systems analysis in their plan for the adoption and utilization of science and technology to reduce crime through deterrence. Being focused on law enforcement, the plan was premised on connecting information and computer application elements within the system. Computers would be used to collect data, which would then be quantified and analyzed. Decision-makers would be able to use the data to identify problems, such as delays in apprehension by police and delays in case processing by the courts. It was also believed that data collection and analyses could be used by correctional agencies to make agency decisions and aid rehabilitation of inmates. Ultimately, the report has become widely known for advancing the "system" model of the overall criminal justice process. Relying on data from the FBI's Uniform Crime Report (UCR) for the (then) seven Index crimes, the system model depicted the flow of arrested offenders as they were processed through police, court, and corrections subsystems. As authorities made decisions subsequent to the reporting of an index crime, cases were depicted as being funneled away from the system at the decision points of arrest, filing of charges, sentencing, and prison (See Figure 2 in Introduction.).

Meanwhile, in the general field of organizational study, three paradigms or system-level perspectives of organizations eventually emerged: rational systems, natural system, and open systems. **Paradigms** are models that provide a framework of basic assumptions or ways of thinking which are commonly accepted by members of a discipline, group, or scientific community. Accordingly, "the rational, natural, and open system perspectives are, in this sense, organizational paradigms" (Scott & Davis, 2007, p. 33). These perspectives or paradigms provide three approaches through which to view organizations. They resemble each other in that they each serve to conceptualize the same phenomena and partially overlap, yet they also partially conflict and complement each other.

Rational and Normative Systems Approaches

Initial efforts of describing and analyzing organizational forms of administration and management followed the works of Weber and Taylor by taking a **rational systems** approach. A rational system is defined by two distinctive features: specific goals and formal structures (Scott & Davis, 2007). The rational perspective theorizes that organizations collectively coordinate activities to achieve specific goals which are explicitly and "clearly defined, and provide unambiguous criteria for selecting among alternative activities" (p. 28). The structure of the collective is likewise formal in that the rules governing behavior are precisely and explicitly formulated. The roles of personnel are dependent on the formal position or title within the organization, rather than personal characteristics or informal relationships of the individuals holding a position.

The rational, as well as normative, perspective has dominated the literature on criminal justice administration and management. In particular,

Weber's (1954) description of bureaucratization in modern Western societies is a main staple in the discussion of criminal justice organizations (See Crank, 2003, p. 110–13). In modern, industrialized societies, **bureaucracies** were believed to achieve multiple goals and objectives by effectively coordinating and controlling an organization's activities. Generally, a bureaucracy is administered by non-elected officials and relies on a hierarchy of authority, specialized functions, and fixed rules. Administrators focus on staffing and structure as a means of handling clients efficiently (Thompson, 2008). Efficiency is maximized by "defining offices according to jurisdiction and place in a hierarchy, appointing experts to offices, establishing rules for categories of activity, categorizing cases or clients, and then motivating proper performance of expert officials by providing salaries and patterns for career advancement" (p. 5). Just as rational theory proposes that criminals are rational-thinking beings who perform a cost-benefit analysis prior to committing crime, rational theory holds the "idea that an organization controls its behavior and sets its goals independent or fully cognizant of external influences" (Crank, 2003, p. 110). "The central idea of these models is straightforward: the behavior of organizations can be understood by what the organization states that it does. Consequently, to understand organizations, we should look at its formal goal, policies, organizational chart, and the like" (p. 110).

The normative perspective has also been pervasive in the criminal justice literature. Like the rational approach, the **normative perspective** assumes that criminal justice agencies are created to reduce crime and their policies and practices are designed to achieve that goal (Crank, 2003). It is assumed that each decision made by officers, prosecutors, judges, and corrections are rational processes based on criminal law wrought to a foregone conclusion of decreasing crime and improving public safety. According to Crank, criminal justice practitioners, academic educators, and researchers have had an "uncritical acceptance of the status quo, and its preservation" (p. 112). Practitioners perceive their work to be good for society and fail to consider negative consequences. It is assumed that interventions such as arrest, prosecution, and punishment will result in only a reduction of crime. There is little consideration given as to whether jails and prisons may increase the exposure of juveniles to criminogenic factors or whether adults will be less employable. In the case of education, instructors focus on teaching the functions and processes of the justice system. Likewise, research begins "with the premise that doing something about crime [is] the most important police goal" (Crank, 2003, p. 112). From the normative perspective, it is presumed that particular police tactics result in crime control, arrests bring about only desirable outcomes, government should intervene in citizens' lives, the results of intervention are "good," and the tactics of justice agencies are morally superior (pp. 113–114).

The rational and normative perspectives are limited, however, by their idealistic assumptions about internal human and organizational rationality. The modernization of industrialized societies in the early 20th century advanced the idea organizations may find "one best way" to efficiently organize tasks by studying workers and production processes (Thompson, 2008). It was believed that collective activities should be organized like manufacturing companies wherein goals and products are known and quantifiable, tasks are repetitive, and efficiency should be maximized. Administrative management scholars assumed specialization, departmentalization, and control was determined by a master plan. Hence, specialized tasks were grouped into departments and managers were assigned responsibilities according to a span of control.

Rational choice theorists incorrectly assumed that decision makers have complete control and knowledge of factors affecting the consequences of their actions (Thompson, 2008). Critics of the rational approach noted that optimal decision-making for agents of organizations is subject to **bounded rationality and uncertainty** (Thompson, 2008). As March and Simon (1958) first pointed out, rationality requires that the decision-maker have complete knowledge about the factors affecting their anticipated outcomes. However, decision makers are incapable of obtaining perfect knowledge. Humans can gather and process partial amounts of information upon which to make decisions. Rather than making optimal decisions which maximize efficiency, agencies make satisfactory decisions based on known alternatives and beliefs.

Natural Systems Approach

The second major paradigm of examining organizations is the **natural systems** approach. According to Thompson (2008), scholars of human relations challenged the rational view of work and workers. From their perspective, informal and interpersonal relationships were seen to be of more importance than the formal structures espoused by rational theorists. Analyses of managers and workers at the micro-level demonstrated that participants are not solely motived by the goals of the organization. Rather, individuals within an organization are motivated by their own interests. Managers and workers strive to use the organization as a resource to obtain their personal goals, making organizations much more diverse and complex. For those inside the organization, maintaining and strengthening the organization becomes and end in itself, regardless of whether the organization is accomplishing its formal goals. Scott and Davis (2007) define the natural system perspective of organizations as "collectivities whose participants are pursuing multiple interests, both disparate and common, but who recognize the value of perpetuating the organization as an important resource" (p. 30).

At the macro-level of analysis, Chester Barnard and Philip Selznick took an adaptive system perspective similar to that of biology (Thompson, 2008). Along the natural system vein, it was theorized that organizations must adapt to the system to survive within their environment. Whereas the rational system perspective emphasized planned and controlled organizational design, the natural perspective viewed organizations as organic systems that evolved through indeterminate processes, and survival of the organization within the system was the true underlying goal.

Closed System Approach

The rational and natural system perspectives take a **closed system** approach of examining organizations (Scott & Davis, 2007). A closed system assumes that organizations contain a set of stable and easily identified participants. Presumably, "all elements and processes of interest are internal to the system being examined" (Thompson, 2008, p. xviii). The closed system perspective assumes the elements or variables of the organization being studied are few and sealed off from the environment, so the relationships between the variables may be controlled. Environmental forces outside the organization are seemingly fixed and predictable. However, just as individuals are whole units comprised of many systems (e.g., cardiovascular, digestive, and lymphatic) directly influenced by the environment, organizations are entities comprised of various systems or elements also heavily influenced by external factors of the environment. Enter open systems.

Open System Approach

Open systems or general systems theory recognizes that organizations are open to and dependent on their environment for information, personnel, and other resources (Scott & Davis, 2007; Thompson, 2008). There is an emphasis on the interdependent flows and activities between organizations. In general, this perspective assumes a system contains more variables than we can comprehend, measure, or control. Organizations are analogous to other scientific phenomena, such as microorganisms and plants, in that they operate as systems with a complex set of interdependent parts that each contribute to the whole. Systems, generally, vary in their levels of complexity, reactivity, and degree of coupling. In applying the open system perspective to the study of organizations, researchers have found that they are highly complex due to their numerous interdependent parts and wide variety of reactions. The system components or elements tend to be loosely rather than tightly coupled with each other, a topic more thoroughly addressed in our chapter on IORs. The open system perspective "… is less concerned with distinguishing formal from informal structure; instead, organizations are viewed as a system of interdependent activities" (Scott & Davis, 2007, p. 31). Activities are coordinated *between* organizations in a system, as well as *within* them between sub-systems. Moreover, open system has led to the development of concepts of organizational sets, populations, and fields which will be addressed in our discussion on organizational ecology.

Six Major Categories of an Organization

Pursuant to the open system approach, organizations are comprised of six major categories which allow us to examine the interdependencies both *between* and *within* organizations. These six basic characteristics are linked internally, as well as externally, and include: the environment, strategy and goals, work and technology, formal ways of organizing, informal ways of organizing, and people (Scott & Davis, 2007). Each of these categories contains distinct elements or factors which may be more directly observed and shared within and between organizations.

Environment

The first major category of an organization is the **environment**. It includes those "elements outside the organization that influence its ability to survive and achieve its ends" (Scott & Davis, 2007, p. 19). The environment is the "specific physical, technological, cultural, and social [surroundings] to which [an organization] must adapt" (p. 19). The environment has been defined in criminal justice as any external phenomenon, event, organization, group, or individual, which may bring to bear legal, political, economics, technological, or cultural forces which impact an organization (Stojkovic, Kalinich, & Klofas, 2015). The **external elements** outside of an organization include the clients, customers, or constituents that the organization serves, as well as other resources needed for survival. Moreover, personnel, information, and other resources inside the organization also come from

Figure 3.1: Six Elements of Organization

the environment. Criminal justice agencies depend on environmental elements such as statutory laws from legislators, resource allocations from politicians, and legitimacy, incident reports, and cases from citizens. Because an organization depends on its environment for resources, the environment influences the organization by providing both opportunities and constraints. From the open systems perspective, external elements to the organization may be more important than internal components (Scott & Davis, 2007).

In the world of for-profits and non-profits, organizations are capable of defining their domain within the environment. An organization's **domain** is the range of products sold, populations served, and services rendered that an organizations stakes out for itself (Levin & White, 1961). Government organizations, however, are more restricted in claiming or altering their domains. Governments must ask whether they should and can get involved, and are generally constrained by their police powers of protecting public health, safety, morality, and general welfare (McCarthy & Reynolds, 2003). Regardless of organizational type, they all connect to their **task environment** which refers to parts of the environment which are "relevant or potentially relevant to goal setting and goal attainment" (Thompson, 2008, p. 27). The four major sectors of a task environment include customers, suppliers, competitors, and regulators (Dill, 1958). "The relationship between an organization and its task environment is essentially one of exchange" (Thompson, 2008, p. 28). According to Levine and White (1961), the three main elements of exchange from the environment include the following: referral of cases, clients, or patients; giving or receiving labor services or training personnel; and sending or receiving resources other than labor, including funds, equipment, case and technical information.

Goals and Strategy

The second category of organizations is **goals and strategy** (Scott & Davis, 2007). The "goals" of an organization are the outputs or outcomes it is trying to achieve. "Strategy" refers to the choices an organization makes about the clients or markets it intends to serve, methods by which it plans to rival its competitors, and specific tactics it will employ to reach said goals. Using prosecutors as an example, their goals may be closing cases and controlling crime. Both of these goals may be achieved strategically through plea bargaining practices. Plea bargaining closes cases more quickly by avoiding trials and controls crime via specific deterrence and incapacitation, at least theoretically. Some organizations, such as for-profit corporations and non-profit charities, are able to choose their outputs, such as innovative products and services, as well as selecting their geographical and customer targets. In contrast, public agencies, such as sheriffs, courts, and jails, are limited or constrained in terms of services, clientele, jurisdictions, and budgets. As we will learn in the final section of this text, devising strategies and output objectives such as 'reducing citizen complaints of excessive use of force by 20% in three years' are key in planning, measuring, and obtaining criminal justice agency goals.

Work and Technology

The four remaining major components of organizations are all internal. **Internal elements** are contained within the organization. They are all linked to or interdependent upon each other inside the organization itself. And, as conceived by open systems, they are also linked to the external environment of various resources. It is through the component of "goals and strategy" discussed above that the organization and its internal elements are linked to the environment's resources or external elements.

One of the major components within an organization is **work and technology** (Scott & Davis, 2007). "Work" refers to the tasks required for the organization to obtain its goals. Applied to the courtroom, work consists of the tasks and functions of prosecuting defendants, defending the rights of the accused, and presiding over court hearings and trials. The term "technology" is used very broadly in the organizational literature. Technology can be defined as "the extent that the activities thus dictated by man's beliefs are judged to produce the desired outcomes" (Thompson, 2008, p. 14). It is a "mechanism for transforming inputs into outputs" (Scott & Davis, 2007, p. 22). Whereas some organizations process material inputs to produce outputs of goods to be sold, others process people to produce outputs such as educated children, healthier individuals, or law-abiding citizens. It is important to keep in mind that technology includes *all* methods of getting work done; it is not limited to current references of advanced electronics, such as computers and smart phones. Moreover, there is variation in the extent to which organizations utilize the technologies available, a matter further developed in our chapter on Criminal Justice Informatics.

Formal Organization

Another internal category generalizable to all organizations is the **formal ways of organizing or formal organization** (Scott & Davis, 2007). The formal organization is the explicit methods by which work gets done, and includes human resource practices, job design, and organization structure. "Human resources" refers to the practices used to recruit, hire, train, compensate, and promote employees and administrators. Public policing agencies, for example, typically use civil service processes for screening and recruiting potential candidates. In Florida, minimum standards include no felony convictions, submission to fingerprint and background checks, passing a medical examination, and successful completion of basic training and certification (Doerner, 2015). To retain officers, promotions and benefits, such as health insurance and pension, are often exclusive to the agency and are not transferrable to another agency.

"Job design" describes the tasks required of a single job (Scott & Davis, 2007). Prior to the modern industrial period, skilled craftsman performed the work of producing goods after learning their trade through lengthy apprenticeships. The labor of producing goods became divided, however, to increase production. Functions were broken down to repetitive tasks coordinated along a production line, as in the case of Henry Ford's Model T's in Detroit. The division of functions has likewise been adopted by criminal justice agencies. In the courtroom, the disparity between the large number of cases and limited court resources, as well as the lack of individualized justice, has been widely dubbed "assembly-line justice." Prosecutors' offices typically divide cases according to types of cases, with more experienced attorneys handling more serious crimes. Large offices in big cities are likely to divide attorneys' functions further by using "horizontal prosecution" which assigns prosecutors to specific stages of the case process, such as initial appearances, preliminary hearings, grand juries, trials, or appeals. Accordingly, attorneys could earn promotions to more difficult stages.

The final dimension of the formal organization category is "organizational structure" (Scott & Davis, 2007). After dividing functions and assigning the work to individuals as discussed above, the organization then groups those jobs into larger units, such as departments. The grouped units are typically coordinated by establishing a hierarchy with formal authorities and patterns of communications or chains of command. Whereas a corporation may be grouped according to functions, such as engineering, manufacturing, and marketing, criminal justice policing agencies group officers according to ranks (e.g., police officer, detective specialist, sergeant, lieutenant, captain, deputy chief, and chief) and specialties (patrol, detectives, vice, traffic, juveniles, special services, and training). In addition to grouping functions and establishing hierarchies, criminal justice organizations are notoriously divided according to jurisdictions. Court jurisdictions are defined along boundaries of geography (e.g., federal, state, circuit, and county), subject matter (e.g., traffic, misdemeanors, and felonies), and hierarchical functions (i.e., original and appellate). Jurisdictional boundaries directly affect the functions and groupings of the work performed by criminal justice organizations. Here, we have begun to conceptualize the internal structure of an organization. Later in this chapter, we will further develop the general levels of organizations and conceptualize structure in association with the environment (i.e., other organizations). It is the division of labor and subsequent coordination, both internally and externally, which defines organizational structure.

Informal Organization

In contrast to the formal organization component, the next internal category of an organization is **informal organization** (Scott & Davis, 2007). It is the fifth of our six overall major categories, and refers to the informal characteristics or ways of organizing. Whereas formal organizing characteristics are made explicit, informal organizing is not. "Informal organization refers to the emergent characteristics of the organization that affect how the organization operates" (p. 23). Most notably, informal characteristics of an organization include its culture, as well as internal and external social networks.

Broadly defined, "culture" refers to a group's general customs, beliefs, or way of life transmitted through human interaction. People convey notions of knowledge, meanings, beliefs, values, attitudes, ways of behaving, social hierarchies, and roles across generations within social, ethnic, and age groups. Organizations too have patterns of expectations, values, and beliefs shared by members (Scott & Davis, 2007).

Studies of culture in criminal justice are certainly not lacking. Police culture, for example, has been described as one of cynicism, secrecy, and insulation, and is widely known as the "blue curtain." The police sub-culture has been associated with covering up bad practices, such as excessive use of force in policing. Research has also shown that criminal justice agents across the system learn the shared norms of "normal crimes" that fit patterns of typical incidents, criminals, and victims (Sudnow, 1965). This shorthand categorization of normal crimes is deeply entrenched in criminal justice way of life. Literature on the cultures of criminal justice officials is beyond the scope of this text, and we do not seek to reiterate it here.

"Social networks" is another dimension of the informal organization (Scott & Davis, 2007). It refers to informal connections and communications between individuals. Members of an organization may seek others outside of the formal "chain of command" for information, advice, career advancement opportunities, or development of creative or innovative programs and services. Of course, there's the informal groups who lunch together or participate in other social activities outside of work. These informal social networks transpire between individuals of the same organization, as well as those of differing organizations.

Prosecutors, defense attorneys, and judges may be characterized as a network. Each is independent of the other due to their separate administrative structures and functions. In Florida, for example, State Attorneys, Public Defenders, and Circuit Judges are each elected separately at the circuit level. Although they are independently administered, these three main characters in the courtroom are interdependent in their mutual goal of closing cases. The dynamics and interactions between prosecutors, defense attorneys, and judges has been labeled the "courtroom workgroup" (Eisenstein & Jacob, 1991). This network relationship is characterized by informal plea bargaining processes, rather than idealistic adversarial traditions. In addition to learning the formal rules, workgroup newcomers are socialized as to the informal rules of behavior, such as expeditious closing of cases. Outsiders are often surprised to observe cooperation and social familiarity between the work group actors, as opposed to pointed arguments over evidentiary processes and determinations of guilt.

People

The final essential organizational category is **people** (Scott & Davis, 2007). Individuals who participate in an organization may do so in varying degrees. The decision as to whether organizational leaders, employees, clients, suppliers, lawmakers, and other stakeholders constitute "participants" may be difficult to define and vary according to the situation or program. Individual participants bring with them characteristics that influence the organization. These traits include the knowledge and skills suited to the performance of their tasks, as well as their needs and preferences, broader experiences, and demographics such as age, gender, and ethnicity. Characteristics of leaders, in particular, have a direct impact on the organization. Authorities are often categorized according to Weber's typology of traditional, rational-legal, or charismatic leadership.

Conclusion

We just identified and described the six general categories of an organization: environment, goals and strategies, work and technology, formal organization, informal organization, and people. These components are not mutually exclusive; they interact with each other both inside and outside the organization to create interdependent systems and sub-systems. As mentioned earlier and discussed in more detail later, administrators are responsible for determining their agency's goals and strategies. It is the category of goals and strategies through which an organization (and its four internal elements) is primarily coupled with and legitimized by its environment.

At this juncture, it may be prudent to note the organizational components that are and are not emphasized in the remainder of this text. First, we do not directly address individual characteristics or interpersonal relationships which operate at the individual level. As such, we do not review the characteristics of "people," such as age, race, gender, and experiential background, which are imported into an agency or courtroom workgroup. Likewise, the "informal organization" and its dimensions of culture and social networks are not explicitly addressed. This includes topics such as individual perceptions by citizens and victims, excessive use of force, violations of civil and Constitutional rights, job stress and burnout, misconduct, promotional aspirations, or staff-inmate relations. By extension, group relationships and perceptions based on observations of individuals, such as collective efficacy and procedural justice, are not included. The literature in these areas is extensive and perhaps more applicable to management rather than administration. We do not seek to repeat it here.

Two of the three dimensions of the "formal organization" component have also been heavily researched and published. The criminal justice literature is saturated in the two areas of human resource practices and job design. Questions as to how officers, prosecutors, judges and the like obtain their positions of authority, as well as descriptions of their roles, have been thoroughly vetted. In fact, numerous introductory texts serve to educate the reader on these topics. Again, we see no purpose in regurgitating the general qualifications and functions of criminal justice personnel.

Now for those components we do emphasize. The focus of this text is administrative decision-making as it relates to planning and managing change at the organizational level. Criminal justice administrators exist at the highest echelon within an agency, making decisions about the organization's goals and strategies regarding clients served, specific tactics, and competitors. An understanding of administrative decision-making in criminal justice agencies beyond normative and rational assumptions is sorely lacking. Accordingly, the organizational components addressed in this text focus on administrative choices related to the areas of agency goals and strategies, environmental ties, the work and technology of the organization, and the third dimension of formal organization—structure.

Key Words

Bounded rationality
Bureaucracy
Closed systems
Culture
Domain
Environment
External elements
Formal organization
Goals
Human resources
Informal organization

Internal elements
Job design
Levels of analysis
Macro
Meso
Micro
Natural systems
Normative perspective
Open systems
Organizational structure
Paradigm

People
Psychological perspective
Rational systems
Social networks
Sociological perspective
Strategy

System
Task environment
Technology
Uncertainty
Work

Organizational Basics: Structure and Strategy

Learning Objectives:

1. Define organizational structure.
2. Describe and differentiate external structure and internal structure.
3. Identify, describe, and analyze the three major internal levels of organizations.
4. Identify, describe, and analyze the three types of organizational technologies and describe how each is related to achieving outcomes.
5. Apply the three types of organizational technologies to criminal justice, particularly as they relate to outcomes.
6. Describe and analyze the association between an organization's task environment and subsequent contingencies and constraints.
7. Describe and differentiate inputs and outputs.
8. Define strategy and describe its association with defining outcome preferences and specifying cause-effect relations.
9. Analyze the four strategies of computation, judgment, compromise, and inspiration and apply them to criminal justice agencies.
10. Define strategic planning and how it is used to manage interdependencies between organizations.
11. Define and describe controlling strategies. Be sure to include the concepts of sanctions, consent decrees, incentives, alternative sources, and prestige.
12. Define and describe cooperative strategies and distinguish them from controlling strategies.
13. Discuss how criminal justice organizations may use controlling or cooperative strategies to reduce environmental contingencies and constraints.
14. Discuss how administrators use strategies to shape their organization's internal and external structures. Be sure to include the concepts of tools

(informal and formal), slack, domain, total institution, departmentalization, and hierarchy.
15. Describe and analyze organizational strategy and structure as they are applied to police agencies.
16. Describe the responsibilities of criminal justice agency administrators and what happens if there is a failure to make a clear distinction between institutional and managerial functions.

Introduction

In this chapter, we begin to build-out the components of organizations outlined in the previous chapters. One of our themes in the text is that criminal justice organizations (CJOs) are increasingly utilizing non-CJOs to assist in achieving organizational goals. This "interorganizational" approach requires different ways of planning, implementing and evaluating organizational efforts than required in "command and control" settings. This chapter begins the discussion of aligning strategies and operations (structure). This also requires discussion of constraints and contingencies on one of the potentially most powerful sectors in the civil government. This chapter provides the foundation on which much of Section Two is built. It sets the stage for returning to how such alignments can be achieved in Section Three. It may be one of the "thickest" chapters in the text, so be prepared to read it more than once; but, it is important information. It will all come together soon!

Structure

This chapter will more thoroughly define and describe organizational structure and strategy, both generally and as they apply to criminal justice agencies. "The **structure** of an organization can be defined simply as the sum total of the ways in which it divides its labor into distinct tasks and then achieves coordination among them" (Mintzberg, 1979, p. 2). It is the dividing of tasks and re-coordination of said tasks that defines an organization's structure both internally and externally. In an effort to understand differentiations in organizational structure, researchers have studied variations both within and among organizations. Theorists have described the general levels and characteristics of organizations and how they relate to their environment. These general theories have been applied to the study criminal justice organizations, particularly large police agencies. This chapter will review the general descriptions of external and internal structures, organizational levels, and various characteristics. Then, we'll learn how administrators use strategies to coordinate the structures of their organization. Finally, the application of these theories to the structures of large police agencies will be reviewed.

Organizations are open systems in the sense that they are externally connected to each other. Criminal justice is often portrayed as a system in which police, courts, and corrections are connected by cases. Often, we limit our perceptions of the criminal justice "system" to the flow or processing of offenders through these three primary agencies. However, agencies are linked together in a number of ways. As discussed earlier in the description of external elements, organizations depend on each other for many resources, such as funding, personnel, and information.

Thus, an organization's **external structure** is determined by its environment and linkages with other organizations, otherwise known as interorganizational relationships. In general, organizations are connected to each other through systems of multiple technical flows of inputs, throughputs, and outputs (Scott & Davis, 2007). Organizations are linked not only through technology, but also tasks, territories, positions, offices, responsibilities, opportunities, rewards, sanctions, intentions and actions, events, means and ends, processes and outcomes, and hierarchical positions such as staff and administrators (Weick, 1976). The linkages among organizations tend to be more varied in more complex environments, which means greater variation in organizational structures (Lawrence & Lorsch, 1967). Accordingly, more complex environments increase the need to devote more resources to coordinating tasks with other organizations. Likewise, a less complex environment is associated with easier integration of elements between organizations. The linkages amongst organizations vary in not only complexity, but also in the length of reaction times to each other and tightness or looseness of coupling among system components (Boulding, 1956).

In general, organizations structure themselves to obtain the resources they need from an environment often fraught with uncertainty (Thompson, 2008). More complex environments require greater coordination of elements between organizations, which increases the number of variables and degree of uncertainty in decision-making. Uncertainty in decision-making creates problems administrative leaders must solve. Contrary to the rational perspective, organizations have limited capacities to gather and process information to solve problems. Making decisions between alternative resources requires the development of processes for searching and learning (i.e., problem solving processes). Rather than making optimal decisions which maximize efficiency, the decisions made by administrative leaders are subject to bounded rationality or limited information. Thus, an organization's structure may be merely satisfactory, rather than optimally efficient.

In addition to external relationships with other organizations, researchers have studied variations of **internal structures** within organizations. Organizations are comprised of various subcomponents or sub-units with various responsibilities and functions. Parsons (1956a, 1956b) asserted that three general structure levels exist within organizations: production or technical core, management, and institutional. In 1967, Thompson (2008) incorporated these three levels to develop his contingency theory of organizational design and structure. He asserted that organizations face problems which need to be solved at each of these levels, with technologies and environments being major sources of uncertainty. According to contingency theory, an organization's design and structure would be dependent upon its internal technologies and environmental domain, as well as the contingencies and constraints imposed by the organization's task environment. Let's describe each of the three internal structure levels in more detail. Then, we will define and describe organizational contingencies and constraints.

Technical Level

Thompson (2008) proposed that each of Parson's three organizational levels varied in uncertainty, as well as criteria for rationality. The technical functions or tasks are found at the organization's first internal level, the **technical core.** This level includes the technology or work to be done, as well as the materials or people to be processed. According to Thompson, uncertainty increases with the number of variables or technologies to be coordinated; therefore, it is advantageous for an organization to use a rational or closed system of logic to protect its technical core from external influences or exogenous variables. Ideally, the organization wants to eliminate uncertainty to have full knowledge about cause/effect relationships. Since organizations have expressed goals and **outcomes**, decision makers want to achieve what Thompson calls "*instrumentally perfect technology*" in which the technical core always produces the desired outcomes. In comparison "*less perfect instrument technology*" produces the desired outcome only part of the time due to a lack of knowledge or certainty. (*Instrument rationality* refers to whether actions produce the desired outcomes, and should not be confused with *economic rationality* which refers to obtaining results with the least amount of expenditure of resources.)

Organizations have desired outcomes (we return to this in the final section of the text). In the case of criminal justice, outcomes may be reducing crime or recidivism or increasing public safety. The degree of certainty in achieving an organization's desired outcomes may lie in the variations of different types of technology. According to Thompson (2008), there are three types of technologies: long-linked, mediating, and intensive. Organizations with **long-linked technologies** produce standard products at a repetitive, constant rate. Products are created and assembled through a series of linked inputs and outputs, and organizations may be linked wherein one organization's output is the input for another. For example, a manufacturer may acquire steel from a supplier to forge an engine block, which becomes an output to be sold to a car repair shop. Long-linked technology is the original depiction of technical rationality—the mass production line. In comparison, a **mediating technology** links multiple clients or customers to a service that is standardized. For example, large numbers of depositors and borrowers are linked to commercial banks, which are regulated according to standardized accounting practices (p. 16). Other mediating technologies include insurance agencies, telephone companies, and employment agencies.

The third and final type of technology, categorized according to uncertainty as to outcomes, is **intensive technology** (Thompson, 2008). Organizations with intensive technologies use a variety of techniques to "achieve a change in a specific object; but the selection, combination, and order of application are determined by feedback from the object itself. When the object is human, this intensive technology is regarded as 'therapeutic' but the same technical logic is found also in the construction industry" (p. 17). These organizations provide custom technologies designed for a specific project or individual case. Successful outcomes require organizations to possess the capacities needed to do the job. Those capacities are applied to the individual person or project in a customized order in consideration with multiple situational factors. Additional examples of intensive technologies include general hospitals, research teams, and military combat teams.

When considering the application of these three general categories of technologies to criminal justice, we must consider not only the processes of coordinating tasks, but, perhaps more importantly, the certainty of desired outcomes. For those working at the technical core, otherwise known as street-level bureaucrats (Lipsky, 1979), the technology of criminal justice may appear similar to the long-linked or mediating categories. In fact, the courts have been likened to an "assembly line." Police officers close cases by making arrests. Prosecutors close cases by obtaining a guilty plea or conviction. Correction officers maintain custody and control over incarcerated offenders. The work of criminal justice officials is regulated through laws, making the processes quite standardized. Large numbers of offenders are processed through the system continuously. Seemingly, there appears to be a high level of certainty about outcomes.

The biggest problem with the above application of criminal justice to long-linked and mediating technologies, however, is in the "outcome" definitions or expectations. From the organizational perspective, processes and outputs should not be confused with outcomes—arrests, closed cases, and custody and control of inmates are steps in a process. They are the tasks which must be coordinated between criminal justice agencies in a complex system. The true outcomes of the system are reductions in crime and increased public safety, as expressed in most criminal justice agency mission statements. (This is a matter we will discuss further in the section on organizational planning.)

Criminal justice more aptly fits into the intensive technology category based on expressed agency outcomes of reducing crime and increasing public safety. These outcomes are not "instrumentally perfect." The desired outcomes are not reliably or inevitably produced. Rather, criminal justice is a "less perfect" technology. Desired outcomes are produced only part of the time; our knowledge and control over the variables that cause criminal behavior is admittedly uncertain; and the technologies of police, prosecutors, judges, public defenders, parole and probation officers, corrections officers, and other service providers, such as mental and physical health, are complex in their coordination.

The technology of criminal justice is similar to that of public health. Just as the public health system exists to improve population health, criminal justice exists to improve public safety. Public health and criminal justice are socially supported so they may prevent and intervene in the factors that produce poor health outcomes and criminal behavior, respectively (Akers, Potter, & Hill, 2013). Policymakers' efforts to impose the rational model of perfect technology standards to criminal justice outcomes is misleading, if not disingenuous, and should be resisted by administrators, practitioners, and researchers alike. The efficiencies and certainties of for-profit corporations are nothing like those of criminal justice. We are, however, capable of planning, implementing, and assessing outcomes—matters addressed later in this text.

Management Level

The first internal level of an organization is that of technology, which we just covered. The second level is managerial services (Thompson, 2008). **Management** mediates between the two other organizational levels. It serves the technical group by allocating resources, and controls it by carrying out administrative decisions about tasks, employment, scale of operations, policies, and the like. In essence, it implements the decisions of top-level administrators. Parson's (1956a, 1956b) conceptualization envisioned management as a mediator between the two extremes of the closed-system qualities of the technical core and open-system qualities of the institutional environment. According to Thompson's theory of contingency, the management level is not a primary source of uncertainty and variation, unlike technology and the environment. Organizations with different technologies would, theoretically, have different management and administrative structures. Likewise, organizations with different environments would call for different structures at all three internal levels.

Institutional or Administrative Level

The final level of an organization is the **institutional or administrative level** (Thompson, 2008). Unlike managers, administrators possess the right to control and spend resources outside the organization, as well as making commitments on behalf of the organization they represent. The administrative level has the greatest amount of uncertainty due to its exposure to the environment. Those with administrative authority interact and negotiate with outside organizations and groups on a continuous basis. Uncertainty looms large as they have little, if any, formal authority or control over environmental elements, such as codified laws, best practice standards, or public interest and opinion. Hence, this level is much more open to the system, as compared to the technical and managerial levels.

Parsons (1956a, 1956b) initially dubbed this the "institutional" level, meaning that society must perceive it as being legitimate. To be successful, the organization and its administration must be established as a fundamental part of culture, behaving in socially acceptable ways. The concept of institutional legitimacy is common in criminal justice literature (e.g., Crank, 2003; Crank & Langworthy, 1992, 1996; McCorkle & Crank, 1996). Institutional legitimacy and its implied connection to administrative decisions is an underlying theme in most discussions of criminal justice agencies.

The structure of an organization is shaped by its dependence on inputs and outputs. Being dependent on the environment for supplies of inputs and demands for outputs generates multiple sources of uncertainty for organizational administrators (Thompson, 2008). At this level of an organization, administrators are tasked with managing their dependencies by developing and maintaining relationships with other organizations to exchange resources.

According to Levine and White (1961), the three main elements of exchange from the environment include: 1) referrals of cases, clients, or patients, 2) giving or receiving labor services or training personnel, and 3) sending or receiving resources other than labor, such as information, funds, or equipment.

Organizations exchange elements with each other, forming a network of interdependence (Thompson, 2008). Administrative management of these interdependencies requires that organizations adapt to the resources within their environment. The network of organizations upon which the organization depends (i.e., **task environment**), may restrict access to resources through contingencies and constraints.

Contingencies and Constraints

The exchange of organizational elements, such as information or clients, may be subject to certain contingencies, such as laws. **Contingencies** occur when the task environment finds it "necessary or desirable to discontinue support to an organization" (Thompson, 2008, p. 30). Recent changes to state laws concerning the legality of marijuana, for example, would greatly impact therapeutic drug courts that divert first-time, non-violent users away from traditional court processes. States that legalize recreational use of cannabis may substantively reduce or completely eliminate the utilization of drug courts designed to target marijuana users.

Organizations may also find their access to resources to be constrained. **Constraints** are limits on the capacities of supporting organizations within the task environment and the lack of feasible alternatives. County or circuit courts, for example, may be financially constrained if their budgets are dependent solely upon local taxes. Rural communities, in particular, are heavily impacted by economic factors and inadequate tax bases (Weisheit, Falcone, & Wells, 2006). Taking a single death penalty case to trial could bankrupt a local government due to budgetary constraints, making it necessary for administrative leaders to secure additional funding or an alternative venue for prosecution.

Contingencies and constraints create sources of uncertainty for organizational **inputs** (Thompson, 2008; Sylvia & Sylvia, 2012). Within the systems theory framework, organizations receive inputs from the environment. Inputs are those elements needed for survival. Some organizations may have many alternative sources for inputs in their environment, while others do not. If there is a high demand for particular inputs or the environment does not have the capacity to provide them, then resources are constrained. This would be particularly relevant to criminal justice agencies, as they rely on legislators or local government for their budgets. Ironically, local police, courts, and corrections must work cooperatively to achieve their goals, while simultaneously competing with each other for the same tax dollars.

In general, organizations are also dependent on their environment for **output** demands (Thompson, 2008; Sylvia & Sylvia, 2012). Organizational survival depends on whether its outputs are sufficiently valued by actors in the environment. If not, it will fail to procure the inputs it needs. Outputs may include goods, services, regulations, or support for other organizations or programs. It may be that a single organization is the sole provider of a particular output, or they may be competing with many organizations to sell their output.

In varying degrees, police, courts, and corrections may be the sole provider of their services. However, competition is found in the private sector for services in policing and corrections. Correction agencies are particularly vulnerable to lawmakers' privatization efforts. Administrative decision-makers of for-profits and non-profits (e.g., CoreCivic, The GEO Group, Inc., Pride Integrated Services, Inc., and Judicial Correction Services, Inc.) have greater control over their interdependencies on others, as they have more latitude in changing and negotiating their services provided and populations served, as compared to government agencies bound by legislative and jurisdictional constraints. As we will learn in our section on organizational planning, successful program planning and evaluation requires a full account of inputs, as well as well-defined and measurable outputs (Sylvia & Sylvia, 2012).

Strategy

The administrative designs of organizational structures are not determined solely by the environmental contingencies and constraints, however (Thompson, 2008). Organizations have developed multiple strategies to manage their dependencies on others. **Strategy**, in general, describes the abstract process of managing interdependencies by coordinating organizational structures (Alexander, 1995). Earlier, we defined it as the choices an organization makes about the clients or markets it intends to serve, methods by which it plans to rival its competitors, and specific tactics it will employ to reach organizational goals (Scott & Davis, 2007).

According to Thompson (2008), strategies are often made by a dominant group that makes decisions based on two major factors: *outcome preferences* and specificity of *cause-effect associations*. If the outcomes to be achieved can be ranked in preference and there is a clear understanding of cause and effect relations in achieving those outcomes, the group will use a *"computational strategy."* If the relationship between cause and effect is not clear, whereas the outcomes are, then the group will use their best judgment or *"judgmental strategy."* If the group or organization faces conflicting outcome preferences, as in the case of prison goals of both custody and rehabilitation, then the strategy is to *"compromise."* Finally, if there is uncertainty in both cause-effect relationships and outcomes preferences, the decision-makers are likely to use an *"inspirational strategy."*

The clarity of cause-effect associations and desired outcomes is often lacking in criminal justice planning. Our institutions and programs typically rest on the soft strategies of compromise and inspiration stemming from philosophical beliefs about deterrence, incapacitation, rehabilitation, retribution, as well as due process and crime control. Police are expected to use force when public safety is threatened, while simultaneously upholding individual rights. Likewise, court officials must follow due process procedures for individuals while controlling crime in the community. Correctional institutions are expected to severely deprive inmates, yet release well-adjusted citizens back into the community. We will delve into the topic of cause-effect relationships in later discussions of research, data, and planning. Administrative decision-making can and should be based on clearer understandings of preferred outcomes and factors that are more likely to bring them about.

Strategic planning is one method of defining outcomes and the methods for achieving them. **Strategic planning** is the mapping of broad agency goals, such as program jurisdiction, interest group relationships, congressional allies, agency domain, agency functions and clientele, and maximizing resources (Sylvia & Sylvia, 2012). Strategic plans include variables that can be manipulated to achieve organizational goals, and are used to plan for and reduce external contingencies and constraints on inputs and outputs—i.e., managing interdependencies between organizations (Thompson, 2008). Interdependencies are managed by gaining the power or independence to act without regard for external pressures or actions of outsiders. In plain terms, organizations want to decide on their own goals and don't want to depend on other organizations to get what they need. (Don't we all?)

Controlling Strategies

The structural planning strategies for coordinating resources and activities between organizations may be controlling or cooperative (Alexander, 1995; Thompson, 2008). **Controlling strategies** (also known as competitive strategies) seek to reduce environmental contingencies or constraints by controlling critically needed resources. This strategy may include efforts to control the behavior of another organization or group by somehow "biasing their decisions to produce action which they might otherwise not have taken" (Alexander, 1995, p. 37). Controlling strategies may include methods for invoking *sanctions*, such as withholding resources or exerting external oversight. In the case of criminal justice agencies accused of corruptive or racially biased practices, sanctions routinely include federal investigations.

Investigations of criminal justice agencies have been conducted over the last several decades (O'Hara, 2012). More recently, government officials of Ferguson, Missouri, were investigated by the Department of Justice (DOJ) after Officer Darren Wilson shot and killed Michael Brown, an unarmed African American male (Berman & Lowery, 2015; Department of Justice, 2015). The incident grabbed national headlines as protests resulted in the mobilization of the National Guard and the use of tear gas, rubber bullets, and mass arrests. In 2015, the DOJ found that several local government and criminal justice agencies engaged in racially biased practices which violated the First, Fourth, and Fourteenth Amendments of citizens. Five local officials were subsequently fired or resigned, including the city manager and municipal court clerk, as well as a municipal court judge, police captain, and police sergeant (Ferguson Manager, 2015; Graham, 2015).

The Ferguson, Missouri, investigation is an extreme example of local intervention by federal authorities. Typically, controlling strategies against criminal justice agencies involve civil law suits by stakeholders for violations of civil rights, such as prison overcrowding or biased hiring practices. Criminal justice agencies may enter into "consent decrees" when they are sued. A **consent decree** is a court settlement to resolve a dispute between two parties without admitting to criminal guilt or civil liability. The plaintiff is granted injunctive relief since the defendant agrees to make changes to the organization. In the meantime, the court maintains jurisdiction over the case.

In addition to sanctions, controlling strategies may provide *incentives*, such as funding or access to service populations. The federal government frequently incentivizes criminal justice agencies and researchers at the local level to plan, implement, and assess innovative programs. More specifically, the Department of Justice provides numerous grants annually through the Office of Community Oriented Policing Services, Office of Justice Programs, and Office on Violence Against Women to support innovative practices for crime control and prevention programs at the state and local levels.

Another controlling or competitive strategy is the development of *alternative sources* of inputs and outputs (Thompson, 2008). For instance, universities increase the number of students and tuition as a means of reducing reliance on state tax dollars. An organization that obtains a resource from multiple sources or provides its products or services to multiple target populations reduces its reliance on any single entity. Absolute control over inputs and outputs are limited by law, however. For instance, commercial laws prohibit monopolistic competition in the marketplace. Federal and state antitrust laws, such as the Sherman Act of 1890 and Clayton Act of 1914, regulate the organization of corporations to promote fair competition.

Other types of organizations, such as universities, government agencies, and law firms, compete with each other by acquiring influence and power through *prestige* (Thompson, 2008). Prestige is the projection of a favorable image, and allows organizations to wield informal power by ensuring a sufficient number of clients, donors, or investors. For example, prestigious non-profits may be able to raise funds on their own more easily. Independent fund raising means a non-profit can resist the need to partner and be subject to an umbrella organization, such as United Way. In the case of universities, faculty publications and research grants elevate the school's academic prestige in higher education. In the field of criminal justice, criminal defense attorneys must typically build a reputation prior to opening a private practice. Otherwise, they depend on government funds while practicing as public defenders.

Cooperative Strategies

Cooperative strategies may also be used to manage interdependencies and reduce environmental uncertainties (Thompson, 2008). Cooperative strategies are voluntary commitments made between organizations to exchange elements. Unlike controlling strategies, organizations are not coerced or biased into the activities. Rather, there is an effort to build consensus. Cooperative commitments require that exchange partners demonstrate the capacity or ability to uphold their end of the deal. The general organizational literature describes a spectrum of cooperative strategies, which include public-private partnerships, contracts, coalitions, alliances, joint ventures, federations, and associations (Alexander, 1995; Thompson, 2008).

Competitive and cooperative strategies for managing interdependencies vary in degree of commitment (Alexander, 1995; Thompson, 2008). Greater commitments between organizations results in greater constraints. For example, informal exchanges of information between the prosecutor and defense attorney require less time and effort, as compared to following formal discovery procedures. Thus, organizations seek relationships with the least commitment or constraints possible. They are more likely to choose the simplest, least constraining structure toward managing their interdependencies with other organizations (Scott & Davis, 2007). In other terms, they prefer to be loosely coupled, rather than tightly coupled with each other. The choice of strategy suggests the need to balance "autonomy and adaptability on one hand, and stability and certainty on the other" (p. 240).

The Relationship Between Strategy and Structure

At this point, you may have noticed that organizational strategies and structures are theoretically related (Alexander, 1995; Scott & Davis, 2007; Thompson, 2008). Indeed, the popular phrase "form [forever] follows function" refers to the principle that the shape of a building should be based on its intended purpose. It is at the institutional level where decisions of strategy and structure are made. Administrators use strategies to shape the internal and external structures which, in turn, affect each other. Below, we discuss how administrators' strategic decisions affect the organization both internally and externally.

While theories explaining the external structures or links between an organization and its environment are well-established, empirical studies in criminal justice are rare. We'll describe these theories (e.g., resource dependence, institutional, and transactional cost theories) in more detail in our chapter on IORs. For now, we will conceptualize the diverse spectrum of structured activities through which organizations interact with each other (i.e., external structure). Administrators use these activities to manage their dependence on other groups for the exchange of various elements the organization needs (i.e., strategy).

Interactions between organizations make up the external structure. These activities vary along a continuum, ranging from the simple, single transaction to the full merger of two organizations (Alexander, 1995; Guo & Acar, 2005; Scott & Davis, 2007). The general organizational literature often refers to coordinating structures such as coalitions, joint ventures, federations, and associations. Organizations can link their activities for acquiring inputs or outputs such as information, clients, labor, technology, specialized functions, or the like through **tools** (a more concrete or specific term, as compared to "strategies") (Alexander, 1995). Tools may be *informal*, such as interpersonal information exchanges during meetings or telephone calls. These are the most commonly used tools for coordination, and often coincide with formal tools.

Tools used to coordinate activities between organizations may also be *formal*, and link organizations through mechanisms such as contracts, overlapping board memberships, or co-locations. The government is also linked to organizations through its use of tools, such as regulations, tort laws, loans, contracts, grants, taxes, fees and charges, insurance, and government-sponsored enterprises (Salamon, 2002). Essentially, tools "can be 'nested' in or used in the framework of strategies" (Alexander, 1995, p. 41). Therefore, tools serve as manifest evidence of the relationships and interactions between organizations. Tools form the structure by which organizations formally or informally share decision-making, resources, and information.

As we learned earlier, the internal structure of an organization typically consists of three general levels: technical core, management, and institutional (Parsons, 1956a, 1956b). Institutional leaders are responsible for designing the technical and managerial levels for the processing of inputs and outputs. The technical core, which produces the goods or services to meet the organization's goals, relies on the top administrative level to provide the necessary conditions for success. Likewise, administrators rely on the technical core and managerial level to provide what March and Simon (1958) call "slack" (Thompson, 2008, p. 150). **Slack** refers to the capacities of an organization to do more. By developing the capacities of those at the technical and managerial levels, administrators create an ability to take advantage of opportunities from the environment. If an organization can respond to opportunities as they arise, they may subsequently make demands on the environment.

Strategic planning for the future likely involves changing the organization's structure. Restructuring often occurs at the technical level through the adoption of more functions, which expands the organization's domain (Thompson, 2008). **Domain** is the work claimed to be done by the organization, and it is shaped by the range of products it provides, services it renders, and the population it serves (Levine & White, 1961). Therefore, administrators plan structural changes by modifying the technologies included, populations served, and services rendered (Thompson, 2008).

Expanding an organization's domain may be shaped by its type of technology. According to Thompson (2008), organizations using intensive technologies (in which processes are customized and outcomes are not guaranteed) tend to incorporate the object worked on. That is, the organization becomes a **total institution** whereby residents are cut off from society for a period of time (Goffman, 1961). Total institutions would include correctional facilities such as prisons, jails, youth detention centers, and juvenile residential facilities. In the case of mediating technologies, such as banks and insurance companies, organizations expand their domains by increasing the populations served (Thompson, 2008). Long-linked technologies, such as an assembly-line, are more likely to combine the successive stages of production by expanding control over resources and manufacturing technologies.

Overall, simple organizations have fewer linkages and less specialization, whereas complex organizations have a number of different components which are departmentalized and connected. Two common methods of coordinating or structuring larger, more complex organizations are through departmentalization and hierarchy (Thompson, 2008). **Departmentalization** refers to the grouping of positions or components within an organization. Departments may be grouped according to common purposes, common processes, a particular clientele, or a particular geographic area. **Hierarchy** refers to degrees of highness and lowness, but also includes the "clustering or combination of interdependent groups to handle aspects of coordination which are beyond the scope of any of its components" (Thompson, 2008, p. 59). Departmentalization and hierarchy are both familiar concepts in the literature on the quasi-militaristic style of policing. As early as 1970, Egon Bittner argued that the bureaucratic military structure of the police, with its hierarchical and departmental command structure, was inconsistence with the goal of developing "professional discretionary methods for crime control and peacekeeping" (Kappeler, 2006, p. 191).

Structure and Strategy: A Criminal Justice Example

In criminal justice, the conceptualization of external and internal agency structures and their associations with strategies (or lack thereof) have been well established (Kappeler, 2006; Stojkovic, Klofas, & Kalinich, 2010). Empirical examinations of agency structures, however, have focused primarily on internal characteristics. In the area of policing, studies of police structures and strategies have been best developed and serve as an illustration of how general organizational concepts may be applied to criminal justice agencies, both theoretically and empirically. Let's review the assumptions upon which police organizations were built and the study of police agencies at the organizational level of analysis.

The modern police organization was born in London out of Sir Robert Peel's Metropolitan Police Act of 1829 (Walker, 2011). The first of Peel's nine principles of law enforcement stated police should prevent or deter crime and disorder. Moreover, there was a clear connection made between the public and the police in that each relied on the other and each were one and the same. The belief that a visible police presence would deter crime was a core principle, and most accepted this idea on faith. Police foot patrols, and later vehicle patrols, became a main function upon which police agencies were structured.

The good faith beliefs of using police patrols to deter crime held true until the 1970s as research in criminology and criminal justice came of age. In 1973, the landmark Kansas City Preventive Patrol Experiment tested the deterrence effect of police vehicle patrols (Kelling, Pate, Dieckman, & Brown, 1974). After matching 15 beats on community characteristics, such as median income and number of calls for service, and randomly varying the levels of preventive patrol, the researchers found that level of patrol had no effect on either crime rates or citizen's fear of crime. A similar experiment was used to assess the effectiveness of foot patrol in Newark, New Jersey, which confirmed that varying levels of foot patrol had no effect on the crime rate (The Police Foundation, 1981). Citizen fear of crime, however, was improved.

The patrol studies of the 1970s "shattered traditional assumptions about patrol strategy" (Walker, 1984). As a result, administrative leaders and theorists began to propose new strategies or styles of policing. Notably, Wilson and Kelling's (1982) proposal to return to a "watchman" style of policing sparked debates as to the changes in police-citizen contacts brought on by the "technological revolution" from foot to car patrol.

Since the 1980s, four policing strategic models have been well conceptualized (Greene, 2000). Traditional policing is the original quasi-militaristic model which has existed in the U.S. since the early 20th century. The other three models, community-oriented policing (COP), problem-oriented policing (POP), and zero-tolerance policing (ZTP), typically emphasize reforms through greater interactions with the community. Theoretically, each model varies in its interactions or activities between police and community stakeholders. For example, the exchange of information for traditional policing and ZTP theoretically flows downward from police to community. In contrast, information flows horizontally between police and community in COP and POP. Interactions with outside agencies are described as being "poor and intermittent" under traditional policing. Under COP and POP, policing agencies are conceptualized as "integrating" their activities with other agencies.

Overall, the implications for changing the structure of a police agency are different for each of the four policing strategies (Greene, 2000). The two most extreme or juxtaposed models are traditional and COP strategies. Under the traditional model, the internal structure of a modern police agency would be characterized as having a command and control hierarchy, centralized authority, specialized departments, and elaborate rules and policies. External relations would require that a traditional police agency only fend off the environment. Accordingly, most U.S. police agencies would need to make few, if any, structural changes to fit the traditional strategic model. In contrast, a COP (and to a lesser degree, POP) agency would have an internal structure that was flatter and less specialized. Officers would be generalists and their training would be more community-focused. External relations would require partnerships and greater interactions with other agencies and stakeholders. A typical U.S. police agency adopting the COP strategy would need to make many changes, as the organization would work closely with the environment (i.e., citizens and other agencies).

In addition to theoretical debates, researchers have empirically examined police agency structures. In the general literature, sociologist Peter Blau (1965) proposed that an organization's structure could be empirically measured according to various dimensions such as size (e.g., number of employees, total assets); complexity (e.g., number of objectives, number of locations); specialization (e.g., number of occupational positions, distribution of members, number of functionally specialized departments); bureaucratization (e.g., proportion of personnel in administrative or staff positions); and hierarchy (e.g., number of hierarchical levels, average span of control, proportion of personnel in managerial positions). Theoretically, more complex environments would result in more complex organizational structures with more departments, specialties, and the like.

Relying heavily on the work of Blau, Robert Langworthy (1986) pioneered the examination of how organization size, task, and environment each related to structures of police agencies. Langworthy found that police agencies were not "significantly constrained with respect to agency size, technology, population size, change, complexity or local government" (p. 279).

> The empirical fact that all types of municipal police agencies are found policing all types of populations and in all kinds of local governments makes it amply apparent that it is not impossible to place any type of police agency in any setting. The criteria for police organization thus becomes purpose (p. 279).

Langworthy (1986) extended the general literature on organizations to criminal justice, paving the way for others to follow.

Theoretical debates as to policing strategies and breakthrough findings of patrol and agency structure set the stage for funding and research on policing strategies and structures. Community policing advocates argued that agency structures needed to change (Redlinger, 1994). Twentieth century traditional policing structures were centralized due to technological advancements, such as radios and motorized vehicles, during industrialization (Skogan, 1990). Moreover, police narrowed their focus to serious crimes and sought efficiency by measuring officer "outputs" such as response time. It was argued that officer-citizen interactions had weakened under these traditional structures, and COP was the better strategy.

In an effort to plan and implement COP at the local level, federal funding was provided to designated sites in the 1980s. Two such sites were Houston and Newark. Wesley Skogan (1990) evaluated the Houston and Newark COP projects using a mixed methods approach of interviews, observations, and administrative data. Data were collected on key elements which included "decentralization, police-citizen interaction, information-sharing, responsiveness to civilian input, and support for local self-help efforts" (p. 95). He found that Houston's plan consisted of small teams of officers who operated autonomously, and their interactions with citizens were informal and less visible. In comparison, Newark's program was more formal and visible. Citizens were three times more likely to remember having an officer visit them at home, and more citizens were aware of Newark's storefront office.

Skogan (1990) was also able to identify the problems with COP. First, officers felt COP was inefficient, as police-citizen interactions were time-intensive and not rewarded in traditional performance evaluations. Second, decentralizing decision-making threatened the role of middle managers. Finally, community input was not binding. Based on findings like these, it would seem that police agencies resist external efforts to alter their structures and functions.

Other researchers have examined the structural changes of police agencies. For example, Maguire, Shin, Zhao, and Hassell (2003) used quantitative analyses to examine changes in large municipal police agency structures during the 1990s. It was assumed that any changes which were consistent with community policing strategies were the result of reform efforts. Measuring seven dimensions of police agency structures related to dividing labor and controlling officers, the researchers found three had changed significantly, indicating that community policing reforms may have taken hold. Large municipal agencies decreased centralized decision-making (i.e., centralization) and the proportion of organizational resources committed to administration (i.e., administrative intensity). There was also a significant increase in the degree to which civilian workers were used (i.e., occupational differentiation).

However, the other four dimensions of police structures did not change during the 1990s (Maguire et al., 2003). Notably, the signature "flattening" of the police hierarchy (i.e., vertical differentiation) did not transpire. More specifically, the number of command levels (i.e., segmentation) and percentage of personnel located at various levels (i.e., concentration) did not change significantly. A third dimension of vertical differentiation, height, actually increased. That is, there was a greater social distance between the lowest and highest rank employees, which directly conflicts with COP strategies. Two other dimensions of agency structures that did not change included the extent or percent of formal policies (i.e., formalization) and number of special units (i.e., functional differentiations), which theoretically would have decreased under a COP strategy. Finally, the extent to which an organization is spread geographically (i.e., spatial differentiation) was mixed in that there were a greater number of stations, but their beat coverage was about the same. Maguire and associates concluded that there were mixed findings to suggest community-policing reforms had taken place.

At this point, we would like to pause for a moment to analyze the system perspectives and research methods used by Skogan (1990) and Maguire and associates (2003). If you recall, there are three system perspectives: rational, natural, and open (Scott & Davis, 2007; Thompson, 2008). The rational or normative system approach focuses on formal structures of the organizations. The natural system approach emphasizes the informal relationships within an organization. Both rational and natural systems are characterized as being closed system perspectives which do not account for environmental factors. In comparison, open systems or general systems theory recognizes that organizations are open to and dependent on their environment for information, personnel, and other resources.

Both Skogan (1990) and Maguire (2003) claim to study the changes in police agencies associated with community-oriented policing reforms. Yet, only Skogan included data which assessed the exchange of elements between policing organizations and their environmental stakeholders (i.e., information-sharing). In contrast, Maguire and associates restricted their measures to characteristics of agencies' internal structures, which included methods of dividing labor (i.e., differentiations of functions, occupations, space, and height) and control mechanisms (i.e., centralized decision-making, formal rules and policies, and administrative overhead). In other words, Skogan included variables related to police internal and external structures, whereas Maguire relied solely on internal structure measures and assumed that structural changes were associated with COP strategies. Two of the three organizational dimensions that changed significantly in the Maguire study were a reduction in resources spent on administration and a greater reliance on civilian workers. These changes could as easily be attributed to tightening budgets, rather than COP strategies.

We would argue that Maguire's study took a natural system approach due to its exclusion of any measures related to interactions or element exchanges with the environment. The advantage of this approach was a much larger sample size (ranging from 230 to 353 depending on the data set and variable) which allowed for inferential statistical analyses. The disadvantage of using a natural system perspective is the exclusion of any variables of the organization's external structure. In other words, there is nothing measuring the assumed association between the COP strategic reforms and organizational structure. Unfortunately, both authors herein have anecdotally noted that this is an all-to-common weakness in the current literature on criminal justice organizations and evaluations of programs professing to be founded on interorganizational partnerships.

Unlike Maguire's measures of internal police agency characteristics, Skogan took an open system approach which included the exchange of elements, as well as officer-citizen activities. Interactions and exchanges outside an agency affect an organization's external structure. The advantage of including variables of external structures is a more honest assessment of the relationships between criminal justice organizations and their environmental stakeholders. The disadvantage of including variables of external structures is that they are relatively cumbersome to obtain. They do not typically exist in secondary data collections. Hence, the analyses tend to contain small samples with qualitative measures and descriptive statistics. This is not to say that the relationships between organizations cannot be quantified using larger samples. We merely note the lack of empirical development in the criminal justice literature.

Conclusion

The theories that explain organizational strategies and structures have existed for decades (Alexander, 1995; Himmelman, 1996; Scott & Davis, 2007; Thompson, 2008). An organization's strategies and structures should be aligned. Strategies are used to express an organization's goals and preferred outcomes based on currently established knowledge as to cause-effect relationships. Strategies are also used to plan for the acquisition of inputs and demands for outputs. Administrative leaders may use controlling or consensual relationships with other organizations to exchange elements, such as information, clients, technology, services, training, and the like. These interorganizational relationships or linkages make up the organization's external structure; they are the conduits through which inputs and outputs flow.

Like the external structure, an organization's internal structure consists of the division and coordination of tasks. It includes the sub-units of various responsibilities and functions within the organization. Within organizations, there are three general structure levels: production or technical core, management, and institutional (Parsons, 1956a, 1956b). In addition to devising strategic relationships with external groups to exchange elements, institutional leaders are tasked with organizing the technical core and managerial levels to process inputs and outputs. Everyone, at all levels, rely on the lower levels to meet the organization's immediate goals. Future goals, however, require administrators to build the capacity of the technical core to meet and take advantage of the demands of a changing environment.

Meeting the demands of a changing environment, now and in the future, requires administrators to solve problems, such as finding and maintaining viable technologies and relevant partners in the task environment (Thompson, 2008). Generally, organizational strategies for change involve alterations to the technical core and changes in the services provided, population served, and geographical boundaries. In the case of for-profits and non-profits, they are capable of various alterations such as mergers to create hierarchical efficiencies or expansion of populations or territories (Alexander, 1995; Pfeffer & Salancik, 2003). Yet, many restructuring tools, like mergers, are not an option for criminal justice agencies due to constitutional mandates or jurisdictional restrictions. Criminal justice administrators simply do not have the flexibility of expanding the territory or populations they serve due to legislative controls. Moreover, the services provided are almost equally restricted by legislative, judicial, and budgetary constraints.

That being said, criminal justice administrators do need to think and plan strategically. Although most public agencies do not "go out of business," they are capable of failing nonetheless (O'Hara, 2012). It is up to administrators to shape their agency's goals, objectives, interorganizational relationships, and technical core capacity. Rather than relying on decision-making strategies of compromise and inspiration wherein outcome preferences and cause-effect associations are unclear, criminal justice leaders of today are tasked with developing a clearer understanding how to achieve desirable outcomes.

Agency administrators are also responsible for providing greater capacity and flexibility at the managerial and technical levels (Thompson, 2008). Criminal justice agencies do not merely react to the pressures of the environment, such as laws and citizen satisfaction. Moreover, organizational hierarchies do not exist for the sole purpose of establishing rules for the levels below. Institutional leaders can take advantage of opportunities afforded by the environment by increasing capacity and creating slack at the core. As a result, the agency can resist or even make demands on its environment. In fact, ignoring the development of technical core's capacity, particularly in understanding cause-effect relationships and assessment of behavioral outcomes, may leave the organization vulnerable to privatization efforts seeking financial efficiencies.

Criminal justice organizations are more likely to be poorly administered if there is a failure to make a clear distinction between the functions and demands of the institutional and managerial layers (Thompson, 2008). The differences between these layers are often clouded by the use of a "uniform chain of command which makes each successive rank different only in degree from the preceding one" (p. 153.) Decisions made at the managerial level are limited and typically involve supervising the technical core, searching for problems, and assessing efficiency. In comparison, administrative decisions involve: strategic planning based on a clear hierarchy of expressed outcomes; evidence-based knowledge of cause and effect relationships; seeking out and planning for opportunities from the environment; and assessing the internal and external organizational system of inputs, throughputs, and output activities. Traditional administrative writings and courses taught from an ideal rational system perspective fall short in teaching decision-making due to the lack of systematic understanding of complex post-industrial organizations. The remainder of the text seeks to address current gaps in administering criminal justice organizations.

Key Words

Cause-effect associations
Compromise strategy
Computational strategy
Consent decree

Constraints
Contingencies
Controlling strategies
Cooperative strategies

Departmentalization
Domain
External Structure
Hierarchy
Inputs
Inspirational strategy
Institutional/Administrative level
Instrumental rationality
Intensive technology
Internal structure
Judgmental strategy
Long-linked technology

Management level
Mediating technology
Outcomes
Outputs
Slack
Strategic planning
Strategy
Structure
Task environment
Technical level/core
Tools
Total institution

Interorganizational Relationships (IORs): Motivations for IORs

Learning Objectives:

1. Identify the organizational level that controls resources to coordinate activities and exchange elements between organizations.
2. Define and describe partnerships.
3. Describe how partnerships are being used as a strategy in criminal justice and apply it to the field of corrections.
4. Define and describe interorganizational relationships (IORs).
5. Define and describe "levels of commitment" to IORs.
6. Identify the type of IOR structure organizations are more likely to choose.
7. Describe Himmelman's (1996) theoretical framework of IOR levels, and distinguish its four dimensions, particularly linked elements and activities.
8. Identify and describe the organizational theory that dominates criminal justice.
9. Identify, describe, and distinguish Oliver's (1990) six determinants for the creation of IORs.
10. Identify and describe the theories upon which voluntary IORs are grounded.
11. Describe how mandatory IORs for CJOs may be different from non-CJOs.
12. Identify, describe, and distinguish partnership members' governance structures.
13. Discuss how federal grants and constitutionally mandated police powers may affect CJO partnerships.
14. Define domain similarity and describe its theoretical effect on IORs.

Introduction

One of the major themes of this text is the interorganizational relationships that characterize our current criminal justice system in the United States. We would argue this reliance on other organizations is also characteristic of the criminal justice systems of most western democracies of any substantial population. As we have learned, administrators are responsible for strategically planning for the future of their organization. This includes the expression of the organization's goals and preferred outcomes based on currently established knowledge as to cause-effect associations. Strategic planning also includes coordinating inputs, throughputs, and outputs both inside and outside the organization. Administrators must work with other organizations to obtain elements they need from the environment, such as clients or constituents, information, personnel, funding, and training. As a result, organizations affect each other and become connected to each other through technologies, tasks, territories, actions, events, laws, and the like (Weick, 1976). The effects organizations have on each other and the linkages between them are an underlying theme throughout the remainder of this text.

In this chapter, we delve further into various types of interorganizational relationships (IORs) and motivations for developing IORs. Interactions between criminal justice agencies and other organizations are established at the institutional level. Unlike managers, administrators are distinguished by their ability to control and make decisions about the organization's resources. Within the context of IORs, they deploy resources to coordinate activities and exchange elements with other organizations. Like relationships between individuals, IORs vary according in the level of commitment and the types of activities and resources they share.

In addition to examining types of IORs, we will address the administrative motivations for developing relationships with other organizations. Motivations for organizations working together may be the result of controlling or cooperative strategies as a means of managing their interdependencies. In short, we are examining the IORs that form an organization's external structure and motivations that explain IORs.

Criminal Justice IOR Strategies: Policymaker and Researcher Assumptions

The concept of interorganizational relationships (IORs) or **partnerships** has yet to be clearly defined, operationalized, and applied in the field of criminal justice.[1] According to Rosenbaum (2002), "there is no single definition of a partnership, but essentially, we are talking about a cooperative relationship between two or more organizations to achieve some common goal" (p. 172). Alternatively, Roman, Moore, Jenkins, and Small (2002) limit criminal justice partnerships to interorganizational relationships consisting of at least one criminal justice agency and one community organization that share a goal related to community justice. Moreover, they assert that member organizations must make a commitment to invest resources to "bring about mutually beneficial community outcomes with regard to public safety and community health" (p. iii). Typically, criminal justice administrators and researchers tend to lump all IORs into the same category, as evidenced by the fact that the term partnership is often used interchangeably with terms such as initiative, alliance, collaboration, and coalition (Roman et al., 2002).

Partnerships, or IORs, have become a common strategy to achieve criminal justice outcomes. Strategies such as community-oriented policing, problem-solving courts, and offender reentry are grounded in the development of partnerships between CJOs and non-CJOs. It is premised on the belief that partnerships between criminal justice agencies and community organizations will bring about better results. In our chapter on structure and strategy, we examined community-oriented policing (COP) and its related research. As you may recall, study findings were mixed, at best.

These strategies are supported and advanced by federally funded programs requiring the development of interorganizational partnerships. Using the field of corrections as an example, offender reentry initiatives such as the Reentry Partnership Initiative (RPI), Prisoner Reentry Initiative (PRI), Second Chance Act, and Serious and Violent Offender Reentry Initiative (SVORI) were all premised on the development of partnerships between correctional and community entities.

In the past, changes in the field of corrections, such as community corrections and intensive supervision programs, took a natural systems approach by focusing solely on correctional agencies. In comparison, the

---

1 This chapter draws heavily from the dissertation of Gail Diane Sears Humiston entitled "Offender Reentry: A Mixed Model Study of Interorganizational Commitment to Partnership"

reentry movement has taken more of an open systems approach. Reentry is presumably different in the strategic use of partnerships between criminal justice agencies and community-based organizations (Backer, 2005; Bassford, 2008; Byrne, Taxman, & Young, 2002; Jannetta & Lachman, 2011; Jucovy, 2006; Rossman, 2003; Visher, 2007; U.S. Department of Education, 2009; Wilkinson, Bucholtz, & Siegfried, 2004; Yoon & Nickel, 2008). Policymakers and administrators assume that the creation of reentry partnerships allows offenders to continue receiving services after being released to the community.

Researchers also make assumptions about partnerships between CJOs and non-CJOs by limiting their program evaluations to measures of outcomes. Despite the belief that partnerships are critical to the success of a program, evaluators often fail to measure the existence and levels of commitment to IORs (Humiston, 2014). Instead, it is assumed that the partnerships between organizations exist at sufficient levels to bring about desired outcomes. Moreover, researchers assume that organizations want to be fully integrated or tightly coupled at the system level. By relying on outcome evaluations, researchers ignore the factors which may explain why a program worked and are crucial to implementation (Chen, 1990). These "black box" program evaluations are performed with the goal of determining whether a specific program works, rather than explaining why it works or fails to work.

Theories that explain relationships between organizations are well established. In comparison, empirical literature on IORs in criminal justice are only now beginning to emerge. We don't really know whether the existence of partnerships between CJOs and non-CJOs yield better outcomes. Nor do we know what level of commitment is needed between organizations to obtain the desired results. Keeping in mind that CJOs do not have the same options for altering their IORs and external structures, let's review the conceptual framework for organizations' interactions and reasons for partnering, as well as relevant research examples.

Levels of Commitment to IORs: A Framework for CJ

Policymakers and researchers have assumed that partnerships are necessary between CJOs and non-CJOs. Many assume that successful outcomes require highly integrated systems or tightly coupled organizations. However, the development of IOR measures and their association with desired outcomes have yet to be thoroughly validated. Here, we seek to advance the general understanding of IORs and its application to CJ.

Earlier, we defined **interorganizational relationships (IORs)** as "cooperative relationships between two or more organizations to achieve some common goal" (Rosenbaum, 2002, p. 172). IORs are broadly defined as the "relatively enduring transactions, flows, and linkages that occur among or between an organization and one or more organizations in its environment" (Oliver, 1990, p. 241) and is used synonymously with terms such as "partnerships" or "collaborations." Organizations "see different aspects of a problem to constructively explore their differences and search for solutions that go beyond their own limited visions of what is possible" when they work collaboratively (Gray, 1989, p. 5). Theoretically, partnerships, collaborations, and IORs allow organizations to reach beyond their own boundaries, both horizontally and vertically, to access resources and engage stakeholders to achieve organizational goals (Alexander, 1995; Crawford, 1997; Rosenbaum, 2002).

Like individuals, organizations vary in their levels of commitment to their relationships. The term "**level of commitment**" refers to the variations of relationship complexity. Although some researchers have used labels such as "strategies" for collaboration (e.g., Delany, Fletcher, & Shields, 2003; Himmelman, 1996) or "integration" of services or activities (e.g., Fletcher et al., 2009; Konrad, 1996), the common conceptualization is that relationships vary in their levels of formality (Fletcher et al., 2009) and commitment of resources (Roman et al., 2002).

The relationships that criminal justice agencies develop with each other, as well as non-criminal justice organizations, will differ according to each organization's level of commitment (Roman et al., 2002). Research has shown that partnerships vary in their structures and levels of commitment (Delany et al., 2003), levels of integration (Konrad, 1996), degree of formality and accountability (Backer, 2005), and ability to implement transformational changes within the system or community (Fletcher et al., 2009; Roman et al., 2002). Moreover, the relationships between organizations reflect stakeholders' commitment to integrating social services, improving cost-effectiveness, and actually addressing issues of social justice, such as class and racial discrimination (Himmelman, 1996).

The key factor in developing interorganizational relationships is interdependence, or at least a perception of interdependence (Alexander, 1995). Organizations may be dependent on others for clients, labor, technology, specialized functions, or various inputs or outputs. Managing these interdependencies produces a diverse spectrum of structured activities, which vary along a continuum, ranging from the very simple to the very complex

(Alexander, 1995; Guo & Acar, 2005; Scott & Davis, 2007). IORs are structured through tools that link their activities. Tools structure the interactions between organizations to informally or formally share decision-making, resources, and information. Organizations are more likely to choose the simplest, least constraining structure toward managing their interdependencies with other organizations (Scott & Davis, 2007).

Himmelman (1996) provides us with a theoretical framework for the conceptualization of various IOR levels of commitment. He acknowledges that organizations vary in their relationships with each other. The processes by which organizations partner with each other "build upon each other along a continuum of complexity and commitment" (p. 26). They range from informal, less structured activities to more formal, structured activities. He conceptualized the levels of commitment along this continuum to include the following dimensions: networking, coordination, cooperation, and collaboration. Let's describe Himmelman's four theoretical dimensions of IOR levels and examples of its empirical application to offender reentry.

Networking

The first type of interorganizational relationship is **networking**, which requires the lowest level of commitment due to its high degree of informality and ease of employment (Himmelman, 1996). Networking is defined as "exchanging information for mutual benefit" (p. 27), and it reflects an initial level of trust. This type of relationship is best when linkages between organizations are in the form of person-to-person connections, rather than organization-to-organization. Examples of networked relationships include making referrals through personal contacts and meeting with other organizations to discuss their missions, goals, major programs, and types of services.

Himmelman's (1996) framework of IORs has been applied empirically to offender reentry, which includes the activities and programming during and after incarceration to prepare ex-convicts to return to the community. One study of reentry partnerships between correctional facilities and substance abuse treatment providers supported the assertion that sharing information on offender needs and services was the most common low structure activity between criminal justice agencies and substance abuse organizations (Fletcher et al., 2009).

Another study of jail reentry partnerships surveyed diverse types of organizations about their levels of commitment to partnering with local jails (Humiston, 2014). Whereas other studies in reentry focused on the connection of offenders to services, this study focused on a variety of elements that connect organizations to each other. Accordingly, the study examined the linking of clients, services, service providers, data, program evaluations and grant funding, and management functions. At the networking level, the element of "clients" was found to link two organizations together simply through informal person-to-person contacts. The networking activities that linked organizations to the jails by sharing clients included the following: referring clients/offenders on a case-by-case basis; sharing information on offenders' needs for services and treatment provisions on a case-by-case basis; and informally agreeing to provide services to offenders in the jail or community (without making any alterations to the services).

Coordination

The second type of interorganizational relationship is **coordination**, which necessitates more organizational involvement and commitment than networking (Himmelman, 1996). Coordination is defined as "exchanging information and altering activities for mutual benefit and to achieve a common purpose" (p. 27). Coordination is distinguished from networking in that any information sharing must result in organizations changing their activities. According to Himmelman, coordination is an important change strategy for those who consider human services to be essential for well-being, but find 'systems,' such as education, to be fragmented and unfriendly. The primary human service systems of today were not originally designed to work in accordance with the current societal needs and governance structures. Over the years, "countless public and private 'refinements' have been piled one on top of another... without any overall plan" (p. 27). An example of a coordinated relationship includes the sharing of information about program activities, which results in a mutual decision to change the program. Two or more organizations may agree to change the content or schedules of their respective programs to improve services for common clients or customer service areas.

Prior studies have attempted to measure or observe coordination between correctional agencies and other organizations. In the study of jail reentry, Humiston (2014) confirmed Himmelman's construct of coordination as being one of low formality linking the element of "services" between organizations. Administrators coordinated program content and schedules to improve services for common clients, signed formal agreements to provide services to offenders in the jail or community, and met to discuss missions, goals, programs, and types of services. In their study of prisons and substance abuse treatment providers, Fletcher and associates (2009) had several measures of coordination, which included: employing similar requirements for program eligibility, using written agreements to provide space for services, holding joint staffing/case reporting consultations, modifying program protocols to meet the needs of each agency, coordinating policies and procedures to accommodate each other's requirements, holding joint staff meetings, and having written protocols for sharing offender or client information.

Cooperation

Cooperation is the next level of interorganizational relationship, requiring even greater commitment from organizations and possibly involving formal legal agreements (Himmelman, 1996). Cooperation is defined as "exchanging information, altering activities and sharing resources for mutual benefit and to achieve a common purpose" (p. 28). Coordination would be a necessary step to achieving cooperation. However, cooperation is distinguished by the sharing of resources. At this level of commitment, organizations are willing to contribute human, technical, and financial resources (e.g., staff, physical property, and money) to the relationship. According to Himmelman, it is important to recognize that intangible resources, such as linkages to the community, are as vital to system change as tangible resources. Therefore, those who supply financial resources are not to be given greater power than partner members. Examples of cooperation include the same activities of coordination, but, in addition, organizations may decide to share physical space for programs and vehicles for transportation. Cooperation may be indicated by the development of joint policy and procedure manuals or the pooling of funds to provide services (Fletcher et al., 2009). Activities may also include the construction of standard intake and assessment process forms, the pooling of resource data to create a joint directory, and the joint hiring of advocates to address community needs and build trusting relationships (Kovener & Stark, 2002).

Humiston's (2014) exploration of the cooperation construct found that these moderately formal IOR activities linked organizations to jails by sharing the elements of service providers and data. "Service providers" were linked between organizations by attending or hosting cross-training events and the informal reporting of problems with released offenders between service providers. Organizations shared "data" elements through the following activities: informal and formal agreements to adopt the same standardized assessment tool for offenders; agreeing to participate in a case management system with the jail; contributing case data for the creation of an online case management system to be used by the organization, jail and other re-entry partners; and contributing to the costs of hiring an information specialist for the creation of said case management system.

The concept of cooperation is distinguished from the lower levels of commitment, (i.e., networking and coordination) in that organizations are willing to contribute their own resources to the relationship. We should note, however, that the exchange of resources as an indicator of an interorganizational relationship should be carefully examined and interpreted. In the case of one study on reentry partnerships, several programs paid community organizations to provide guardians and advocates (Young, Taxman, & Byrne, 2002). Theoretically, the reentry strategy conceptualized these community guardians and advocates as being volunteers provided (or paid for) by the non-CJO service providers. In other words, the non-CJOs were to contribute the human resources, rather than being paid to provide human services.

Himmelman's (1990) concept of cooperation suggests that organizations make contributions of resources within the context of improving public and social services. This is distinctive from an economic market whereby money and services are exchanged according to supply, demand, and price (Anderson, 1995). It is up to researchers to tease out the differences and interpret interorganizational relationships within the context of the partnerships and appropriate theoretical framework.

Collaboration

The final form of interorganizational relationship is **collaboration**, which demands the highest level of commitment and participation from an organization (Himmelman, 1996). Collaboration is defined as "exchanging information, altering activities, sharing resources and enhancing the capacity of another for mutual benefit and to achieve a common purpose" (p. 28). At this level, the relationship transcends the direct benefits of self-enhancement to include action for the betterment of others. Collaboration includes all of the activities of networking, coordinating, and cooperating, but also consists of enhancing the capacity of another organization through the sharing of "risks, responsibilities, resources, and rewards" (p. 28). Organizations may sponsor cross-training workshops on professional functions (Himmelman, 1996); agree to joint program and impact evaluations (Council of State Governments, 2007); implement cross-agency evidence-based assessments to identify clinical, supervision, and social service needs for offenders (Belenko, 2006); implement a cross-agency online case management system to eliminate duplication of intake, improve follow-up referrals, and share case records; design and implement a shared online resource directory which is administered and managed by an information specialist; and extend their services to neighboring, underserved communities (Kovener & Stark, 2002).

In their study of partnerships between prisons and substance treatment providers, Fletcher and associates (2009) found measures that that indicated higher levels of structured activities, which included the sharing of budgetary oversight over treatment programs, sharing operational oversight of treatment programs, and cross-training of staff on substance abuse issues. Humiston's (2014) jail reentry study had similar findings of highly formalized structures. Organizations partnering with jails reported sharing management decisions, as well as grants and evaluations. The activities linking "program evaluations and grant funding" included the following: dedicating personnel or contributing to the cost of a grant writer to apply for grant funding; agreeing to a joint impact evaluation on offender outcomes; and contributing to the cost of hiring a dedicated project director for a partnership between the jail and its re-entry partners. The element of "management" linked organizations through activities of sharing budgetary and operation oversight with the jail over a treatment program and developing universal performance measures for the jail and its re-entry partners.

In sum, policymakers, practitioners, and researchers espouse the strategic development of IORs between CJOs and non-CJOs. Theoretical frameworks conceptualizing IORs are generally well established, but need to be evaluated in their application to CJOs. Emerging research confirms that organizations have varying levels of commitment or couplings which can be measured (Fletcher et al., 2009; Humiston, 2014). The simplest form of linking organizations, networking, does not require administrative decision-making, as it does not involve the formal exchange of resources. Information may be exchanged between employees of different organizations on a case-by-case basis. As predicted, networking is the most common IOR.

The other three levels of commitment to IORs, coordination, cooperation, and collaboration, operate at the administrative level due to the more formal exchange of resources. Organizations engage in various activities to pursue the exchange elements, such as services, service providers, data, program funding and evaluations, and management oversight (Humiston, 2014). As predicted, the sharing of activities and linking of elements becomes progressively formal and less frequent at each level due to the greater commitment of resources from partnering organizations.

The goal of this section has not been to provide a thorough review of the current research. Rather, we sought to describe a theoretical framework suitable to CJOs and provide examples of how measures of IORs have been explored in offender reentry. Future research should seek to confirm these measures in their application to other CJOs and organizational populations and determine whether IORs affect desired (and undesired) outcomes. Current research suggests they may not. For instance, in the National Criminal Justice Drug Abuse Treatment Study, researchers found that IORs were not related to the increased provision of services to female offenders (Oser, Kundsen, Staton-Tindall, & Leukefeld, 2009). Rather, organizational size and culture were significantly related to community services being provided. We have yet to link valid measures of IORs to service provision, which theoretically lead to improved offender behavior and reductions in criminal behavior.

Motivations for IORs

So far, we have learned that organizations need resources from their environment. They must fit into their environments by exchanging elements, such as information, clients, funding, services, and the like. In the case of CJOs, one of the resources it needs from the environment is legitimacy and authority to enforce the government's power to police. Generally, if an organization needs a resource, it is dependent on and must interact with the environment to obtain the resource it needs.

Observing organizations' interactions with others can be accomplished using two levels of analysis—system and organizational. Metaphorically, the system and organizational levels of analysis provide us with two distinctive lenses through which to view organizations. The view of the 'bureaucratic world at 50,000 feet is very different from the view at 50 feet' (Akers, Potter, & Hill, 2013, p. xxxv). Both are useful for analyses, and one cannot supplant the other.

At the system level, we can view organizations using the rational, natural, or open system paradigms. System theories are useful in describing how organizations fit into their environment (Aldrich & Pfeffer, 1976). They give us a macro or ecological view of where organizations are situated within their environments. It takes a holistic, collective view that allows us to describe where an organization fits in relation to other organizations. It is, however, a limited view. Systems theory is limited because it does not explain *why* organizations work with each other. If an agency is able to obtain a resource from more than one source, what motivates it to decide which organization to work with? To explain organizations' choices in IORs, we need to operate at the organizational level of analysis.

To explain *why* organizations work with each other, we need theories that operate at the organizational or meso level of analysis. Organizational theories provide a lens through which to examine decisions made on behalf of an organization. As you can imagine, these theories also serve to plan and manage organizational change. Theories provide a decision-making perspective to study variations in organizations and explain how organizations change in response to their environment. As we know, the environment consists primarily of other organizations. Organizational theories purportedly predict why organizations form IORs with each other or share certain activities or elements. When organizations exchange elements, they form interorganizational relationships (IORs) which make up their external structures.

Thus far, criminal justice literature relies heavily on a single theory—institutional theory (Meyer & Rowan, 1977; DiMaggio & Powell, 1983). Simply stated, institutional theory as utilized proposes that organizations become similar rather than diverse, in an effort to attain legitimacy and resources from environmental constituents. The structure of a CJO may be neither effective nor efficient because tasks may not align with the agency's goals, yet the agencies are motivated to create certain structures to maintain public support (Crank & Langworthy, 1992, 1996; McCorkle & Crank, 1996). In criminal justice, agencies often rely on good faith and good intentions, rather than optimal structures, to avoid losing legitimacy.

Rather than relying heavily on CJ's dominant theory of institutionalization to explain organizations' motivations, we will provide a more balanced approach to describing the general theories that explain organizations' motivations for working with each other. In criminology, we learn that no single theory can explain all criminal behaviors. The same holds true in the examination of organizations' motivations and behaviors. To examine why organizations form IORs, we need a diverse set of theories. Organizational behavior is complex due to the desire to maintain independence while managing interdependencies.

Building on the work of others, Oliver (1990) provides an integrated theoretical framework of diverse theories. She asserts that there are six critical contingencies which cause organizations to involuntarily or voluntarily create interorganizational relationships. The six determinants (i.e., necessity, asymmetry, reciprocity, efficiency, stability, and legitimacy) are premised on four organizational theories. These theories include resource dependence (Pfeffer & Salancik, 2003), transactional cost (Williamson, 1981, 1985), institutions (DiMaggio & Powell, 1983; Meyer & Rowan, 1977; Scott, 2008), and social exchange (Emerson, 1976; Levine & White, 1961).

Oliver's (1990) integrated framework for the motivations to develop interorganizational relationships is detailed below. There are two major categories which consist of motivations for mandatory relationships (i.e., necessity) and motivations for voluntary relationships (i.e., asymmetry, reciprocity, efficiency, stability, and legitimacy). Although the focus is on voluntary relationships, it is important to first distinguish them from mandatory relationships.

Mandatory IORs: Necessity

The first step in determining the factors which influence voluntary interorganizational relationships is to distinguish them from relationships which are mandated, or limited, by higher authorities. Oliver (1990) uses the term "**necessity**" in her conceptualization of relationships between organizations which may be required through legal or regulatory mandates. These types of relationships are distinct from those born out of voluntary agreements. "The mandated versus voluntary distinction is important because the explanations and consequences of relationship formation associated with each are fundamentally different" (p. 243). Organizational linkages mandated by higher authorities, such as government agencies, legislators, or professional regulatory bodies, are obviously coercive in the formulation of exchanges which may not have transpired otherwise. Like many organizational theorists, however, Oliver fails to see the other side of the coin. That is, the government is equally capable of limiting the ability of organizations to form voluntary exchanges. Examples include the limitations on cartels or trusts (i.e., Sherman Act of 1890), collusions (i.e., Clayton Act of 1914), and mergers (i.e., Celler-Kefauver Act of 1950) (Scott & Davis, 2007, p. 239).

CJOs may be affected by mandates differently than non-CJOs. For instance, the distinction between mandated and voluntary interorganizational relationships is unique within the context of offender reentry due to the application of statutory laws and agency regulations. The traditional conceptualization of "necessity" within the organizational literature typically refers to laws and regulations which impose an expansion of linkages between organizations. For example, in the United Kingdom, the central government has mandated the development of crime reduction partnerships between various health and social care agencies (Williams, 2009). In the U.S., the federal government may require that grant recipients incorporate community service coordination efforts across community organizations (e.g., Banks, Dutch, & Wang, 2008).

However, in the context of reentry, the concept of necessity, as a legal or regulatory mandate, may also structure interorganizational relationships by restricting or prohibiting the provision of certain goods and services to offenders (Petersilia, 2003; Travis, 2002). For example, public housing units may have adopted policies that prohibit them from allowing convicted felons from residing in public housing. Even private housing may be required to exclude particular offenders, such as convicted sex offenders, depending on the residence's proximity to schools and day cares. Hence, legal and regulatory mandates within the context of reentry may actually cut the ties of collaboration, rather than developing interorganizational cooperation within a community.

Motivations for Voluntary IORs

In contrast to mandated interorganizational relationships, organizations may engage in voluntary interactions. These are often explained by the theory of resource dependence. Resource dependence theory, in general, allows researchers to explain a variety of organizational strategies and tactics used to manage exchanges in response to turbulent environments (Pfeffer & Salancik, 2003). More specifically, resource dependence explains latent goals, such as a desire to increase power or reduce dependence and uncertainty (Scott & Davis, 2007). Political scientists argue that analyzing the management of interorganizational relationships is based on three premises: 1) social context, 2) the ability of organizations to draw on varied strategies to pursue their interests and augment their autonomy, and 3) "power—not just rationality or efficiency—is important for understanding what goes on inside organizations and what external actions they take. The emphasis on power ... is the distinctive hallmark of resource dependence theory" (Scott & Davis, 2007, p. 233). Organizations may be willing to incur transactional costs, such as time spent negotiating relationships, in return for power, such as resources or information. Moreover, this framework is advantageous due to its ability to explain behaviors which are not based solely upon profit or efficiency, and can be used to explain the behavior of for-profits, non-profits, and governmental organizations (Pfeffer, 1987).

Resource dependence may be used to elaborate upon two of Oliver's (1990) determinants of interorganizational relationships that follow: asymmetry and stability.

Asymmetry

Resource dependence includes "asymmetry" as one of the motivations or determinants for voluntary interorganizational relationships (Oliver,

1990). **Asymmetry** refers to an organization's desire to enter into an IOR for its own self-interest. Organizations are motivated to use strategies which would allow them to exploit an opportunistic situation to obtain scarce resources and even limit competitors' access to those resources. In the criminal justice arena, agencies seeking supplemental funds and assistance from federal authorities are required to compete for those resources (Brewer, Jefferis, Butcher, & Wiles, 2007). Gaining power through control of resources and information exemplifies efforts to control interdependencies (Oliver, 1990).

In addition to controlling interdependencies, organizations are motivated to retain their independence (Oliver, 1990; Wakefield & Webb, 1979). Partnership members may be concerned about losing their independence through the blurring of organizational boundaries, loss of agency autonomy, and shifts in professional roles (Crawford, 1997; Murphy & Lutze, 2009). Moreover, the formation of relationships may also be predicted by the reluctance to lose autonomy in areas such as discretion and decision-making (Oliver, 1990). For example, Wakefield and Webb (1979) found that, contrary to prediction, smaller agencies with fewer resources were less likely to engage in interorganizational relationships, as compared to larger agencies with more resources. The researchers speculated that smaller organizations may have been more concerned about maintaining autonomy and that smaller entities perceived a greater risk of losing their independence as a result of working cooperatively with larger and more financially sound organizations. Therefore, "both the desire for control and the reluctance to relinquish control reflect asymmetrical motives in the organization's decision to interact" (Oliver, 1990, p. 244).

This conflict of managing interdependencies and independence, therefore, influences the structure of IORs. Power is more symmetrical and decentralized if decisions are made regardless of a member's size, resources, or performance (Provan & Kenis, 2007). Conversely, power is more asymmetrical and centralized if a single participant makes key decisions, controls or retains resources, and coordinates the activities of the members.

The asymmetry or symmetry of a partnership is manifested in the members' **governance structure**. First, participants may be "participant-governed" which allows all members to meet formally or informally to make decisions regarding strategies, functions, and implementation (Provan & Kenis, 2007). Second, participants may prefer to broker a single entity, which is not a member of the coalition, to administer, manage, and coordinate products and services as a means of improving perceptions of legitimacy and efficiency in handling complex network problems. Third, the partnership may use multiple agencies for planning, but allow a single member organization to implement services (Rosenbaum, 2002). Finally, alliances with a large membership may use a model in which a single participating member assumes the responsibilities of making key decisions and coordinating the activities of all members (McGarrell, 2010; Provan & Kenis, 2007). With this final method of governance, resources may predominantly be supplied by the leader organization; however, it may also receive contributions from network members or control external government funding or grants. Integrated service systems with a dominant agency may reduce conflicts in service delivery (Alter, 1990). This model is utilized more often by hospitals in community health and police agencies in community policing.

Within the context of CJO partnerships, the concept of asymmetry may be affected by federal grants and constitutional mandates. First, federally funded projects may shape the structure of criminal justice partnerships. Federal grants may require that entities share decisions and service implementation, yet a single agency is often responsible for applying for the grant, administering the program, and managing the funds (Lane & Turner, 1999). At first blush, this may be viewed as an asymmetrical relationship mandated by grant funders. However, it is possible that the interorganizational relationships are more symmetrical in nature. Several organizations within a CJO partnership could take a leadership role in multiple grant applications and administration. In reentry, for example, a community's local jail may take the lead on a reentry grant for correctional agencies, while a partnering police agency focuses on a reentry grant for law enforcement and a non-profit agency administers a mentoring grant.

Second, the concept of asymmetry is also distinctively tempered by the criminal justice system's inherent governmental function—the power to police and use force against citizens. Public safety is clearly a government function (McCarthy & Reynolds, 2003). Allowing non-governmental entities to use force against citizens as part of providing service to clientele may not be a power or resource readily negotiated or bartered (Salamon, 2002). Therefore, CJOs may be more likely to retain a centralized position within any IOR involving police powers.

Stability

In addition to asymmetry, resource dependence theory also includes the concept of "**stability**" or predictability as a determinant of voluntary interorganizational relationships (Oliver, 1990). Organizations may form relationships as a response to uncertainty within the environment, such as resource scarcity and a lack of knowledge. Relationships are fashioned as a strategy for coping with uncertainty and managing risk by establishing reliable patterns and flows of resources and information from multiple, diverse sources. For example, separate agencies may agree to work together to plan and implement programs to reduce the risks associated with mounting new programs, particularly if the social service or outcome is complex.

By working cooperatively with other community entities, organizations may be more stable and capable of achieving their goals by connecting their clients with goods and services beyond the organization's individual capacity. "The stabilizing effects of commitment to a social problem are especially relevant in nonmarket settings in which the moral imperative of social responsibility is fundamental to organizational goals" (Oliver, 1990, p. 256). Organizations may enter into a partnership with a CJO if they believe the benefits, such as obtaining information and resources, outweigh the costs (Rosenbaum, 2002). The concept of organizational stability has received very little attention in the criminal justice literature, and measures that indicate stability, such as organizational age, may be treated primarily as a control variable (e.g., Guo & Acar, 2005).

Reciprocity

The next determinant of voluntary IORs, "**reciprocity**," is based on the premise that organizations are motivated by consensus and cooperation in pursuit of mutual goals (Oliver, 1990). This is in direct contrast with asymmetry which assumes motivations of power, domination, and control. Reciprocity stems from exchange theory which depicts the formations of linkages as being harmonious, equitable, and mutually supportive, as opposed to being coercive, conflicting, and dominating. Typically, parties to the exchange will anticipate a greater degree of benefits which far exceed the potential costs (Molm, 1997).

Reciprocity between organizations may be formed through former cooperative exchanges that develop trust; however, these exchanges are more likely to be developed and maintained when organizational domains are 'moderately similar.' **Domain similarity** refers to the sameness of organizational goals, funding sources, services, staff skills, and clients (Van de Ven, 1976; Van de Ven & Ferry, 1980; Van de Ven & Walker, 1984). Organizations with 'very similar' domains are likely to be aware of each other which may facilitate exchanges, but it is more likely that organizations which are almost identical will compete for territory or perhaps become a single organization. At the other end of the spectrum, organizations with 'very dissimilar' domains are much less likely to be aware of each other, and thus less likely to develop an exchange relationship. Therefore, organizations which are 'moderately similar' in domain are more likely to interact and form mutual exchanges due to their complementary resources, awareness of each other's interdependence, and tempered levels of competition and territorial disputes.

Legitimacy

Another motivator for creating interorganizational relationships is "**legitimacy**," which is derived from institutional theory (Oliver, 1990). The implementation and sustainability of CJO partnerships relies on whether the members perceive it as a legitimate way to provide services, reduce recidivism, and improve public safety. Generally, legitimacy is defined as "a generalized perception or assumption that the actions of an entity are desirable, proper, or appropriate" (Suchman, 1995, p. 574). The perception that actions of an entity are proper is based on external rule-making, internalized moral norms, or socially shared cultural beliefs (DiMaggio & Powell, 1983; Meyer & Rowan, 1977; Scott, 2008; Scott & Davis, 2007). More simply stated, legitimacy refers to the authority vested in persons or organizations to exercise power or perform a function. Moreover, from the institutional perspective, legitimacy is not a resource which can be possessed or exchanged; nor can it be treated as an input to be transformed to an output (Scott, 2008). Both organizations and partnerships rely on legitimacy, which allows them to continue to operate as long as they are supported by professionals, scientific authorities, and the public.

The institutionalization of interorganizational relationships as a legitimate strategy for implementing CJO partnerships, such as offender reentry, is critical to the survival of voluntary IORs. Organizations and professionals who purport to represent the interests of the community exercise enormous influence over the planning and implementation (Scott & Davis, 2007) of CJO community-based partnerships. When representatives of multiple organizations in the public sector collectively recognize the importance of working together to address complex issues, they are more likely to work collaboratively with other agencies (Solansky & Beck, 2009).

The specific issue of legitimacy for CJOs is whether partnerships are the proper way to "do business." The question is whether the formation of partnerships between government and community organizations is equally or more desirable than traditional direct government bureaucracies (Provan, Kenis, & Human, 2008). Formal, bureaucratic organizations are more readily legitimized (Meyer & Rowan, 1977) than partnerships and networks which are a relatively new form of organizing work and achieving goals (Provan et al., 2008). Organizational perceptions as to whether the actions of a community partnership are desirable and proper may be evaluated by comparing the acceptance of collaborations or networked services versus direct government service provisions (Human & Provan, 2000).

Efficiency

Thus far, the determinants of voluntary interorganizational relationships have been derived from theories which predict organizational behaviors in relation to their environment. However, transactional cost theory asserts that motivations are also fashioned by the rational consideration of "**efficiency**," which emphasizes the individual organization's specific goals and structure (e.g., resources, information, personnel, and technology) (Scott & Davis, 2007). "Efficiency contingencies are internally, rather than externally, oriented" (Oliver, 1990, p. 245). Organizations may enter into a partnership as a strategy for reducing its costs through efforts such as joint training, joint purchasing of resources, or coordinating services to address service gaps or redundancies (Mellow, Christensen, Warwick, & Willison, 2011; U.S. Department of Education, 2009).

The decision to participate in a relationship may be affected by an organization's desire to reduce costs, and organizations must therefore decide whether to "make or buy" a good or service (Scott, 2008). In recent years, the public sector has adopted the private sector's managerial methods by focusing on outcomes of efficiency and economy, as well as effectiveness (Crawford, 1997). In other words, organizations, both public and private, must decide whether to provide a particular good or service themselves or pay someone else to do it.

The decision to enter into an implied or expressed agreement with another entity for the provision of those goods or services results in transactional costs (i.e., the costs associated with planning, adapting, and monitoring a contract), which must also be taken into consideration (Scott & Davis, 2007; Williamson, 1985). If the costs of maintaining a relationship with an organization are not perceived as being cost effective, an organization may move the provision of goods or services "in house." Alternatively, if the organization feels it can "do without" and participating in the partnership is too costly due to expenditures such as human resource time, money, or equipment, an organization may rationally choose to not participate (Alexander, 1995; Williamson, 1981, 1985).

Efficiency considerations have been found in previous studies on interagency relationships in criminal justice. Some agencies or professionals may perceive that the costs of maintaining implied or expressed agreements to be too great. For example, Crawford (1997) found that both police and probations officers felt that interagency crime prevention initiatives "diverted energies" away from their principal functions of "real policing" and "client-based work," respectively (p. 113). Likewise, Humiston (2014) found a negative relationship between efficiency and the development of jail reentry partnerships.

Indeed, the cost savings accrued as a result of a criminal justice partnership may be externalized (Roman, Brooks, Lagerson, Chalfin, & Tereshchenko, 2007). In the case of the Maryland Reentry Partnership Initiative, a cost-benefit analysis showed a benefit of approximately $21,500 per participant, but most of this benefit resulted from a reduction in victimization. The internal benefits to public agencies were small and non-significant. Externalized efficiencies may not sufficiently motivate organizations, as they are not able to directly benefit by reducing their own internal expenditures.

Distinguishing Motivations for Voluntary IORs

Oliver's (1990) determinants of interorganizational relationships are likely to interact with each other, but each may be sufficient cause for the formation of organizational relationships. Exploratory factor analysis of the voluntary motivations for IORs has shown that the five constructs described above can be empirically measured and distinguished (Humiston, 2014). See Table 5.1 for a summary of the five organizational motivations for developing voluntary interorganizational relationships (i.e., reciprocity, stability, efficiency, asymmetry, and legitimacy). The measures of organization's motivations for developing IORs shown came from surveys of administrative leaders about their intentions and activities at the institutional level. For example, the construct of asymmetry can be measured according to the importance of retaining decision making over various elements or activities, such as clients, services, or grant funds on a five-point Likert scale.

TABLE 5.1: MOTIVATIONS FOR VOLUNTARY INTERORGANIZATIONAL RELATIONSHIPS (IORs)

Asymmetry—organizations form relationships to acquire scarce resources to minimize interdependencies or retain independence. An organization may be motivated to work with another organization if they can:
Retain decision making over service coordination
Retain decision making over sharing of client information
Retain decision making over leadership
Retain decision making over grant funds
Stability—organizations form relationships in response to environmental uncertainty or complexity. An organization may be motivated to work with another organization if they can:
Expand services to clients
Diversify funding sources
Learn from others
Expand client base
Reciprocity—organizations develop cooperative relationships to pursue mutual goals together. An organization may be motivated to work with another organization if they have:
Mutual goals
Mutual clients
Mutual services
Legitimacy—organizations will engage in partnerships as long as they are socially supported as a proper way to do business. An organization may be motivated to work with another organization if they believe:
Partnerships are better at assessing offender needs and risks (as compared to a single CJO)
Partnerships are better at implementing case management (as compared to a single CJO)
Partnerships are better at monitoring the behavior of released offenders (as compared to a single CJO)
Efficiency—organizations engage in relationships that reduce costs or redundancies. An organization may be motivated to work with another organization to:
Reduce costs through joint purchasing
Reduce costs through joint training
Reduce unnecessary redundancies in services
Increase services to offenders without increasing costs to the organization

Conclusion

In this chapter, we examined Himmelman's (1996) theoretical framework of interorganizational relationships (i.e., networking, coordination, cooperation, and collaboration) and its application to CJOs. One of the major strategies of CJOs has been the utilization of partnerships or IORs with other organizations (e.g., community-oriented policing and offender reentry). There is an assumption by administrators and researchers alike that partnerships are necessary and organizations must be highly committed or tightly coupled to bring about desired outcomes. Research indicates that administrators make various levels of commitment to IORs (e.g., Humiston, 2014). The application of a theory that is useful to CJOs and the utilization of valid measures becomes imperative for assessments (instrumental, outcome evaluations, and process evaluations) to determine whether desired outcomes are being achieved through predicted causal factors (various levels of IORs).

In addition to describing IORs, we examined Oliver's (1990) integrated framework for understanding organizations' motivations for developing IORs (i.e., necessity, asymmetry, reciprocity, efficiency, stability, and legitimacy). Except for necessity, these determinants were built on the four theories of resource dependence (Pfeffer & Salancik, 2003), transactional cost (Williamson, 1981, 1985), institutions (DiMaggio & Powell, 1983; Meyer & Rowan, 1977; Scott, 2008), and social exchange (Emerson, 1976; Levine & White, 1961). While Oliver's (1990) determinants of IORs most likely interact with each other, a single determinant may be sufficient cause for the formation of relationships between organizations. Empirical applications indicate that the constructs can be discriminated or measured separately (Humiston, 2014).

This prepares us for the topic of how administrators and others will gauge the success or failure of IORs and the programs related to them. In the next chapter, we will canvas these issues and relate them to the logic and techniques of organizational planning to be covered in Section Four. Especially as we continue to operate in times of relative fiscal (financial) austerity, being able to develop effective and efficient IORs to accomplish the outcomes expected of the CJS will remain important.

Key Words

Assumptions
Asymmetry
Collaboration
Cooperation
Coordination
Domain similarity
Efficiency
Governance structure
Institutional theory
Interorganizational relationship
    (IOR)

Legitimacy
Levels of commitment
Mandatory IOR
Motivation
Necessity
Networking
Partnerships
Program evaluation
Reciprocity
Stability
Voluntary IOR

CHAPTER 6

Assessing Organizations

Learning Objectives:

1. Describe how outcome preferences and knowledge of cause-effect associations, as well as instrumentally perfect and less perfect technologies affect the types of assessments used by organizations.
2. Identify, describe, and distinguish the three types of assessments used by organizations and apply them to CJO strategies.
3. Compare the similarities between organizational strategies and assessments to social research evaluations.
4. Describe outcome evaluations.
5. Describe process evaluations and identify their goal.
6. Explain why social tests are the poorest form of assessment and identify examples of social reference groups.
7. Define and describe symbolic research and relate it to instrumental and social tests.
8. Relate instrumental rationality and economic rationality to organizations promoting "smart" approaches to the criminal justice system.

Introduction

In the previous chapter, we examined the motivations for criminal justice organizations (CJOs) to engage in relationships with non-CJOs to accomplish desired social and/or organizational outcomes. As we noted, sometimes these interorganizational relationships (IORs) are due to the demands of an organization other than the CJO. Grant applications that require participation of non-CJOS are a good example of this sort of "necessary" IOR. At other times, however, the IOR may be initiated by the CJO because the administrators perceive it would be of benefit to the CJO alone ("asymmetrical"). Many volunteer programs in jails and prisons would fit this description.

In this chapter, we want to examine some of the strategies that administrators might use, based on the motivating reasons, for engaging in the development of an IOR. This leads to the manner in which CJO administrators, as well as those in the partner organizations, can determine whether the IOR is achieving the outcomes desired. As part of that determination, the various elements of decision-making will be identified.

Strategies, Outcomes, Causal Factors, and Appropriate Assessments

In Chapter Four, we talked about strategic decisions being based on two major factors: outcome preferences and knowledge of cause-effect associations (Thompson, 2008). Accordingly, strategies can be ranked as to clarity of outcomes and causal factors (i.e., computation, judgment, compromise, and inspiration). In the field of criminal justice, outcome preferences are well established and typically consist of increasing public safety, preventing crime, or reducing crime or recidivism. In comparison, outcomes at the organizational level may become more ambiguous if goals are conflicting, as in the case of custody and control versus rehabilitation in corrections. When goals conflict, strategies of compromise may be used and outcomes may be ranked in preference.

In addition to outcome preferences, strategic decisions are made in accordance to administrators' knowledge of *cause-effect associations* (Thompson, 2008). In criminal justice, our knowledge as to the factors which are necessary and sufficient to bring about the desired results is lacking. From the open system perspective, causal actions and effects vary greatly. There are multiple outcomes stemming from multiple causes. Open systems approaches tell us that "effects within the system may stem from action outside it" (p. 85).

Many of the laws enacted by legislatures that affect the CJS can be used as examples here. For example, criminal justice researchers and practitioners have gradually introduced technologies associated with criminogenic risk assessment of sex offenses. Although research has shown that sex offenders vary in recidivism and valid assessments that predict risk exist, we have met resistance from legislators. Even in the face of solid empirical evidence, these legislators have simply rejected that evidence. For them, belief in deterrence, and that sex offenders are almost uniformly going to re-offend, outweighs the empirical evidence provided by academic and government researchers. Their beliefs in cause-effect association leads to statutory requirements that increase custodial sentence lengths and reduce access to quality programming to reduce the likelihood of re-offending. Perceptions of constituent demands, coupled with their own cause-effect beliefs, have substantial impacts on strategies adopted by CJS administrators.

In addition to discussions of outcomes and cause-effect relationships, we have also described the difference between instrumentally perfect and less perfect technologies in our analysis of different types of organizations. Organizations such as manufacturers strive to always produce their desired outcomes; they endeavor for instrumentally perfect technology (Thompson, 2008). In comparison, some types of organizations, like CJOs, may produce the desired outcomes only part of the time; they have less perfect instrument technology. As you may recall, instrument rationality (perfect and less perfect) is different from economic rationality. Whereas **instrument rationality** refers to whether actions produce the desired outcomes, **economic rationality** refers to obtaining results with the least amount of expenditure of resources.

> ### "SMART JUSTICE": THE INTERSECTION OF INSTRUMENTAL RATIONALITY AND ECONOMIC RATIONALITY?
>
> In the early 1990s, Osborne and Gaebler (1992) published a text that would serve as the blueprint for the Clinton-Gore administration's "reinvention" of government. The Vice-President was the driving force behind what was originally known as the National Performance Review, and then the National Partnership for Reinventing Government (Kamensky, 1999). Kamensky wrote: "We started our work with a clear set of principles and an inspiring vision of what government should look like. We said we would create a government that works better and costs less by putting customers first, empowering employees to allow them to put customers first, cutting the red tape that held back employees, and cutting back to basics." This was an approach to government at least initially embraced by the Bush-Cheney administration. The events of September 11, 2001 led to a different reinvention of government at the federal level.
>
> The reinvention of government seemed to stall at the federal level, but started to kick into high gear at the state level, it seems. We would note that the "national accountability movement" in education, begun in 1990 and eventually expressed in the No Child Left Behind Act of 2001, reflected a similar sentiment of holding public agencies to sets of measurable performance standards and outcomes. These "movements" provided a template for the involvement of commercial

interests (businesses) and citizens' groups to begin placing government agencies under the microscope in terms of becoming more economical and responsive. In the reinvention of government, we see the potential cause-effect associations beginning to yield to a more "evidence-based" approach over other, non-rational approaches.

In the world of criminal justice another organizational player can be included in the mix of non-CJOs pushing the economic rationality and instrumental rationality mantra. This organization was the American Legislative Exchange Councils (https://www.alec.org/). Through a series of "model policies" many of the ideas of accountability, cost-saving, and public safety merged in a conservative approach to reforming the CJS. Given that most criminal justice operations are based at the state and local government levels, the model policies were adopted by several state governments.

At about the same time, the idea of "justice reinvestment" was taking hold. The Center for State Governments' Justice Center defines justice reinvestment as: "a data-driven approach to improve public safety, reduce corrections and related criminal justice spending, and reinvest savings in strategies that can decrease crime and reduce recidivism" (https://csgjusticecenter.org/jr). This strategy can be traced back to early discussions of the value of prevention versus late-stage interventions such as incarceration. This strategy was a part of the re-entry programming that was beginning in the late 1990s: take the money saved from stopping the return of previously incarcerated individuals to prison and re-invest it back into prevention and other early-stage programs designed to reduce the number coming into the system on the front-end.

Using a combination of solid empirical research and the personal stories of those who have been involved in the CJS, a new set of organizational convergences began in the early 2000s around issues of economic rationality and instrumental rationality in the CJS. Representatives of "liberal" CJ reform organizations found that they shared interests in the same sorts of evidence-based programs in CJ as did those from "conservative" reform organizations. Notions of "smart justice," "right on crime," and so forth became rallying points leading to the formation of coalitions and non-profit organizations at many state levels. For example, leading the way, the Texas Public Policy Foundation (along with the American Conservative Union Foundation and Prison Fellowship) opened the Right on Crime office in 2005 (http://rightoncrime.com/about/). Not to be outdone (remember that isomorphism stuff?), here in Florida we developed the Center for Smart Justice at

Florida Taxwatch (http://old.floridataxwatch.org/Research/centers/csj.aspx; early associated with the Collins Center at the University of Miami). Probably just about every state in the United States has some affiliated "smart justice" office. Even the Canadians, who provide one of the most succinct statements of purpose (or mission):

"Smart Justice is a way of addressing criminal justice issues that solves the problems of crime rather than simply punishing the criminals: it addresses the profound connections of crime to mental health, addiction, employment, education, housing and social inclusion. Smart Justice doesn't spend money on ineffective responses to crime. Instead, it clears clogged courtrooms and overcrowded prisons, supports victims and protects families, empowers communities and improves safety through programs proven to reduce crime and help people lead law-abiding lives" (http://smartjustice.ca/).

It is this focus on economic rationality and instrumental rationality that characterizes the logic of this movement for CJ reform. As the National Association of Counties (NACo) states: "Smart Justice projects enhance partnerships among public, private and philanthropic leaders along with national experts to promote safer communities and utilize taxpayer money more effectively and efficiently." For the NACo folks, there are several steps in this process:

- "Promoting evidence-based, data-driven local justice policies and practices throughout the nation's counties;
- Taking a leadership role in exploring and implementing local justice reforms;
- Developing strategies to save counties money while creating safer communities; and
- Providing education and assistance to counties to assess their adult and juvenile systems to explore opportunities for efficient and effective use of public dollars" (http://www.naco.org/resources/programs-and-initiatives/smart-justice).

Common to all of these approaches is the emphasis on using taxpayer dollars effectively and efficiently to produce public safety outcomes.

At Smart Justice conferences the authors have attended, there are often discussions about whether the actions being proposed are focused primarily on the cost-savings aspects of many programs in

> contrast to actually making a difference in the lives of people. Critics generally tie the politically conservative focus on fiscal reform to a lack of attention to the impact on individuals and communities. However, it has been our experience those discussions generally end with an acknowledgement that public safety is about the people and communities, and that such must be balanced against the costs. This has been one area, much like the Prison Rape Elimination Act work described elsewhere, where we have seen politically different organizations find common ground and use their organizational voices for a common purpose. For now, at least...
>
> Our purpose here is to demonstrate one area in criminal justice where the emphasis on economic rationality and instrumental rationality have come together through a variety of interorganizational relations. That this confluence brings a variety of organizations with often very different organizational philosophies (e.g., conservative, liberal, libertarian, etc.) together, helps us move toward the next set of chapters in the text. As we move forward, we will begin to discuss how a variety of groups within the CJS, and a range of groups outside the formal system, come together at times, conflict at other times, and at times become oppositional to CJOs.

In short, administrators use strategies and knowledge about cause-effect associations to bring about desired outcomes. Applying this to criminal justice organizations, current strategies include the use of IORs between CJOs and non-CJOs, and desired outcomes, such as crime reduction, may only be achievable part of the time. Our current knowledge of how IORs affect outcomes is lacking. So, how do we know if our strategies of developing IORs between CJOs and non-CJOs (i.e., external structure) are resulting in preferable outcomes at an acceptable rate?

Determining whether outcomes are being achieved requires assessments. According to Thompson (2008), there are three categories of organizational assessment: efficiency, instrumental, and social tests. Using the appropriate method of assessing an organization's ability to achieve its expressed outcomes is based on whether knowledge about cause and effect is complete and the clarity of outcomes.

The first form of assessment, **efficiency tests**, may be used for those with instrumentally perfect technologies (Thompson, 2008). As in the case of manufacturers, these organizations are capable of producing the desired outcome nearly every time. This allows them to be assessed in economic terms of efficiently producing those outcomes for the least cost. As we have already argued, however, CJOs are not like production lines. CJOs cannot be expected to consistently produce the same outcomes when dealing with human behavior. Therefore, using tests of efficiency may not be the most appropriate form of assessing them.

The second method of assessment is the **instrumental test** which refers to assessing whether a desired outcome was achieved (Thompson, 2008). Instrumental tests are less strict than efficiency tests. An instrumental test is the appropriate method to use when outcomes are known but empirical knowledge of causal factors is incomplete. Social researchers may refer to this type of assessment as an *outcome evaluation*. An outcome evaluation measures the impact of a program on cases that have been processed (Bachman & Schutt, 2015). Organizations implement programs with multiple intended outcomes, such as higher rates of job retention, lower rates of poverty, and fewer criminal offenses. However, programs are also capable of producing unintended outcomes which should also be assessed, such as higher incarceration rates of non-violent offenders and their commission of violent crimes after release.

In social research, outcome evaluations can and should be accompanied by process evaluations. *Process evaluations* assess whether a program is working as planned (Bachman & Schutt, 2015). In a process evaluation, assessors measure the inputs, processes, and outputs which lead to outcomes. (These terms should sound very familiar from our discussion of organizational structure!). *Inputs* are the resources, raw materials, clients, and staff that go into a program (Bachman & Schutt, 2015). *Processes* are the steps taken by employees to deliver a service or treatment. *Outputs* are the completed services or products produced, which may become an input for another organization. Finally, *outcomes* are the final results, the same results used for an outcome evaluation.

The goal of a process evaluation is to provide feedback to decision makers to make improvements to the program and, by extension, the organization. For example, if the program is not recruiting the population they intended to target, administrators can take corrective action. We'll address this more in our discussions of logic modeling, evidence-based practices, and managing organizational change. For now, we are focusing on the similarities between organizations' structural elements, assessing organizations, and social research evaluations.

There is one final method of assessing an organization, according to Thompson (2008). In situations where both outcomes and cause-effect associations are ambiguous, organizations may resort to using **social tests** as a standard for evaluation. When empirical knowledge is absent or lacking on outcomes and causal factors, organizations turn to social reference groups to make comparisons. Social tests of reference groups' satisfaction is the poorest form of assessment because measures of satisfaction are used in place of valid, relevant measures of outcomes and causal factors. The question then becomes which reference group to satisfy, as there may be multiple groups to be satisfied and opinions may differ accordingly. In the case of a prison evaluation, "prisoners, guards, and legislative groups emphasize different aspects" (p. 88). In higher education, the criteria of satisfaction would vary for alumni, faculty, and employers of a university's graduates.

Social tests allow evaluators to choose from numerous social reference groups (Thompson, 2008). For example, satisfactory performance may be demonstrated by organizations showing historical improvements. In this case, the organization uses itself as a reference in comparing its current status to earlier periods of time. Another social test may be a comparison to one's peers. For example, for-profits compare market shares and stock prices to satisfy investors and shareholders. Universities compare increases in the number of students and faculty as some measure of quality, rather than measuring and reporting long-term educational and graduate outcomes. Police agencies may survey citizens about their beliefs in legitimacy to detract accusations of misconduct.

One final example of using social tests as a form of assessment is accreditation (Thompson, 2008). Organizations may have external professional groups perform accrediting evaluations as a visible measure of quality. The external evaluation may be important for internal purposes and public relations. However, according to Thompson, organizations use the accreditation process primarily due to its visibility to constituents, not necessarily because administrators want to improve the quality of their organization or program. Organizations that are subject to or use accreditation include criminal justice organizations, as well as schools, universities, and hospitals. We'll address issues of accreditation and professional social reference groups in more detail as it applies to criminal justice in later chapters.

It is not uncommon for organizations to resist instrumental tests in favor of social tests. Nor is it uncommon to supplant evaluations using valid measures with symbolic research (Thompson, 2008). *Symbolic research* avoids the development and utilization of valid measures of outcomes and processes. It uses invalid or poor measures, such as "number of cases seen, frequency of remission and cures, and testimonials about the value of a practice by clients and their families" as some indication of success (p. 92). Valid research would require that 'number of cases processed' be used as a measure of a program's output, rather than being used in place of an outcome. CJOs do not express 'case processing' as their ultimate outcome. Their outcome would be to reduce crime. Also, as we learned earlier, 'satisfaction' measures of social groups, such as staff or clients, are the poorest measure of performance. Rather, instrumental assessments that measure real and expressed outcomes should be used. Both researchers and administrators abdicate their roles by not developing and utilizing instrumental measures of performance related to an organization's outcomes.

Conclusion

In this chapter, we examined the various types of assessments organizations can use, and we compared them to the outcome and process evaluations used by social research. Instrumental assessments of desirable outcomes should be used by CJO administrators to make decisions about their organizations. Likewise, social researchers must develop and utilize valid measures to IORs in research. There are practical implications of researching partnerships. By exploring the associations between organizations' motivations and varying levels of commitment to IORs, CJO officials will better understand who will partner, why and to what extent. As a result, we may better understand the extent to which organizational changes can be successfully planned, implemented, and sustained. In the remainder of our text, we will continue with the underlying theme of understanding the CJ environment and interactions between CJOs and other types of organizations.

Key Words

Cause-effect associations
Inputs
Instrument rationality
Instrumental tests
Economic rationality
Efficiency tests
Outcome evaluation

Process evaluation
Processes
Outcomes
Outputs
Social tests
Symbolic research

CHAPTER 7

The Organizational Core of Criminal Justice and Other Government Organizations

Learning Objectives:

1. Identify the key decision points in the United States' criminal justice system and the core criminal justice organizations involved at each level.
2. Discuss the issue of privatization within the criminal justice system and its implications for criminal justice organizations.
3. Identify points at which criminal justice organizations may need to involve non-system partners and the issues associated with such partnerships.
4. Discuss how mission statements can be used to identify the values, activities and orientations of different organizations across the criminal justice system.
5. Identify the three areas addressed by organizational ecology and how each helps to explain variation and similarity ("isomorphism") in the criminal justice system.
6. Discuss how non-criminal justice organizations within government can exercise control over criminal justice organizations.

Introduction

Up to this point we have focused primarily on the foundations of the organizations that form our United States criminal justice system (CJS). These include the legal foundations of the formal CJS as it exists in most US states. We have outlined key organizational theories that help to explain how these organizations interact with each other, and with other sorts of organizations in the social environment. We will continue to focus on the organizational and interorganizational levels of analysis. In this way, we hope to begin to develop that "organizational sense" we wrote of earlier—seeing organizations as actors in their own right as they work together to achieve "justice." In the next section of the text we will begin to examine a variety of other organizations in the environment and how they work with or against the CJS to achieve "justice." In this chapter, we want to begin to develop a picture of the organizations/agencies that comprise the system at various levels of authority.

Levels and Organizational "Players"

From a sequential experience of the CJS, we can illustrate three levels of the CJ organizations (CJOs) as experienced by alleged offenders, victims, CJ personnel, and the public. At the County (misdemeanor) level, there are police/sheriff agencies, county jails (maybe some local lock-ups), prosecutors, defense counsel (public and private), the County courts, and county-level probation.

At the felony level, all of these same organizational players are involved except county-level probation. A different level of Court is involved. These are generally organized at the circuit or district level, depending upon the state. Likewise, the enhanced penalties associated with conviction bring the state prison system and state probation organizations (sometimes within the same agency; sometimes different) into the picture.

When federal charges are involved, the organizational players may change again. That is, a federal law enforcement agency is likely involved, as well as local law enforcement agencies. Depending upon where one is located, the US Marshalls Service may operate a detention center; or, they may house detainees in a contracted county jail facility. A similar set up is found for cases that involve Department of Homeland Security agencies. The court structure will be different in terms of the involvement of a federal prosecutor, public defender, and judges. If convicted, incarceration is likely to be in a Federal Bureau of Prisons facility. Here medical services are likely to be provided by the Public Health Service, an organization of the Department of Health & Human Services. If placed on probation, jurisdiction switches to the Federal Courts.

There is an old saying that "where one sits determines what one sees." That means for us that the level of the system from which one looks can reveal a very different picture of what happens in the CJS. This becomes important when we talk about selecting a "focal" (or "index") organization from which to make our observations. For example, viewing the CJS from the local versus the federal perspective means that we will see things very differently. Even within a particular level, looking at the CJS from the perspective of law enforcement versus corrections can produce very different conclusions about a particular issue. Add in the various professional viewpoints (officers versus lawyers, treatment staff versus custody, line versus administration, etc.), and the perspective changes yet again.

Decision Points and Organizational Actors

Figure Intro. 1 provides a tour through the CJS decision-points provided by the Bureau of Justice Statistics. This was developed originally by the President's Commission on Crime in the early 1970s and revised in the late 1990s. We have added an additional decision-point given the widespread attention to inmate/prisoner re-entry since the turn of the century. Building around our notion of the "core" government agencies/organizations involved in the CJS, we can tour Figure 7.1 to identify not only the core agencies, but the variety of other government and non-governmental organizations (NGOs) with which they interact. We divide NGOs further into for-profit organizations (FPOs), non-profit organizations (NPOs), and faith-based organizations (FBOs). Some authors may lump all NPOs and FBOs into the category of community-based organizations (CBOs). This lumping occurs because the assumption is that both NPOs and FBOs have a primary mission of service to the community(ies) where they serve, rather than any profit motive. The bases of the NPO are likely to be more secular (non-religious-based) than that of the FBO, which is assumed to have a religious base for its activities. In fact, the services provided by NPOs and FBOs may be identical, only the motivation for providing the services and the source of authority for operation may be presented as different.

Table 7.1 is a general coverage of the types of formal organizations involved in the CJ decision-making process. If we take each of the organizations involved as the "focal" organization at each point, the result of the decision to be made can be quite different. As mentioned in the table, the decision to report a criminal act by an organization can produce different results for the organization. The classic example is the under-reporting of embezzlement by banking organizations. We are told this is to avoid consumers of the services of the organization losing faith in the bank or investment company, for example. Reporting embezzlement might open the organization to public scrutiny and embarrassment. If faith in the organization is lost, consumers will withdraw their business and the organization might fail. Thus, some organizations may choose not to report crimes against or within the corporation. We have seen this recently in several high-profile computer "hacking" cases against major corporations such as SONY.

TABLE 7.1: VARIETY OF FORMAL ORGANIZATIONS INVOLVED IN THE CRIMINAL JUSTICE DECISION-MAKING PROCESS

Law enforcement (Policing)
    Federal
    State
    County
    Municipal

Corrections
    Local Jails & Metropolitan Detention Centers (US Marshalls)
    Pre-trial release programs
    Prisons (State and the Federal Bureau of Prisons)
    Probation (County [Misdemeanor], State and Federal)
    Parole

Prosecutors
    Solicitors (Local)
    District/State Attorneys
    Federal

Public Defenders

Judges
    Misdemeanor
    Felony
    Appeals Courts
    Supreme Courts

Clerks of Court

Court Administrators

Missing from Table 7.1 are the formal (contractual, memoranda of understanding, etc.) and informal connections each focal agency has with other organizations in the community. The formal connections are important ways to connect the focal organization with other organizations. These represent obligations to and from other organizations in the environment. These may be as seemingly unrelated to the core mission of the agency as a contract for janitorial services—as opposed to using "trustee" labor—or provision of an employee cafeteria or sandwich stand.

By the time we move into various aspects of corrections, the potential for complex and complicated interorganizational relationships can skyrocket. In some states legislators seem intent on "privatizing" as many functions of correctional agencies as possible. Whether it is wholesale contracting of the management of prison facilities—but not whole prison systems—or a piecemeal approach to services such as laundry, health care, prisoner transport, etc., a correctional system and individual facilities can have a wide range of relationships with other NGOs. In the area of health care, for example, those "private" agencies can include medical schools from state universities—though most medical schools are trying to get out of the business—to national-level FPOs. Small jails may contract with the local emergency services organization and a local physician (almost always incorporated), and hire their own nurses for daily services.

Let us pick on misdemeanor probation services for a moment. In Georgia between 1991 and 2015 we saw widespread privatization of misdemeanor probation services. This resulted in charges of "tolling" or keeping individuals on probation longer than sentenced due to inability to pay fees to the private providers. In 2015 the oversight of misdemeanor probationers was returned to the Board of Community Supervision (http://dcs.georgia.gov/adult-misdemeanor-probation-oversight), a state government agency. In Florida, we have seen a movement to and from private providers at the county level, where misdemeanor probation is organizationally located. Within some counties we have seen movement within government agencies of the misdemeanor probation function to and from the corrections department. Those corrections departments, in turn, are sometimes operated by the County Commission rather than the Sheriff's Office.

As the idea of re-entry from prisons has been applied to jails in recent years, the number of organizations with which a jail might have informal and formal relationships has sometimes multiplied dramatically. One local (large) jail with which the authors work counts more than 60 CBOs as "partners" in providing a range of services to detainees, inmates, and probationers inside and outside the facility. In other (medium) jail systems it is not unusual to have 20 or more CBOs attend meetings around service provision. The mix of NPOs, FBOs, and even some FPOs showing up to re-entry meetings varies by county.

One area we do not include in the Figure Intro. 2 or Figure 7.1 is *crime prevention*. Depending upon the type of crime—e.g., property versus violent—not only policing agencies are likely to be involved. Faith-based and other civic organizations most likely provide the core prevention messages against crime. At a more targeted level, we find multiple health-related organizations involved in violence prevention and some types of substance use prevention. The role of the private security sector (e.g., https://www.asisonline.org/Pages/default.aspx) nationally and internationally in the prevention of crimes is another area where we have less information than desirable.

FIGURE 7.1: ORGANIZATIONAL INVOLVEMENT IN THE CRIMINAL JUSTICE PROCESS DECISION PROCESS

Decision to be made	Organizational involvement	Description	Outcome	Leads to...
Commission of crime	Criminal organization or corporation acting criminally	Criminal organizations or legitimate corporations may engage in criminal activities	Commission of a crime	Reporting?
Reporting of a crime	Victim corporation	Some corporations may have policies that restrict reporting of criminal victimization for a variety of reasons	Under-reporting of crimes, especially "white collar" crimes; costs of crime passed on to consumers	If reported to law enforcement, investigation may occur
Investigate or not?	Police agencies	Not all reported crimes will be investigated or reacted to	Some reports do not rise to probability of a criminal charge being sustained	If investigated and found to be substantiated, arrest may occur
Arrest or not?	Police agencies	Some offenses may be handled without arrest, such as civil citations or notices to appear	Some organizational policies may restrict arrest to only more serious charges	If citation used, case referred to a Court; if arrested, booking comes next
Booking	Police agency, jail, health provider organization, bonding organization	Initial charge filed based on police report; jail processes individual including possible health screening	Some jails do not book misdemeanor charges; some Courts have set bond schedules to allow swift processing; bonding agency may be involved	If booked and detained, the next step would be some form of "first appearance."

(continued)

FIGURE 7.1: ORGANIZATIONAL INVOLVEMENT IN THE CRIMINAL JUSTICE PROCESS DECISION PROCESS (*CONTINUED*)

Decision to be made	Organizational involvement	Description	Outcome	Leads to...
First Appearance	Court (including Clerk and/or Administrator), prosecutor, defense counsel, jail, bonding organization	Whether probable cause exists and whether bond should be provided, as well as amount	Policies of prosecutor and defense organizations may dictate process from those organizations; court may have set criteria; bonding organization may have risk schedule	If no probable cause found, case may be dismissed; sufficient cause found and alleged offender can "make bail," release to await plea or trial; if no bond available, sent back to jail for classification and detention
Diversion	Court, prosecutor, defense counsel, service provider(s)	If a diversionary program is available pre-trial, negotiations may occur	All organizations involved will have policies related to eligibility, performance, and outcomes	If diverted, the case may be dismissed on successful completion; if not, prosecution must decide how to proceed
Pre-trial detention	Jail, health care provider, other service providers	Classification for housing purposes, assignment to cell area, may dictate access to programming	Assuming the jail is not too small, jail will utilize a classification scheme for cell or facility assignment	Detainee awaits either plea agreement or trial
Formal charge	Prosecutor	Determining the charge(s) with which to proceed against the defendant	Some offices may have charging standards; some may engage in charge bargaining	Once charge is clear, negotiations and please may result or move forward to trial

(*continued*)

FIGURE 7.1: ORGANIZATIONAL INVOLVEMENT IN THE CRIMINAL JUSTICE PROCESS DECISION PROCESS (*CONTINUED*)

Decision to be made	Organizational involvement	Description	Outcome	Leads to...
Arraignment	Prosecutor, Defense counsel, Court, Investigative agency	Official recognition of charges, potential plea entered and/or summary judgement	The bargaining positions of the prosecution and defense organizations and the acceptance of plea agreement by the court	If plea offered and accepted, sentencing may be immediate or later
Trial	Prosecutor, Defense counsel, Court, Investigative agency,	Determination of guilt	Court hears arguments from both sides, jury or judge makes decision on guilt	If guilty, sentencing may be immediate or later
Sentencing	Prosecutor, Defense counsel, Court, Investigative agency, Service providers, Probation, Corrections (Jail or State)	Type of sentence (custodial versus probationary); requirements of sentence (e.g., completion of programs, etc.), length of sentence (will influence location where served), etc.	Sentencing will be affected not only by legislated requirements, but by service options available in a given system or jurisdiction.	Sentence will affect service decisions and length of time the convicted will be under formal control of the State; this is especially true of "truth in sentencing" and "minimum-mandatory" states.
Community Corrections	Court, Probation agency, service providers, Law enforcement	The types of conditions of probation (conditional release) will be influenced by services available in a jurisdiction, the length of sentence, and the role of law enforcement agencies in monitoring probationers	Assuming a quality criminogenic risk assessment, the probation program and community providers will develop a plan to meet client needs to reduce recidivism. Multiple organizations may be involved	If the organizations involved agree that the client has met the obligations under the Court's instruction and agency guidelines, the case may move toward closure.

(*continued*)

FIGURE 7.1: ORGANIZATIONAL INVOLVEMENT IN THE CRIMINAL JUSTICE PROCESS DECISION PROCESS (*CONTINUED*)

Decision to be made	Organizational involvement	Description	Outcome	Leads to...
Incarceration	Court, Correctional Agency (including contractors)	Once the orders of the Court are entered, the correctional authority assumes custody and provides services consistent with the sentence and the custody, care, and control of the convicted	Administrative authority is passed to the Corrections agency, with potential Court oversight. Defense organization may maintain contact. A variety of contract agencies may provide services and/or management of the convicted.	While the sentence may be set, the daily administration of the sentence will rest with the corrections agency. Unless there is indeterminate sentencing and parole, corrections becomes the dominant agency until re-entry planning
Parole	Varies from state to state with regard to whether the parole agency is part of the corrections department or a separate entity, Service providers, Law enforcement agencies	Parole-granting decisions may be made by a board with conditions attached; service providers in a jurisdiction may be involved in release planning; Law enforcement agencies may play a role in surveilling parolees along with parole agency	Parole is another form of conditional release that imposes restrictions on the convicted. The services available in a given jurisdiction may influence the decision-making by the parole agency.	If parole planning is effective and meets the needs of the convicted, successful completion of the parole period should be the end of the case.
Re-entry	Correctional agency, Community Corrections, Service providers, Law enforcement agencies	Based on a combination of criminogenic risk and social welfare needs, organizations plan with the convicted for meeting needs in the community upon release (may be part of a probationary release) to reduce the likelihood of recidivism	Whether termed a continuity of care or wrap-around service approaches, this requires the coordination of needs assessments and matching to community resources to lower the criminogenic risk and meet basic needs of the returning individual	If successful, this stage should reduce the likelihood that the individual will engage in further criminal activity.

We conclude this section with the prevention example because it helps us point out that we have to think more broadly than just the formal, government-based organizations that comprise the CJS when we think about Justice. The variety of organizational relations involved at all levels of the CJS and across the more than 3200 counties in the United States requires that we pay attention to organizational relations more than we ever have. The CJS leaders currently and in the future are going to need this sort of knowledge and interorganizational skills to manage effective public safety programs. And, we have not yet introduced the development of multi-government organizational relations or the increasingly sophisticated criminal organizations and organized criminals and their victims with which such leaders must deal.

Organizational Missions

Organizational mission statements (sometimes accompanied by "values" or "vision" statements) provide a way of understanding the *interests* of different organizations within a particular ecological system. In the text box example, we provide several snippets of organizations' mission statements. We move from local law enforcement through the criminal courts, local corrections to state corrections, and a sampling of key community partners for re-entry. You may note a progression within the formal CJOs from crime reduction and safety to an emphasis on protecting rights, to providing safe and effective corrections to protect the community. Among some key community partners involved in re-entry efforts, the emphasis is on successful life in the community, with little mention of the key role they play in the CJS.

> **MISSION STATEMENTS AS ORGANIZATIONAL VIEWPOINTS:**
>
> "The mission of the Orange County Sheriff's Office is to reduce crime by providing excellent service at a reasonable cost through partnerships that build trust, create a safe environment, and enhance the quality of life in our community."
>
> "Keep Orlando a safe city by reducing crime and maintaining livable neighborhoods."—OPD

> "Our mission is to seek justice for everyone in Orange and Osceola counties."—Office of the State Attorney, Ninth Judicial Circuit.
>
> "The mission statement of the Ninth Judicial Circuit Court is to fairly and impartially administer justice and resolve disputes brought before the court."
>
> "The mission statement of Court Administration is to efficiently and effectively provide comprehensive administrative support to all the judges of the circuit, to manage programs and to act as a liaison between the Court and the people it serves."
>
> "To enhance public safety by operating a safe, secure and humane correctional system"—Orange County Corrections Department
>
> "Provide a continuum of services to meet the needs of those entrusted to our care, creating a safe and professional environment with the outcome of reduced victimization, safer communities and an emphasis on the premium of life."
>
> "Community Corrections' primary function and mission is to protect the community by supervising offenders and reporting non-compliance to the sentencing or releasing authority."—Florida Department of Corrections (Institutions and Community Corrections)
>
> "The mission of Aspire Health Partners is to provide the people of Central Florida with compassionate, comprehensive and cost effective behavioral health care services that lead to successful living and the ability to achieve and maintain healthy, responsible lifestyles."
>
> "Building lives that work."—Goodwill Industries of Central Florida

The primary take-away from this brief side trip is to illustrate ways that we can use statements by organizations to help us understand the interests of each "focal" organization. As we move through the CJS, it is helpful to remember that, while there may be an overall mission of justice, the specific interests of each formal CJO and our allied organizations are often quite different. Whether we can use these differences to build an effective system or allow them to result in segmented justice based on organizational interests remains a key question.

The Social Ecology of Criminal Justice

Most students of criminology and criminal justice are familiar with the Chicago School's "social ecology" approach to crime causation. These are represented by the works of Louis Wirth (1931) on group conflict and Sutherland's differential association ideas (now social learning). The basic idea is that all elements of human social life exist in a broader social environment that affects and is affected by the local ecology of neighborhoods and associations. It is that local social ecology that provides us with our most direct knowledge and reinforcement of proper social behavior. As differential association/learning approaches tell us, an excess of values and attitudes favorable to law-breaking are likely to lead to criminal behavior among individuals and groups.

The idea that local communities (ecologies) contain different groups/organizations that may come into conflict with other groups/organizations makes great sense in criminal justice circles. Perhaps less obvious is that that same ecology includes other groups/organizations among which we might observe collaboration and cooperation. This is, to some extent, what separates the early Chicago School of Social Ecology from the later Chicago School (Shaw & Mckay, 1942; Sampson & Groves, 1989). We will return to some of these ideas of competition and cooperation in the later chapter on criminal organizations.

Less developed in criminology and criminal justice is the application of the social ecology of organizations to the criminal justice system (CJS) and the range of non-governmental organizations (NGOs) increasingly involved with the CJS. Actually, to say that the range of NGOs interacting with the CJS has/is increasing is itself a research question. We would argue that there is a tendency among scholars to treat late Twentieth and early Twenty-first Century criminal justice as if it were an incredibly stable institutional set. In most texts, once the history of the early US CJS is covered, there is little discussion about how the system has changed overall in the past 70 years in terms of the organizations that make up the total system.

For example, Burch (2016) tracks the number of Sheriff's Offices (SOs) in the US between 1993 and 2013. In 1993 there were 3,084 SOs, rising to a high of 3,088 SOs in 1997, and falling to 3,012 by 2007 and maintaining that number in 2013. It should be noted that some of that decline is due to not counting SOs without a primary law enforcement function. This would exclude counties like some in metropolitan Atlanta (Georgia) counties where the SO provides primarily jail and courthouse management services. We will explore further the changes in criminal justice agency populations below.

Sticking to our focus on how organizational theory can assist leaders in the criminal justice world make decisions, we want to concentrate on the primary varieties of organizational ecology. The first of these observes the "diversity" of organizations in the environment; the second involves looking at the "set" of organizations with which one's "focal" agency interacts. The third approach looks at the reasons why organizations within the same sector grow or decline within that sector. Finally, ecological approaches examine why certain organizational forms survive while others fail. We will address each of these themes in more detail and suggest data sources that will allow leaders to make decisions about where their organization "fits" into the social environment and criminal justice ecology.

"Organizational Demography"—Why So Many Organizations?

We introduce this section using Carroll's (1984) term for what others describe as the question of why there are so many different types of organizations in an ecological area (e.g., Hannan and Freeman, 1977; Baum & Shipilov, 2006). So, why are there so many CJOs in the US? As noted in the opening chapter, it is because of the way our federal and state Constitutions generally define responsibility for criminal justice functions—generally vested at the state and local levels. In 2013 there were 3,007 counties and 137 "county equivalents" (i.e., Louisiana and Alaska political boundaries), or 3,144 such entities in the US (USGS, n.d.).

Table 7.2 provides an overview of the number of law enforcement organizations (LEOs) across the nation in 2003 and 2013. Sheriff's offices (SOs) are generally organized at the county level. We see that there were 3,061 SOs in 2003 and 3,012 in 2013—a decline of roughly two percent. As noted above, some of that decline could be due to changing functions of SOs in some counties. Turning to local police agencies (smaller political entities than counties), we can see that there were 12,656 such agencies in 2003 and 12,326 in 2013, or a decline of approximately three percent of such agencies over that decade. We will return to declines in a later section.

Let us contrast this variety of CJOs in the US with some of our closest political allies and common law "cousins." In the United Kingdom (England and Wales, Scotland, and Northern Ireland), there are 52 regional policing agencies reporting up to the three governments involved. In Australia, each of the six states and the Northern Territory have state-level police agencies, with the Australian Federal Police providing services to the Capital Territory and Norfolk Island. It is easy to see that primarily because of differing political structures, the number of policing agencies (as well as other components of

TABLE 7.2: CHANGES IN NUMBER OF LAW ENFORCEMENT OFFICES IN THE UNITED STATES, 2003–2013

Agency Type		Total Agencies 2003	Total Agencies 2013	Total Employees 2003	Total Employees 2013	Full-time Sworn 2003	Full-time Sworn 2013	Part-time Sworn 2003	Part-time Sworn 2013	Total Civilian 2003	Total Civilian 2013 Full-time	Total Civilian 2013 Part-time	Total Civilian 2013 Total
Local Police		12,656	12,326	632,031	604,959	451,737	477,317	25,614	26,745	154,680	127,642	30,572	158,124
Sheriffs		3,061	3,012	354,158	351,904	174,251	188,952	9,498	12,356	170,408	162,952	12,823	175,775
Primary State		49	50	83,212	88,497	56,611	58,421	40		25,561	30,076	1,003	31,079
Special Jurisdiction*		1,376		86,797		46,043		5,083		35,689			
Totals		17,142	15,388	1,156,198	1,045,360	728,642	724,690	40,235	39,101	386,338	320,670	44,398	365,068
Change	Pol		-330	3%	-27,072		25,580		1,131				3,534
	SO		-49	2%	-2,254		14,701		2,858				5,367

Source: Burch, 2016; Reaves, 2015a, 2015b.

the US CJS) are going to be larger than our "relatives" who have chosen to organize at a higher level of political division than we have.

Organizational "Sets"—What Organizations Does Your Organization Interact With?

Using an "organizational set" (Scott & Davis, 2007) analysis, we seek to outline the variety of relationships that an organization has with its various organizational partners. All CJOs have a range of services they provide and types of clients or consumers served and/or processed that are similar. For example, at the county level, the law enforcement agencies will have a relationship with each other, a county jail or detention center, the prosecutor, public defender, and the Court. Yet, in different counties, a variety of other organizational partners might come into play with the "focal" organization—or the organization from which we are looking at the relationships. Most organizational set analyses start from the perspective of an individual organization.

For example, the basic relationship(s) between the county jail and the rest of the CJS will be similar whether we are in Los Angeles County (CA), Osceola County (FL), or Rowan County (KY). Even given the size differences between those counties (LA = 9.8 million; Osceola = 270,000; Rowan = 23,000), and the manner in which jailers are selected (LA—Elected Sheriff who selects jail director; Osceola—County Commission appoints jail director; Rowan—Jailer directly elected), some things have to be done in the same manner at each jail. However, there are aspects of that relationship that will be different in each of the three counties.

Regardless of how alike or different the Los Angeles, Osceola, and Rowan jails might be, each of those agencies will have a variety of relationships with non-CJOs that may differ greatly. For example, the relationship between the Los Angeles County jail and the county health department will be greatly different from that between those same organizations in Osceola and Rowan County. If for no other reason, the health departments are vastly different in the counties. Further, the number of supplier and volunteer organizations that interact with Los Angeles County, Osceola County, and Rowan County jails are greatly different. The county jails may have similar contracts with a given type of supply or volunteer agency, but the scope of those relationships is likely to vary greatly. Figure 7.2 provides a simple example of how external organizational behaviors can affect the average daily population of a local jail. After a quick glance, how many CJOs and external organizations do you count? How many different organizational role sets can you identify?

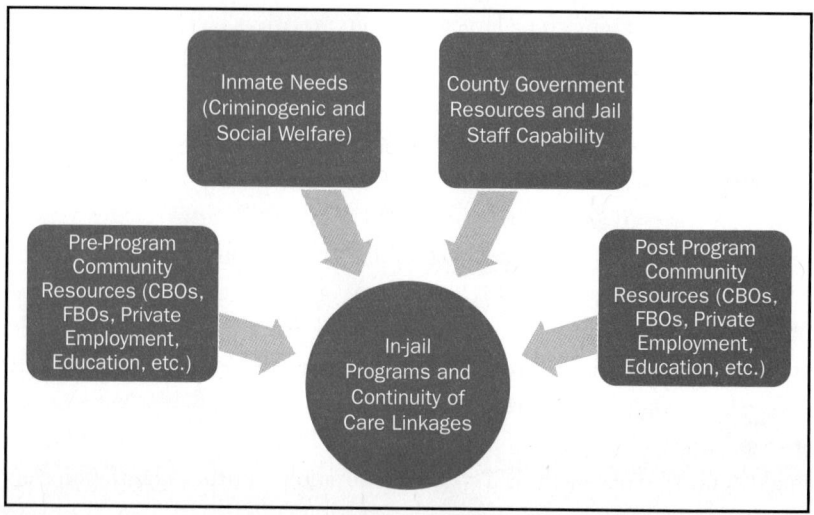

Figure 7.2: The Organizational/Social Ecology of Jail Re-entry Programs.

Narrative: The model proposed suggests that a range of community resources interact with individual characteristics to produce offending behavior. The criminogenic needs of the individual combine with unmet social welfare needs to produce and continue criminal behaviors. The proportion of county government budgets spent on correctional facilities, staff and programs affect the ability to address both criminogenic and social welfare needs of individuals processed through the system (along with the short period of time most people spend in jail). The criminogenic and social welfare needs of the detained individuals are hypothesized to drive the content of the in-jail re-entry programming (and prevention programs in general). The ability to link individual offenders to in-community programs that support and maintain gains (strengths) from re-entry programming and address social welfare needs (deficits) not associated with criminal offending will affect the types of in-jail re-entry programming. In turn, the social welfare needs identified among the individual offenders will shape future community resources needed to meet these social welfare needs.

The role relationships between/among agencies in the focal agency's ecological niche will likely change over time, especially as the criminal law changes. The changing nature of the legal status of marijuana and its effects on the relationships among CJOs as well as non-CJOs is a contemporary example of how the environment can affect the population of organizations and functions of a CJO. Looking at a Drug Court evaluation the first author recently completed, nearly half of the participants were referred because of marijuana. If marijuana is decriminalized in the Court's community, what will happen to the service providers who receive clients from the Drug Court? What will happen to the Drug Court if nearly half of its clientele are no longer subject to CJS supervision? The current move to revisit commercial bail bonds, which exist in 44 states (and the US and the Philippines only), provides another interesting example of how relationships might change if commercial bail is legislated out of existence.

As an exercise, your county jail is your "focal" agency. In this case, you are the newly appointed jail administrator for a troubled jail. You have come in from an agency outside the current county. You need to quickly determine who your CJS "partners" are. Then, you need to determine which non-CJS organizations are also your "partners" in terms of providing services to the jail and inmates, both internal and after release. To do this, develop two network models. First, develop a simple interaction model of the relationships among the key CJOs in your county; think of these as the primary "nodes" in the model. Next, identify at least five key relationships your organizational component has with either a supplier or non-commercial organization. For example, what is the relationship between your component and a janitorial service, health provider, or volunteer organization? Let us keep this simple. If the CJO pays an outside organization for some service, how does that affect the relationship? If the CJO provides the other organization with clients, services, etc., how does that affect the relationship? Once you have developed the two models, you can overlay them and begin to see the range of relationships among the CJOs and other organizations in the local ecology. The document *A Second Look at Alleviating Jail Crowding: A Systems Perspective* (https://www.ncjrs.gov/pdffiles1/bja/182507.pdf) provides an example of such a network model. The role of various agencies in relation to the population of a jail is outlined, along with potential decisions made at organizational levels that affect the people who are housed in the jail.

This "enumeration" of agencies similar to one's own, and the agencies with which one's focal agency deals, helps to reveal the complexity of organizational relationships experienced by US CJOs. Using data from the Law Enforcement Management and Administration Survey (LEMAS) and other Bureau of Justice Statistics (BJS) surveys allows us to examine the variety of formal government agencies there are in the CJS. There are currently no national-level data on the variety and number of non-government organizations (NGOs) that interact with the CJOs. We will return to LEMAS in the next section as we begin to compare CJOs with each other.

"Organizational Populations"—Where Does My Organization Fit?

Hannan and Freeman (1977)—generally credited with the application of ecology to organizations—noted that organizations within a specific ecological domain must have some similarity to each other, or what they termed "*unit character*." That is, what makes my focal organization similar to, or different from, other organizations in my sector? Practically, organizational population approaches suggest that we examine organizations that are relatively alike to determine why some thrive, others muddle along, and some fail. For example, police departments (PDs) would be compared with other police departments; sheriff's offices (SOs) with other sheriff's offices, and so forth. It would make relatively little sense to compare PDs and SOs with State's/District Attorneys, since they do not perform many of the same functions (though some PDs and S/DAs may have their own investigators).

In practical terms, this means being able to "place" one's agency among agencies of like function, size, and structure. In other non-CJS settings, we might think of this as comparing one's home organization with one's competitor organizations. Technically CJOs are supposed to be more cooperative than competitive with each other. But, since they do compete for talent, funding, and other resources, knowing where one's organization fits into the picture may be quite valuable.

Data sets such as the Law Enforcement Management and Administrative Services (LEMAS), and the Census of State and Local Law Enforcement Agencies, collected by the Bureau of Justice Statistics, would be likely the sorts of data that allow you to "locate" your agency among like organizations for information on a variety of comparative information (a matrix of variables). For example, in 2013 there were 12,326 local policing agencies and 3,012 Sheriff's offices in the United States (Reaves, 2015). Of those 12,326 local policing agencies just under half (48%) employed fewer than 10 full-time equivalent sworn officers, and only five percent (5%) employed 100 or more full-time equivalent sworn officers. That five percent of local agencies employed 63% of all full-time officers, however.

If one was trying to compare one's own agency to others, it is likely that the LEMAS data would be the best source to identify similar sized agencies. The LEMAS data also provide a range of other information that can be used to make comparisons even more fine-grained, such as population size served, racial/ethnic diversity of employees, types of specialties (larger agencies only), and so forth. One might construct a matrix of variables such as volume of calls for service, size of the population served, area served (square miles, etc.), cases cleared, and employee size and characteristics, for example. Then, one could add budget information from LEMAS to compare the budgets of the comparison agencies to the "focal" agency's budget. Perhaps then some case might be made that the focal agency is not as well-resourced as comparable agencies and make the case for a budget increase to achieve organizational objectives.

External Control of Criminal Justice Organizations

Just about any United States-based crime drama that features some focus on the executive levels of law enforcement organization (LEO) deals with the "troubles" posed by political and community organizations to the autonomy of the LEO. Among those who are familiar with United Kingdom crime dramas of the 1990s (e.g., "The Bill"), a similar theme on the impact of community advisory boards was a staple of many "police procedurals." Aside from a few references to threats to the political careers of elected prosecutors, we see far less emphasis on the influence of outside organizations on the operations of other portions of the criminal justice system (CJS). The reality of the criminal justice environment is, however, quite different when it comes to the influence and control of criminal justice operations.

A consistent theme in this text is that, while criminal justice organizations (CJOs) are uniquely authorized formal agents of social control, CJOs are also enmeshed in a web of organizational relationships that seek to influence and control CJOs (an homage to Georg Simmel). We have outlined the sources of authority and legitimacy, or at least attempts to achieve and maintain legitimacy, in other sections of the text. Here, we want to provide a brief overview of how other organizational entities attempt to influence, control, and/or conflict with CJOs. Some of these attempts are subtle, while others are quite blatant. Some are the stuff of television and movie lore, and others much less celebrated in the media. In the end, we want to provide the reader with an understanding of constraints on the power of CJOs from a variety of other organizational players and positions (statuses).

In this section we want to pay particular attention to the "regulative" and "normative" pillars of Scott's (Scott, 2008) presentation of Institutional Theory. That is, organizations become similar due to both legal oversight (regulative) and changing social norms (normative). Although CJOs play a core role in legal regulatory processes—they are the "police" in "police powers," they are subject to regulation by other organizations. This is especially true of the political organizations of the government core: Legislative, Executive, and Judicial. As Scott points out, such regulatory control might not be necessarily direct.

For example, the indirectly coercive power of the federal budget can be used to influence a CJO to adopt particular policies. That is, failure to adopt a federal policy might disqualify a CJO from accessing funds to perform some desired function, such as hiring extra police officers. For many years some states resisted the federal requirements to house juveniles in "sight and sound separation" from adults in jails. States had to make decisions about whether the amount of money lost from Office of Juvenile Justice and Delinquency Prevention (OJJDP) block grant funds to the state were less valuable than forcing their county jails to meet the separation requirements.

From 2014 forward, the Prison Rape Elimination Act (PREA) Standards have contained a five percent (5%) penalty on a range of federally-funded grant programs (e.g., Byrne Justice Assistance Grant program, the Juvenile Justice and Delinquency Prevention Act's Title II formula grants, and the Office on Violence Against Women's STOP grants; http://www.ncja.org/issues-and-legislation/prea#sthash.FwoiXlPg.dpuf, accessed September 21, 2016), for states that do not comply with the PREA Standards. Governors of each state must certify that their state prison system and any contract facilities are in compliance on a three-year cycle. As we move forward in the PREA process, Governors and local political leaders will no doubt face decisions about compliance. It will be interesting to observe what role other advocacy organizations play in balancing the costs of compliance with PREA across correctional facilities and the possible loss of funding for other programs. We are likely to see coalitions of organizations supported by those other funding streams pushing their state and local governments to comply in order to avoid loss of funding for their own programs.

Likewise, a county government can influence a Sheriff's Office to perform certain functions by their funding decisions, and a city council or manager can exercise the same influence on a city police department. Crank and Langworthy (1992), following Meyer and Scott (1983), refer to organizational actors who can exercise these influences as "sovereigns." Sovereigns are:

> "agents of authority that are capable of influencing department policy, withholding information or disrupting the flow of resources via such means as litigation, municipal funding or research support for program development; they may also mobilize public sentiment or embarrassing media exposure... Examples of sovereigns in the institutional environment of police organizations include the city council, mayor, police

unions, empowered minority groups, the courts and the voting public" (Crank & Langworthy, 1992, p. 342).

That list can be expanded to include at least the media (Surette, 2013, 2015). And, of course, as we move up the ladder in terms of government oversight, the number of organizations in the "sovereigns" list is likely to grow.

The key point for the reader to remember is that these sovereigns become so primarily because of the organizational position (status) they hold in the environment of the CJO under study. Although the Crank and Langworthy article, along with others, is an application of Institutional Theory, the reader can quickly see how Resource Dependency Theory comes into play. In the end, a key point is that CJOs do not exist in isolation from the rest of the organizational world. CJOs interact not only with individuals in their environment, but with a range of other organizations and organizational fields. CJOs compete for resources of all types, substantive and symbolic, with other government organizations and increasingly with non-government organizations (NGOs). CJOs are also influenced in many indirect ways by these other organizations in the environment. For that reason, we would add "sovereigns" to the list of "stakeholders" who influence CJOs. Sometimes, even the sovereigns have less influence than the "weakest" stakeholders in the community—until those weaker groups organize. We will explore more about a variety of stakeholders in the next section.

Conclusion

This chapter has examined several ways in which organizational theory, especially ecological theory varieties, can be used to study CJOs. We have seen that it is possible to view how CJOs are alike, as well as how they differ from each other. We have discussed ways in which CJOs in similar "sets" can influence each other. This has led to discussions of how CJOs are influenced and controlled by other organizational entities not generally considered part of the formal CJS.

In the next Section we turn to an exploration of other types of organizations in the social environment with which CJOs must deal. These same issues of influence and all of the elements of interorganizational relations detailed in previous chapters will come back into play as we examine CJOs in the broader environment.

Key Words

Census of State and Local Law Enforcement Agencies Survey
Chicago School
Crime prevention
Decision points
Focal/Index agency
Interest
Law Enforcement Management and Administration Survey (LEMAS)
Misdemeanor probation
Normative
Organizational demography
Organizational set
Prison Rape Elimination Act
Privatizing
Regulative
Social Ecology
Sovereigns
Unit character

CHAPTER 8

Applying Criminal Justice/ Criminological Theory to Organizations in the Environment

Learning Objectives:

1. Identify and define five categories of organizations encountered in the larger environment in which criminal justice organizations operate;
2. Apply Merton's modes of adaptation to structural strain ("Anomie Theory") to the five categories of other organizations identified;
3. Apply the concepts from "networked governance" to dealings between criminal justice organizations and other "conventional" organizations in the environment;
4. Discuss how such "conventional" organizations can contribute to the corruption of individuals within the criminal justice organization.

Introduction

We have concentrated on applying organizational theories to criminal justice organizations (CJOs) to this point. In this section we want to begin to look at other organizations in the CJOs' environments. Some of these organizations represent partners, suppliers, and professional organizations dedicated to CJO interests. We will lump these together under the label "conventional" organizations. This should not be taken to mean that there are never conflicts between these conventional organizations and CJOS. However, such conflicts are handled through conventional negotiation and/or legal procedures.

A second category of organizations we are labeling "problematic" in terms of their relations with CJOs. These are often "social movement" groups that may or may not evolve sufficient structure and strategy to become stable organizations. They are often problematic in the sense that they may start out with seemingly or objectively oppositional positions to those of CJOs. Whether the maturing organization adopts non-conventional ways of achieving what are often expressed as socially-desirable goals may be unpredictable. It is this unpredictability of strategy as organizations that we view as problematic, not necessarily the outcomes to be attained.

The final category we have created includes the "anti-conventional" groups. These include both groups that utilize violent revolutionary techniques and criminal organizations. This is grouped primarily around their use of means that are rejected by conventional society to achieve either desired social goals or goals contrary to conventional norms. This is not to suggest that there is not overlap and movement by organizations among these three categories. As we explore more on criminal organizations, for example, we will see how the intersections of criminal organizations and CJOs can lead to undesired outcomes. Perhaps this preliminary overview is starting to seem familiar. That is because we are using a familiar sociological/criminological theory to help explore the relations between CJOs and other organizations in the environment, at least to begin.

Relations with Other Organizations—A Values Approach

Later in this chapter we will discuss networked governance and in Chapter 13 on organizational planning, we will note that the values expressed by formal organizations are often a way of determining what non-governmental/community-based organizations (NGOs/CBOs) make suitable voluntary partners. Here we want to suggest that organizations can be partly differentiated from other organizations in terms of the values they espouse either in word or behavior. That is, we believe it is instructive to take Merton's (Merton, 1967) "modes of adaptation" to structural strain ("anomie theory") and apply it to organizations (see Table 8.1). The basic idea behind structural strain is that there is an imbalance between the socially acceptable goals and the distribution of opportunity to use conventional means to achieve those goals. We generally concentrate on wealth and power as the socially acceptable goals, and then look at the ways in which certain groups' ability to utilize conventional means is blocked.

For our purposes, we want to focus on four of the five modes (ignoring "ritualism") as they apply to five categories of organizations (professional, advocacy, research, social movements, and criminal). Most formal organizations are going to express both their goals and the means for attaining those goals in "conventional" terms. The organization and its members are pursuing socially acceptable ends (goals) using socially acceptable means. Some individuals and groups operating under the umbrella of the conventional organization may indeed act in non-conventional ways. From "dirty tricks" squads in political organizations to industrial espionage to illegal dumping of chemicals, we have many examples of deviance within conventional organizations (Simon, 1996). However, for the most part, these conforming organizations pursue conventional social goals through conventional means.

Revolutionary organizations seek to bring about some substantive difference in social structure. Merton described individuals who adopted the revolutionary adaptation as being alienated from the dominant social structure as most likely to view rebellion as acceptable. Such individuals view the socially prescribed means to achieve socially prescribed as being arbitrary. One of the outcomes desired by the rebellious organization and members is to not only introduce a different social structure, but a social structure in which the goals and means to achieve them are more closely aligned and accessible to all. Rebellion requires a rejection of conventional values. The means to achieve this new social order may be conventional, such as through the political process. The means may also be deviant, as in coups and conflict.

Merton (1967) differentiates "rebellion" from "ressentiment." There are three intertwined components of ressentiment. The first is a diffuse feeling of hate, envy and hostility toward the prevailing conventional social structure. The second is a sense of powerlessness in the ability to express these feelings effectively against the more powerful in the social environment. Finally, the individual(s) must have a continual experience of this perceived powerlessness. Yet, Merton states that ressentiment does not require that the conventional social values be rejected wholly. The focus is more on changing the means by which the desired outcomes can be obtained. This becomes the essential difference between these two inter-related types of rebellion. The ressentiment organization condemns the goals it actually wants to achieve while the rebellious organization condemns what society says it should want. Both view the institutional social system as the problem. Only a change in the social system can bring about the desired resolution.

The mode of adaptation we focus on mostly in criminal justice is "innovation." Innovation occurs when we have the confluence of:

- a cultural emphasis on success and mobility, the blockage of access to the prescribed means to achieve success and mobility for a portion of the society, and;
- individuals who have not been fully socialized into accepting the means-ends linkage in the society.

When an individual desires socially legitimate goals such as money and power, but is blocked from achieving them through access to legitimate means, one path toward the goals involves socially-defined deviant means, such as crime. Merton referred to this as "innovation." We will address the collective strain in Chapter 12 that leads to organized "innovation," or criminal activity.

This brief review of Merton's ideas on structural strain and adaptation allows us to develop a typology of organizations in the environment that interact with, affect, or are affected by criminal justice organizations. This notion of criminal justice organizations being simultaneously affected by other organizations, while affecting the organizations that are affecting it, is a form of "reflexivity" (Mehan & Wood, 1975). In the remainder of this section, we want to explore how other types of organizations in the environment affect and are affected by criminal justice organizations. We believe this will help the reader understand better how treating organizational interaction as a separate level of analysis improves our understanding of the operations of CJOs. It is our notion that the values expressed by organizations—overtly in writing or other statements, or by observed behavior—are important in understanding how CJOs interact with other organizations. In this chapter, we begin with organizations who express agreement with both socially desired goals and employ the socially-approved means to obtain them.

TABLE 8.1: VALUES STRUCTURE OF ORGANIZATIONS ENCOUNTERED IN THE CRIMINAL JUSTICE ENVIRONMENT

Organizational Category	Societal Ends (Goals) +/−	Societal Means +/−
Conventional Organizations:		
Professional Groups	+	+
Advocacy Groups (CBOs/FBOs)	+	+
Research/Think-Tank Groups	+	+
Social Movements (Conventional)	+	+
Problematic Organizations:		
Social Movements ("Ressentiment")	− (+)	+ (−)
Anti-Conventional Organizations:		
Social Movements (Rebellious)	−	−
Criminal ("Innovative")	+	−

Conventional Organizations and CJOs

Throughout the text we have noted how the operational environment in which criminal justice organizations (CJOs) operate has changed since at least 1968. CJOs have moved from being very much "closed" operations to increasingly "open" organizations. Let us use southern prison systems as an example. Because of the climate in the southern states, combined with rural placement of many prisons before the 1990s, southern prison systems have been able to provide much of the food for their prisoners on prison farms. They were relatively independent of commercial supplier most years.

Potter has conducted health accreditation visits to prison farms in one southern state. In that system, one prison provided the egg production for the entire prison system, operated by two prisoners and a supervising correctional officer. Not only did the prison produce enough eggs for the entire state system, but selling the manure from the chicken coop brought in more money to feed back into the operation. Another prison farm provided most of the fresh vegetables and crops such as strawberries for the prison system. At another prison, the furniture for many of the state offices was constructed. Prison industries have often been used to manufacture everything from desks to judges' gavels.

This was one of the reasons per-prisoner operational costs were often so much lower in southern prisons than the rest of the nation. On occasion, however, other businesses have objected to not being able to compete with prison industries because of the low cost of labor in the prisons. In those states, we began to see the erosion of prison industries and the linkages to suppliers from the "free world." Because of his work and research specialties, Potter has also seen and documented the transitions from reliance on prisoners serving as health care providers inside prisons (with or without proper training), to the involvement of state university medical schools providing care (and no use of prisoner labor other than for custodial reasons), to the development of for-profit and non-profit prison (and jail) health care providers in the corporate world. Some of these private health providers function strictly within prisons managed by a private corrections provider, while others operate in state and local facilities as contractors to the systems. Similar patterns can be observed across a range of services that might have once been provided almost completely internal to the prison (or jail) system, but are now "contracted out" to non-governmental agencies.

The point of this quick tour of prison food and health care is that prisons once made it almost as difficult for other organizations, faith-/community-based (F/CBOs) and for-profit, to get into prison as they tried to make it for prisoners to get out of prison. In most places now, F/CBOs and corporate providers have at least controlled access to operate within these facilities. This sometimes includes other government agencies, as well. By the way, Potter also learned that certain types of shoes have metal shanks in the insole while trying to enter San Quentin. Check that before you try to get into a prison… Our point here is that, in organizational terms, prisons (and many jails) have gone from having closed boundary systems to a more permeable boundary—managed, but no longer completely closed.

We have also mentioned the changes in the inclusion of non-CJOs in the operations of the CJS over the course of our professional lives. A basic conundrum is whether we have further "widened the net" of criminal justice (Frazier, Richards, & Potter, 1983), or whether non-CJOs have "penetrated" the CJS. Others may refer to this as "integration" of CJOs with other types of conventional organizations in the community in order to better meet the needs of the community. Operationalizing to answer that set of questions may be difficult. It is clear that the boundaries between CJOs and conventional organizations have become much more permeable, especially since the 1980s.

Networked Governance

At the beginning of the Twenty-first Century, the idea of "networked government" became a new theme. Goldsmith and Eggers (2004) text *Governing by Network* became required reading for those being developed as leaders in the federal government. In many ways, this text reflected trends that had been happening in the state governments for two decades. Goldsmith and Eggers argued that the area of hierarchical government was being replaced by networks of relations between governments and the private sector, for- and non-profit. These networks reflected new demands from citizens, bolstered by the belief that the private sector could deliver the services and products more quickly and cheaply than could government agencies alone. Part of that "cheaper" theme was predicated on the shedding of government jobs and replacing them by contracts with private organizations. Goldsmith and Eggers recommended that we "get past" the debates over whether contracting-out certain services and goods is morally desirable. Rather, it was time to figure out how best to manage the process.

As noted above, the corrections sector—adult and juvenile corrections—was one of the first areas to be subject to contracting in the CJS. We would argue that we still haven't gotten past the "moral" argument on private prisons (and jails). Nor have we decided that contracting-out is necessarily more efficient or effective than government provision, if the 2016 United States Department of Justice announcement it would seek no further private prison contracts is any indication.

Goldsmith and Eggers had warned that the management of networked services would be difficult, of course. However, the ability of private sector organizations to be flexible and to innovate (not in the Mertonian sense; at least, not most of the time) ways of delivering services would be beneficial to the public. Networked providers also allowed for decision-making at the local level, providing a decentralized approach to meeting the needs of citizen consumers at the local level, rather than having to run everything back to the state or federal level for approval.

Among the challenges of networked governance outlined by Goldsmith and Eggers was what we might call the "weak link" problem. If you are relying on a network to deliver the required services, the quality of the service is likely to be threatened by the poor performance of any one provider. Likewise, if your network requires one organization to supply another and the supply relationship breaks down, so does the network. Making sure the correct provider organizations are selected for the network in the first place is a key challenge to the utilization of private sector providers. We discussed some of the more technical organizational issues associated with such coordination in section 1.

This does require an approach to management and leadership very different from when one has hierarchical control. We are not going to focus on the new skills and approaches to such management here, but recommend that the reader look at some of the management and administration texts we have referenced elsewhere. Many of what government types call "knowledge, skills, and abilities," or KSAs, are not found in undergraduate education; perhaps not even in graduate programs in Criminal Justice—unless the programs have a strong Public Administration component. One of the weaknesses in networked governance has been the lack of individuals in the government agencies who can effectively develop, implement, and oversee the operations of a networked provider system. Certainly things have improved since the beginning of contracting-out in the 1980s. It is still imperative that networked governance schemes have capable guardianship provided through well-trained contract managers in order to deliver effective services in an efficient manner and avoid corruption (Wright, 2010).

Improving technology was one key to the types of functions that could be placed in private hands on behalf of governments. In the post-9/11 environment, information sharing across all levels of law enforcement agencies became big business. Whether or not it has become a standard of practice probably depends upon where one is located. We will address this further in Chapter 14.

Corrections, Contracts, and Corruption

We have noted elsewhere that correctional systems are among the most complicated organizations in the CJS. That is because an incarceration facility must meet the needs of those housed within across multiple domains, provide security within and for the community, move detainees, inmates, and prisoners to and from court hearings, and provide a range of other services. All incarceration facilities, both jails and prisons (and some mental hospitals), must provide some of the same functions as other facilities, regardless of size. As size and the duration of incarceration increases, so does the complexity and scope of services that must be provided.

Corrections was one of the first areas of the CJS targeted for privatization—whole or partial—because it was perceived that the private sector could deliver or manage incarceration more efficiently than government. Potter remembers conversations with correctional officials and legislators that featured stories of how airlines had saved thousands of dollars by dropping a single black olive from the salads served to passengers on airline flights. Yes, a meal once came on many flights, along with snacks and drinks. By going private, correctional facilities could avoid government contracts for fuel, allowing them to float with the market and, if prices went down, save money; if prices when up, well… The phrase heard with great frequency was "cut the fat from the bone." While legislators were hearing about "efficiency," academics were arguing about "effectiveness." Guess whose concerns were most important.

Over the past 30 years government-run correctional systems have been challenged to become as financially efficient as their private contractors. As the private providers were able to "cut away the fat" and profit margins shrunk, the costs of incarceration between public and private providers has probably narrowed. Apparently the federal government thought so in the summer of 2016 when the United States Department of Justice (DOJ) (Office of Inspector General, 2016) announced they would seek no further contracts with private prison providers (Savage, 2016). Deputy Attorney General Sally Q. Yates acknowledged that the "private prisons served an important role during a difficulty period, but time has shown that they compare poorly to our own bureau (sic) facilities." Of course, the private providers disagreed with this assessment.

It remains to be seen whether or not other federal agencies, especially the Department of Homeland Security and the United States Marshals Service, state systems, and/or local jail systems will start to pull back on utilization of private incarceration providers. The group not directly mentioned in this discussion—stock holders in the for-profit corporations—at first reacted negatively. *Fortune* (Reuters, 2016) reported an initial loss of up to one-third of the value of stocks among private prison companies after the announcement from DOJ, but a recovery near pre-announcement levels for the companies within a few days. Here again we see how a networked approach to delivery of a criminal justice function extends well beyond the immediate corrections environment to affect organizations in the private sector such as pension funds and university endowments. Yet, our true concern with corrections and incarceration should be on protecting the community and rehabilitating offenders—right? And, in the time since we wrote this paragraph, an election has put much of the discussion of privatization of federal corrections back on the table. This provides a living example of how changes in the broader environment can influence the CJS.

Harding (2001) predicted that the days of wholesale take-over of correctional facilities by private providers would come to an end. In its place would be an incremental approach to contracting-out specific services within facilities. This is observable in regards to health/medical (physical, dental, and behavioral), laundry, food, telephone, communications, and commissary services, in particular. As long as it is perceived that such services can be delivered by private providers with more economic efficiency it is likely that privatization of those services will continue. Exhorbitant costs for commissary products and inmate telephone services allow for large profit margins to contractors and slush fund kick-backs to correctional agencies, This brings us to our final thoughts in this section.

The final caveat about networked governance in the CJS involves the issue of corruption. We have witnessed several high profile instances since 2000 of corruption among high-ranking corrections officials often related to contracts with private providers. While it may be disheartening to believe that "conventional" corporations would use corrupt tactics to make money off of prisoners, our empirical experiences tell us they will. When there is good money to be made, we have witnessed conventional corporate actors using bribes of various types to influence the decisions of correctional officials to benefit the corporation. As long as there is perceived profit to be made from dealing with the CJS, it is likely that we will continue to see instances of corrupt behavior amongst CJS officials.

PRIVATE INDUSTRY CONTROL OVER CAPITAL PUNISHMENT

The death penalty is not just divisive within the United States. According to Amnesty International, around two-thirds (141) of nations had abolished the use of the death penalty by 2016. This places the United States federal government at odds with the majority of other nations and international organizations. In the United States, criminal justice issues are generally left to the states, and 31 continue to have the death penalty as an option in sentencing, while 19 do not. There are a number of non-governmental organizations, both civil and religious, that oppose the death penalty. Despite the sometimes high esteem in which these organizations are held, they have yet to achieve the abolition of the death penalty in the majority of states and the federal government and military.

There is a group of organizations that may put an end to the death penalty in action, though perhaps not in statute—the pharmaceutical industry organizations. In May 2016 Pfizer Corporation announced it would not supply certain drugs used in lethal injections to state correctional systems. This placed Pfizer among 20 or more pharmaceutical companies who had taken similar steps (http://www.nytimes.com/2016/05/14/us/pfizer-execution-drugs-lethal-injection.html?_r=0, accessed September 20, 2016). It has become increasingly difficult for states to obtain the preferred substances for lethal injections.

These are corporations not generally associated with the criminal justice system—though some of their products may be associated with those processed through the system. They are private, generally for-profit companies incorporated not only in the United States, but also European nations, such as Pfizer. The reader may note that all member states of the European Union (including Great Britain) have abolished the death penalty as a sentencing option.

Another organization contributing to the potential de facto abolition of the death penalty in the United States is the American Medical Association (and American Osteopathic Association). Physicians are barred by professional ethics from participating in the execution process, not simply administering lethal substances. The American Pharmacists Association has discouraged their membership from providing the substances favored by correctional systems for lethal injection. While these organizations may not get the death penalty

> sentence removed from state and federal statutes, they will certainly play a role in limiting its implementation.
>
> The involvement of these non-government (and sometimes foreign) organizations in controlling or at least influencing United States criminal justice practice provide a demonstration of control by non-official organizations. In the Scott (2008) Institutional Theory framework, their influence is much more in the cultural-cognitive column. That is, they seek to change the thinking and practice of American sentencing practices through shaming rather than legal or regulatory activities. In our "values" approach, firmly in that cultural-cognitive column, we observe that the values expressed by these corporations and professional associations can directly affect the behavior of CJOs, even when the CJO behavior is expressed as "the will of the people."

Conclusion

This chapter introduced our typology of organizations encountered in the organizational environment occupied by criminal justice organizations. The typology will be developed further in the remaining chapters of this section of the text. We concentrated on the more functional types of organizational relations encountered in the criminal justice system here. Using Goldsmith's and Egger's notions of "networked government," which underlay the "new government" movements of the 1990s, we explored why these inter-organizational relations are increasingly important to criminal justice organizations. These involve many of the contractors and legitimate businesses with which criminal justice organizations interact. In the coming chapters we will explore more "conventional," "problematic," and "unconventional" organizations encountered in the environment.

Key Words

Anomie theory	Networked governance
Closed boundaries	Permeable boundaries
Contracting-out	Privatization
Conventional Rebellious	Ressentiment
Innovation	Structural strain
Modes of adaptation	Widen the net (net-widening)

CHAPTER 9

Professional Associations: Assistance and Enforcement

Learning Objectives:

1. Define the difference between a profession and an occupation;
2. Identify the differences between types of "membership" organizations and "positional" associations;
3. Discuss the role of funding for professional associations and the potential impact on association positions and activities;
4. Identify the variety of services provided by criminal justice professional associations;
5. Identify and discuss the role of conferences, association media, and training programs in the professionalization of criminal justice organizations;
6. Identify and describe different types of accreditation and standards; and,
7. Discuss and critique the role of accreditation in the control of criminal justice organizations by non-criminal justice organizations.

Introduction

In the previous chapter we introduced a typology of organizations ("categories") in the organizational environment occupied by criminal justice organizations (CJOs). We discussed briefly the relationships between CJOs and "conventional" organizations, especially those with some form of commercial relationship to the CJO. In this chapter we want to continue developing the range of conventional organizations that have an influence on, and are influenced by, CJOs. One of the categories of organization we find curiously missing from discussions of criminal justice theory is the professional associations that serve the CJOs. These organizations are very important, in our opinion, because they have the ability to bring about change in CJOs, as well as resist changes imposed by organizations we will discuss later.

Professional Associations: Types and Functions

Professional associations receive mention in most texts on administration and management in criminal justice, but very little attention is paid to their role in assisting and controlling CJOs. We need to spend a moment defining what we mean by a "profession." Jary & Jary (1991) define a **profession** as "any middle class occupational group, characterized by claims to a high level of technical and intellectual expertise, autonomy in recruitment and discipline, and a commitment to public service" (p. 501). Scott & Davis (2007) provide a brief history of "the professions" and what we would term "organized professionals." Those familiar with the history of CJOs will recognize the struggles of different sectors to achieve the recognition of "profession" and any rewards or privileges associated with being a professional. This is the process of "**professionalization**." The term "**occupation**," generally refers to the category of work in which the individual is engaged. There is often a sense of a "profession" occupying a higher social status than an "occupation." Given the humble beginnings of most CJO sectors in the working class, we would argue this process continues. Professional associations play a major role in the professionalization process.

Returning to the definition of profession above, we can characterize **professional associations** as organizations (mostly incorporated as non-profits) that seek to further the interests of those in their sector while maintaining that sectoral interest also serves the public interest. We will return to the issues of professional association certifications in a later section. In the remainder of this section we will focus on some of the services professional associations in the CJS provide to their membership, as well as the role they play in the broader society. Most professional associations among CJOs in the United States are going to fall into the categories of either "membership" or "positional" organizations. We want to take a little space to explain the differences between these two.

The majority of professional associations in criminal justice are **membership organizations**. That is, anyone employed in or interested in the sector can join the association and pay dues. At the broadest level, for example, the American Jail Association does not state that being involved with a jail system is required until one begins to complete the membership application (http://www.americanjail.org/wp-content/uploads/2015/10/Membership-form-10-29-15.pdf; accessed August 29, 2016). Given that they allow academics and students to join, the membership requirements are only to list a jail with which one has an affiliation. The American Correctional

Association states that "membership is open to all individuals and organizations actively working in the corrections profession" (http://www.aca.org/ACA_Prod_IMIS/ACA_Member/Membership/ACA_Member/Membership/Membership_Home.aspx?hkey=582e3c44-b2c1-47e3-be59-3930f0ac5a35; accessed August 29, 2016).

Other membership organizations may require that one hold a particular certification before being eligible to join. An example would be the North American Association of Wardens & Superintendents (NAAWS) whose voting membership is restricted to serving and retired wardens at all levels in the United States and Canada. There is a category of non-voting membership available to "supporters of Wardens" though it represents less than 10 percent of the membership. Several associations have broad membership but subgroups within the association that require passing a particular certification. The National Commission on Correctional Health Care (NCCHC) and the Certified Correctional Health Care Professional (CCHP) are examples of such a relationship.

Likewise, the International Association of Chiefs of Police (IACP; founded 1893) has a broad membership base. "Active membership," however, is restricted to "chiefs and superintendents of police as well as command-level police officers in public law enforcement agencies. Active members have the right to vote to determine official IACP policy and to elect association officers at the annual conference" (http://www.iacp.org/Criteria; accessed August 29, 2016). The "active members" of the IACP are also eligible to be "active members" of the National Sheriffs' Association (NSA). Active membership in the NSA is a bit broader than in the IACP, as it includes sheriffs, sheriffs-elect, sworn employees of sheriff's offices, military police and security, private law enforcement, CJ administrators (including political office holders), and even academics(!) (https://www.sheriffs.org/nsa-membership/requirements-dues; accessed August 29, 2016).

Returning to the idea of organizational boundaries and membership, we can see that what we are referring to as "membership" organizations have boundaries defined by membership criteria. Some boundaries are more permeable than others. Even within the membership organization we find boundaries within boundaries. These are often based on some form of certification or accreditation of either the individual member or the organizational member.

Other organizations are what we are calling "**positional**" **organizations**. That is, membership is generally dependent upon occupying a position in a particular other organization. As an example, the Association of State Correctional Administrators (ASCA) restricts its membership thusly:

> "Membership consists of persons who are appointed to serve on a full-time basis to be directly responsible for the administration of the correctional facilities or correctional system of a jurisdiction. These persons include heads of state corrections agencies, Los Angeles County, heads of Cook County (Chicago), the District of Columbia, New York City, Philadelphia, the Federal Bureau of Prisons, The Correctional Service of Canada, each province of Canada, and any United States territory, possession, and/or commonwealth. ASCA Associate members include former administrators of the above jurisdictions who have successfully served as administrators for an aggregate of at least three years in one or more jurisdictions and who have been nominated and accepted into associate status by ASCA's Executive Committee." (www.asca.net; accessed on August 29, 2016).

At an even broader level, and with increasing influence on the criminal justice system (CJS) over the past two decades, membership in the Council of State Governments (CSG) is restricted to the states and territories of the United States. The representatives of the jurisdictions are appointed by the state/territory governor (or appointee), leaders of each legislative branch, and the highest-raking judge in each jurisdiction. The Council of State Governments does allow for international partners (http://www.csg.org/governance/documents/ArticlesofOrgCSGLeadersGuide2015.pdf; accessed August 29, 2016).

With positional professional associations, one is eligible to be a member only if one occupies a designated position at local, state, federal, or certain other organizations associated with criminal justice. The key point between these two categories of professional associations is that the boundaries become increasingly rigid between the two. One moves from a general membership to a specified set of members and rights. Of course, if an eligible jurisdiction does not wish to participate in a positional association they are not compelled to do so.

Funding: Independence and Control

That leads us to a discussion of how associations are funded. All such organizations collect some sort of "**dues**." For general membership organizations these funds generally come from either individual dues-paying members or from corporate memberships. Such organizations may also receive funding for more specific educational programs and merchandise. We will explain more about the types of services professional associations offer later. For now, suffice to read that dues pay for the administrative costs of organizational offices, magazines and newsletters, websites, and so forth. Some professional associations also have annual or semi-annual conferences that range in price for attendance. Depending upon the nature of the association, they may also feature a "trade show" component where exhibitors pay a fee to display their products or services. We discuss the growth of advertising by certain sectors in the correctional field elsewhere, and those advertisements are usually with media associated with professional associations. Like other organizations in the social environment, diversification in sources of income probably play a strong role in the stability of the organization. That should take you back to resource dependency theory.... .

Positional associations are generally funded by "corporate" membership dues. That is, if the jurisdiction wishes to have representation/participation in the association, they must pay dues; it is not the responsibility of the individual appointed to be in the association. Other sources of support may not be in the form of dues. This is where the overlap between non-member organizations and the positional associations opens them to some criticism. We often observe contract and supplier agencies providing "hospitality suites," golf matches, and dinners to these positional associations at conferences and other gatherings. As we have seen in the area of health care and medical associations, this often draws concerns with influence and leads to restrictions on such relationships.

The role of federal funding for some of these organizations cannot be ignored. We will develop further the idea that these associations play a strong role in the tendency toward "isomorphism" (standardization) later in this section. For now, we want to stress that federal funding for certain aspects of the associations' activities has become increasingly important over the past several decades. This is particularly true for organizations such as CSG who have developed research and technical assistance capacity through increasing receipt of federal funds. Whether those federal funds have been diverted from the academic sector is an interesting empirical question to be examined. The Prison Rape and Elimination Act (PREA) has also pumped new life into several organizations we will examine later as the category of "think tank/advocacy" organizations. The linkages between membership and positional professional associations and the think tank/advocacy organizations will also be explored.

Interorganizational Relations

This leads us to the interactions among professional associations and with other conventional organizations in their environments. We will write primarily from our experiences in the corrections sector. When the ACA ("membership association") holds its summer Congress and winter Conference, we generally find meetings at the front-end of several of the positional associations. At those meetings are often briefings by federal government agencies about current and anticipated policy issues that might affect the organizations being represented at the meeting. These conferences represent one of the few opportunities annually or semi-annually that one can find leaders of prisons, juvenile justice, correctional health care, chaplains, and others gathered in one place and interacting with each other. Likewise, IACP meetings provide an opportunity for leaders from all size police agencies to interact at least annually. Outside of government agencies and universities, professional associations represent one of the few organizations with what Goldsmith and Egger (2004) call the "**power to convene**" a broad range of stakeholders in one place. We would note that universities invoke this particular power on a depressingly infrequent basis.

We want to note that professional associations are also broken out often into "interest group" membership within sectors. Break-outs by ethnicity and gender are among the most common groups. For example, there is the National Association of Blacks in Criminal Justice, the National Black Prosecutors Association, Hispanic American Police Command Officers Association, the National Organization of Hispanics in Criminal Justice, Mexican American Correctional Association (in California), and the Association of Women Executives in Corrections. Table 9.1 provides a sample of key professional associations whose membership is based on ethnic or gender interests in the CJ occupation.

Services Provided by Professional Associations

In several texts on administration and management in the CJS one finds mentions of professional associations primarily in relation to the services and products they provide. Such descriptions are generally devoid of how these services and products fit into organizational processes. There is almost no use of organizational theory to explain the role these services play in controlling organizations in the CJS. We want to at least briefly attempt to address these short-comings in this section.

TABLE 9.1: A SAMPLING OF CRIMINAL JUSTICE PROFESSIONAL ORGANIZATIONS FOCUSED ON ETHNICITY AND/OR GENDER

Organization	Basis of Membership (Interest)	Sector	Social Media Site
National Association of Blacks in Criminal Justice	Ethnicity	System-wide	http://nabcj.org/
National Organization of Hispanics in Criminal Justice	Ethnicity	System-wide	http://www.nohcj.org/
National Black Police Association	Ethnicity	Policing	http://www.blackpolice.org/
Hispanic National Law Enforcement Association	Ethnicity	Policing	http://www.hnlea.org/#Home%20Page
National Latino Peace Officers Association	Ethnicity	Policing	http://www.nlpoa.com/
Hispanic American Police Command Officers Association	Ethnicity	Policing	http://hapcoa.org/home
National Asian Peace Officers' Association	Ethnicity	Policing	http://napoablue.org/
National Association of Women Law Enforcement Executives	Gender	System-wide	http://nawlee.org/
Association of Women Executives in Corrections	Gender	Corrections	http://www.awec.us/en/
International Association of Women Police	Gender	Policing	http://www.iawp.org/
National Organization of Black Women in Law Enforcement, Inc.	Gender & Ethnicity	System-wide	http://www.nobwlenational.org/
Women in Federal Law Enforcement	Gender	Police and Prosecutors	http://www.wifle.org/index.htm#galleryimages/01.jpg
National Black Prosecutors Association	Ethnicity	Prosecutors	http://blackprosecutors.org/
National Hispanic Prosecutors Association	Ethnicity	Prosecutors	https://www.facebook.com/National-Hispanic-Prosecutors-Association-NHPA-122006871156069/

Conferences provide more than just an opportunity to convene representatives together from multiple agencies in one place. Conferences often provide the final step in the governance of the professional association. In short, they are often the official business meeting of the association. Association business may have been discussed through a variety of committees over the course of the year preceding the conference. At the conference, final votes will be taken before the topic under discussion is adopted or rejected by the association. Sometimes an issue can take several years of discussion, committee meetings, reports, and such before the final vote occurs. This is especially true of standards development, which we will discuss later.

Conferences, as noted earlier, also provide a forum for the presentation of new products and services from vendors. We have discussed how technology forms an environment for organizations earlier. In the CJS, technology of all types has developed at an almost dizzying pace over the past 20 years. It is not unusual to attend a CJ professional association meeting and be met by a large "trade show" event. If one looks at a conference guide from a major CJ professional association meeting, it is likely one will find a range of services ranging from weapons, armor, software, hardware, health, food, insurance, and education. By the way, the same food services vendor on our campus serves many correctional systems across the nation. No doubt the mix of vendors changes from sector to sector at conferences. It is unlikely that the same set of vendors will be at a law enforcement (e.g., IACP or NSA) conference as at the National District Attorneys Association meeting.

While not scientific by any means, over the past decade Potter has asked professionals in the CJS where they get most of their information about trends and issues in their particular sector of the CJS, outside of academies and in-service training. The two primary sources identified are conferences and magazines/newsletters provided by professional associations. Experience suggests that the quality of training at conferences is quite variable. This is because it is often provided by members of the association, who may be focused on a rather narrow issue or source of information. As noted earlier, education is one of the services provided by or in conjunction with professional associations. We will explore how this fits into organizational analysis shortly.

Magazines/Newsletters/Social Media

Most professional associations have, at a minimum, a periodic newsletter. Larger associations may have a professional magazine, as well. Access to these media is usually included in the annual dues. These media are increasingly available via a website restricted to membership. They are generally copyrighted materials. Newsletters tend to feature updates and current issues specifically addressed by the association. These are items of interest to the membership, but not necessarily to a broader audience.

Magazines, on the other hand, are "slicker" forms of communication to the membership and about the association to others in the environment. Magazines often feature contributions by authorities outside of the association membership. A reader might find an article from an association member about an issue of interest to the membership, followed by an article by an unaffiliated academic or government representative on the same or a different topic. Articles in association magazines are not necessarily "peer-reviewed," but may be subject to review by an organizational member with expertise in the topic. Contributions from government sources will generally have gone through some "clearance" process at the agency that operates as both a peer-review and a censorship process—making sure the position of the government is clear while disavowing anything written in the article that might become inconvenient at a later date.

Many professional associations in the CJS were a bit late to the social media game beyond a basic website with membership information. However, since around 2010, most have developed not only award-winning websites, but have begun to venture into the worlds of Facebook, Twitter, LinkedIn, and so forth. This is often driven by taking on younger staff who, in turn, demonstrate the importance of these media for attracting and communicating with younger members. This is an area where future students will no doubt find fertile material for research purposes.

Magazines, newsletters and social media are important "organs" of an association. They convey a sense of what is important to the association. In addition, they feature the associations' positions on key elements. These function as cues to the membership about the nature of the issue. Sometimes they become "talking points" for the membership to employ in public discussions about a particular topic. In effect, they are a way of conveying the "normative" position of the association. That normative position should be held by the membership (individual members). Magazines and newsletters are important devices for defining the reality of a given CJS sector, as well as prescribing ways of acting to achieve desired organizational/sectoral goals. We will return to this point later in the section.

Education

Professional associations have played a key role in the "professionalization" of CJOs and their employees, particularly over the past half-century. Because a profession claims "a high level of technical and intellectual expertise" among its membership, educational services are key elements of professional association activities. The issues discussed in earlier chapters about the relationship between strategy and structure is particularly interesting here.

Professional education was once almost exclusively the domain of the members of the association. However, with the increasing complexity of the CJ field and changing technologies for the delivery of educational programs, we have seen the development of several relationships between professional associations and institutions of higher education. While many in the field might say they prefer to receive educational programs in a classroom setting, the development of on-line technology has changed both access to education and the manner in which it is delivered. "Correspondence" courses have given way to on-line webinars and learning management systems that allow association members to access educational materials on their own time. Contrast this with having to attend classes at a particular time and location to receive the content and seek certification or licensure. In fact, some of you reading this may be taking a course on-line for which this is a required reading. Thank you!

The focus of professional education provided through professional associations is different from that provided through formal colleges and universities. The associations' educational offerings are generally oriented toward either a professional certification of some kind (discussed in the next section), or toward a specific issue that has arisen in the sector. The implementation of the Prison Rape Elimination Act (PREA) or "implicit bias" training provide some examples. In a university course, we are likely to touch on these issues and perhaps provide an analysis of research on the topic. In the field, however, professional associations are going to focus on the legal environment surrounding the issue, mandatory or voluntary standards on the issue, solutions to the issue, and enforcement issues. In short, professional education will tend to be much more focused (training) than the university educational experience.

Educational/training programs provided through professional associations are excellent examples of the **normative processes** of organization(s). Topics that are deemed important to the membership of the association—generally decided by a set of elected or appointed members—are developed to meet specific outcomes and pushed out to the membership. Important topics are often the result of some change in the legal or social environments in which the association members operate. The association's educational offerings carry the authority and legitimacy of the sector and become desired among the membership. These educational offerings are not only ways of keeping the association members up to date on the technologies and strategies of the sector, but play a key role in the professionalization process.

Most professional association educational programs result in some form of "**certification**." We want to contrast this with "**licensure**" in a particular area. We often experience some confusion in the academic realms from people who do not understand the difference between a professional certification and a license. A license is generally issued by a government organization. A certification can be issued by just about any organization. The license has the backing of a regulatory process; a certification need not have any backing.

For example, here in Florida you can obtain up to a doctoral degree from at least four state universities. Surely that "certifies" you for something, right? But, you can't become a sworn law enforcement or corrections officer without attending a Florida Department of Law Enforcement (FDLE) certified training academy (or another equivalent for those moving here). The training academies in Florida are operated by what are currently known as "state colleges" (formerly community colleges). It is doubtful that more than a statistical handful of university criminal justice and criminology faculty are certified by FDLE to train recruits (other than as a general exception based on expertise). Every member of the state college academy teaching group must be, however.

Many professional associations offer certification in particular areas. For example, Potter once earned the National Commission on Correctional Health Care (NCCHC) "Certified Correctional Health Care Professional" certification. The certification lapsed due to no need for a Sociologist to do **continuing education**, which is often a requirement to maintain professional association certification. The university department where the authors currently work offers a variety of "certificates" at both undergraduate and graduate levels. These have no backing outside of the department and university. Certifications offered by professional associations, on the other hand, tend to be recognized across the sector served by the professional association. They represent an acknowledgement that the individual has completed an educational process valued by the sector, and that the expectation that the member will continue to develop their knowledge in that area or lose certification. Certification does not carry the weight of government-backed/required licensure. Certification does represent a consensus among professionals in the field that an individual has mastered some level of knowledge required to function effectively in the sector. That is, the individual is or is on the way to becoming a "professional" in the sector, a process of normalization. In the next section, we are going to argue that these professionalizing processes are essentially part of moving organizations toward an isomorphic state. That is, making them all alike.

Standards and Accreditation

When writing about professional education offered through professional associations, the reader might note that we focused on the individual member. Here we want to move back to the organizational level and talk about a key area professional associations offer to CJOs as organizations—**standards development** and **accreditation**. So, what is a standard? It seems like the definition would be pretty obvious, given that standards and accreditation are key to professional associations. Well, it is not that obvious. A wide-ranging search for a concise definition of professional standards reveals little joy. In some instances standards are equated to what we present in the chapter on organizational change and planning as "objectives." Most websites provide an overview of the activities of units dedicated to enforcing professional standards. Yet, other than reference to the set of standards they enforce, they do not define the term "standards." This is not unique to criminal justice, by any means.

Let us take a quick tour of the history of standards in criminal justice and examine some of the ways "standard" is presented in the CJS professional association sector. We begin with the American Correctional Association, the oldest major professional association in the United States criminal justice sector. The ACA website mentioned earlier states that corrections standards were first attempted in 1870, at the founding of what has become ACA. Further development occurred in the 1940s through the 1970s, with a standing "Commission on Accreditation for Corrections" founded in 1974.

ACA now publishes 22 different standards manuals that address all components of correctional operations. These include general operations, correctional industries, food service, and health care services. The American Jail Association (AJA) and that American Probation and Parole Association (www.appa-net.org) defer to the ACA standards on most operational standards, while maintaining separate training programs, initiatives and codes of ethics. ACA standards cover not only prisons and jails, but juvenile and community corrections, as well. In the early days such standards were generally process driven. That is, as long as certain activities were documented, the standard was met. Consistent with the "**quality movement**" to be discussed in Section 4, ACA standards began a process toward becoming "performance-based" standards. That is, "agencies collect, track, and analyze internal outcomes related to each standard in order to gauge their performance and adjust their operations accordingly." Consistent with the ideals of the quality movement, standards are constantly revised through a process of solicitation from the field annually. Of course, like the development of a new standard, revision of standards can take a longer than anticipated time frame.

IACP and the NSA, and all Police Officer Standards and Training (POST) state level offices, participate in the International Association of Directors of Law Enforcement Training (IADLEST; http://www.iadlest.org/Projects/ModelStandards.aspx). Although IADLEST traces the issue of professionalism back to the efforts of August Vollmer, they note that what resembles a standard began to emerge in the POST state-level organizations in the late 1960s. These offices "exist to assure all citizens that peace officers meet minimum standards of competency and ethical behavior. POST organizations also have an obligation to the officers and agencies that they regulate, to adopt programs that are sensible, effective, and consistent with contemporary notions of what standards should be for all officers. It is in this spirit of growth and responsiveness that the International Association of Directors of Law Enforcement Standards & Training have resolved to establish a set of MODEL MINIMUM STANDARDS to which all states may aspire" (emphasis in original). One IACP document devoted to establishing policy-procedure manuals (Orrick, n.d.), defines "standards" as "[g]uidelines or performance requirements that establish benchmarks for agencies to use in developing the organizational structure and measuring its service delivery system" (p. 1).

Standards fall into two primary categories in the criminal justice world—"**voluntary consensus**" and "**mandatory**" standards (http://www.standardslearn.org/lessons.aspx?key=53&okey=10; accessed on September 2, 2016). These terms can become confusing because, even within the voluntary consensus standards, the areas covered mostly by professional associations, generally contain "mandatory" or "required" standards. However, these are usually the professional association standards that a facility or agency must achieve in order to qualify for accreditation by the association.

Voluntary, consensus standards "are standards developed or adopted by voluntary consensus standards bodies, both domestic and international. These standards include provisions requiring that owners of relevant intellectual property have agreed to make that intellectual property available on a non-discriminatory, royalty-free or reasonable royalty basis to all interested parties" (https://www.whitehouse.gov/omb/circulars_a119#3; accessed on September 2, 2016).

There are several "voluntary consensus standards bodies" across the CJS, and all "encourage the participation of federal representatives in these bodies to increase the likelihood that the standards they develop will meet both public and private sector needs." Such bodies are also to have these four attributes: "openness," "balance of interests," "due process," and "an appeals process." That is, the standards development process must be open to those with an interest ("standing") in the behaviors, processes, or products to which the standard applies. Whether it is policing or corrections, the community and affected individuals should be included in the standards development process. Those to whom the standards will be applied must also be guaranteed that the standards against which they will be judged are clear and that disagreements between the agency being accredited and the accrediting organization/association are subject to a clear appeals process. Sounds like something we in the CJS should be familiar with, right?

Truly mandatory standards are almost exclusively the domain of a government agency. They are legally known as "'**Government-unique standards**,' which are developed by the government for its own uses." They often have the force of law and/or licensure to them. For our purposes the Prison Rape Elimination Act (PREA) provides a great example. The PREA standards were developed initially through a consultative process among CJS professionals, survivors, and advocacy groups. All of this was coordinated by the National Prison Rape Elimination Commission (NPREC). Potter chaired one group developing one area of the PREA draft standards. At the end of the process, a "think-tank" group took administrative responsibility for compiling and editing the standards for the NPREC. We will not go into the differences between the draft standards developed by the original committees and those presented to the NPREC and Attorney General here. Suffice to say the differences were substantial and required a prolonged period of negotiation before the Attorney General approved the final standards. The key point is that, once approved by the Attorney General and promulgated (i.e., published as rules) by the United States Department of Justice, the PREA standards have the force of law for correctional agencies across the nation. They have been incorporated into the "voluntary" standards of the ACA as "required" standards, as well.

Each accrediting body in the CJ professional world will publish their monitoring and accreditation process. These can be found at the websites listed in the text. The processes tend to be broken into two types. Some associations employ their own **accreditation teams**. These are generally staff or contractors who are well-versed and certified by the association in the accreditation requirements. These teams will visit agencies or facilities seeking accreditation and assess the site against the standards. A primary advantage of this approach to accreditation is that it is often viewed as more "objective" than the next approach outlined.

The second type of accreditation process involves a form of "**peer-review**" accreditation. This process generally uses association members who have completed special training and certification in the standards of the association. They visit the facility or agency seeking accreditation and conduct an assessment against the applicable standards. The "peers" may be active in the sector or retired; it is their ability to assess against the standards that matters. However, the use of peers has left some to complain about possible "quid pro quo" or deals among peers from different systems to hold each other less liable for deviation from standards. The movement toward performance-based standards, in conjunction with a transparent assessment process, is one way to short-circuit these complaints.

Accreditation is a time-consuming process for the organizations that undergo the process. It is not uncommon in larger agencies to employ an individual whose function is mostly to handle the accreditation issues, from preparation through any appeals that might be lodged. In smaller agencies that seek accreditation, the accreditation manager will often perform this among many other functions. Given the personnel impact, as well as the costs, associated with accreditation, one is likely to ask why an organization would go through the process.

The ACA website (http://www.aca.org/ACA_Prod_IMIS/ACA_Member/Standards___Accreditation/Seeking_Accreditation/ACA_Member/Standards_and_Accreditation/Seeking_Accreditation_Home.aspx?hkey=ed52ffa0-24e4-4575-9242-1aa9d7107e69; accessed September 5, 2016) offers several benefits of accreditation for the organization:

- "Assessment of program strengths and weaknesses;
- Establishment of measurable criteria for upgrading operations;
- Performance-based benefits that provide data that can be used in the day-to-day management of the facility reducing the occurrence of significant events;
- Improved staff morale and professionalism;
- Safer environment for staff and offenders;
- Defense against lawsuits; and,
- Reduced liability insurance costs."

Likewise, the Commission on Accreditation for Law Enforcement Agencies, Inc. (CALEA; http://www.calea.org/content/law-enforcement-program-benefits; accessed September 5, 2016), provides several benefits for law enforcement agencies becoming accredited:

- "Greater accountability within the agency;
- Reduced risk and liability exposure;
- Stronger defense against civil lawsuits;
- Staunch support from government officials; and,
- Increased community advocacy."

The CALEA statement does not contain as many inward ("natural systems") examples as does the ACA list. However, both lists of benefits have a strong external ("open systems") focus for the investment of resources by the agency in the accreditation process. Like so many things, accreditation must be viewed as a strategy for organizational success as much as a good thing to do.

Standards and accreditation of organizations/agencies, along with training and certification of professionals, are key elements of control over organizations. It is rare that this dimension of the processes is discussed. Our brief trip across the standards development and the accreditation process is in contrast to most treatments of this increasingly important form of professional organizational control in most criminal justice texts. In those texts, if accreditation or standards are mentioned, it is generally a replication of the explanation of benefits for the organization. Rarely is the role of organizations outside the CJS brought into the picture. Before returning to the use of organizational theory to examine these processes, we want to explore the involvement of at least one powerful non-governmental (sort of), restricted membership organization in the development of CJS standards and accreditation. This organization is the American Bar Association.

The American Bar Association (ABA) is a professional association with membership open to just about anyone. While the focus is on those in the legal professions, there is an "associate" membership, but without voting privileges (http://www.americanbar.org/membership/dues_eligibility.html; accessed September 5, 2016). For our purposes here, we want to note the influence of the ABA on the development of standards in the law enforcement and corrections sectors of the CJS. On the IADLEST website cited earlier, the role of the ABA in the development of law enforcement standards is listed thusly: "The next major report appears to have been published by the

American Bar Association in 1953. In response to recognition that policing in this country required improved professionalism, the ABA published a 'Model Police Training Act.' The Act outlined eight broad functions that should ideally be performed by police regulatory agencies." It would take until the 1967 President's Report and the funding from the Law Enforcement Assistance Administration (LEAA) to see the standards developed nationally. One is left to wonder how much longer it would have taken without the involvement of the ABA.

In the corrections sector, the ABA teamed with another major professional association, the American Medical Association (AMA), to bring about changes in the administration of health care in correctional facilities. Anno (1991) wrote that, although the first set of correctional health care standards was developed by the American Public Health Association (APHA) in 1976, they were largely unknown and unused. The next set of correctional health standards was published in 1977 by the AMA and included a set of accreditation procedures, which were lacking in the APHA standards (still are). The initial standards were developed for jails, with prison standards coming in 1979. The first prison was accredited in 1982. The ACA adopted the AMA standards in 1977 and continued to use them into the early 2000s, at which point the ACA developed its own health care standards.

From the early involvement of the ABA with the AMA arose a nonprofit organization focused on correctional health care in 1983. In this case, an AMA vice-president who had worked with the ABA's Commission on Correctional Facilities and Services, using funding from the Robert Wood Johnson Foundation along with others, founded the National Commission on Correctional Health Care (NCCHC). The NCCHC continues to develop and publish standards for health care in jails, prisons, and juvenile facilities. It also has several individual-level certifications in physical and behavioral health specialties, and accredits the health care services in jails, prisons, and juvenile facilities (http://www.ncchc.org/time-line; accessed September 5, 2016).

There are three items of interest to organizational theory in this brief discussion of the role of outside organizations impacting the CJS. First, we can see that powerful organizational players in the environment can have significant impact on the rules that govern CJS organizations. In some cases these impacts are welcome by, perhaps even with participation from, CJS organizations. Like the use of lawsuits to force the hand of legislatures to fund certain CJS issues, we view these organizational collaborations as "sweet heart" deals. On the other hand, sometimes the involvement of these non-CJS organizations is unwelcome. Such oppositional situations are cases of true conflict among organizations. As we have seen in earlier discussions of inter-organizational cooperation and conflict, sometimes organizations work together and at other times they compete over resources, both substantive and symbolic.

Next, we begin to see how multiple non-CJS professional associations can band together to induce, coerce, or force changes in the CJS organizations. The NCCHC predecessor originally included 22 organizational representatives, most from the health professions. We also see the involvement of what we will term "think tanks" or advocacy organizations in the next section. These interest organizations join with professional organizations to further the goals of a particular interest segment through the combined influence and power of the larger professional organizations on the CJS sector. Many of these non-CJS organizations by themselves would have little or no influence on the CJS. Aligned properly, however, they can use a variety of resources to bring about both welcome and unwelcome changes in CJS organizations.

Duffee and Allen (2007, p. 8) state that part of the study of criminal justice is determining why a society chooses to use the CJS rather than another social institution to address certain behaviors. Our third point here is that we can examine the competition among professional organizations to "claim" certain behaviors as the domain of a particular set of organizations. We mentioned that the ACA had adopted and used the AMA/NCCHC standards until the early 2000 period. Returning to the section on *organizational ecology*, we want to develop one more idea on the relationships amongst professional associations—they can be competitive. The NCCHC accredits only health care services and facilities in correctional facilities. The ACA accredits all components of correctional facility. Specific health care accreditation standards were developed by the ACA in 1989, but deference was given to NCCHC until 2001. In 2001, the ACA began to publish "Performance-Based Standards for Correctional Health Care in Adult Correctional Institutions." The ACA also began to develop health care certifications for correctional officers ("Correctional Behavioral Health Certification"), Health Services Administrators, Correctional Nurses and Nurse Managers. These placed it in direct competition with the NCCHC certification programs and accreditation. Many facilities around the nation are currently accredited by both NCCHC and ACA. It will be interesting to see how the competition between the two groups affects the size of their health care offerings in the future.

Correctional health practice was not the only area in which health-related professional organizations have sought to supplant or heavily influence CJOs and crime policy over the past several decades. In the 1990s, public health organizations began to make the claim that violent behavior was a "public health issue." This movement to have criminal justice policy on violence more heavily influenced by public health and medical organizations has been more fully developed elsewhere (Akers, Potter & Hill, 2013). For now, it is instructive to note that such attempts to bring criminal justice practices under the province of health-related organizational sectors continue. Certainly substance use and dependency policies have been an area of conflict between criminal justice and health professional associations for the better part of the past 50 years. One of the interesting questions for criminal justice and criminology scholars will be whether society sees fit to choose a different institution to address these problems in the future or continues with the current CJOs.

Standards and accreditation are among the normative control mechanisms of institutionalization discussed by Institutional theorists (DiMaggio & Powell, 1983, 1991; Scott, 1991). Yet, they receive very little attention in most CJ administration and management texts beyond the functions of myth. DiMaggio and Powell focus specifically on the ability of professional associations to move member organizations toward a state of "**isomorphism**," or "sameness." In Scott's (1991) later analysis of many of the ideas presented in Powell and DiMaggio's 1991 collection, we can see how standards and accreditation play a key role in creating the elements of normative expectations for organizations and their members. Likewise, those expectations influence the social identities of those who work in these organizations. Once the standards are set in place, they become very much a core of the regulative "pillar" of Scott's model of institutional pillars and carriers.

■ STATE-LEVEL ACCREDITATION

At the state level, we also see many accreditation processes and organizations. Sticking close to home, we have the Commission for Florida Law Enforcement Accreditation, Inc. (a non-profit corporation; http://www.flaccreditation.org/index.htm; accessed on September 2, 2016). The Commission accredits law enforcement agencies, corrections agencies (Florida Corrections Accreditation Commission, using the Florida Model Jail Standards), pretrial and misdemeanor (County) probation (Association of Pretrial Professionals of Florida and the Florida Association of Community Corrections), and the variety of Inspectors General of Florida government agencies (Chief Inspector General, Inspectors General Workgroup, and Commission Staff). They argue that accreditation provides the following advantages to accredited agencies:

- "Accreditation increases the law enforcement agency's ability to prevent and control crime through more effective and efficient delivery of law enforcement services to the community it serves.
- Accreditation enhances community understanding of the law enforcement agency and its role in the community as well as its goals and objectives. Citizen confidence in the policies and practices of the agency is increased.
- Accreditation, in conjunction with the philosophy of community policing, commits the agency to a broad range of programs (such as crime prevention) that directly benefit the public.
- Accreditation creates a forum in which police and citizens work together to control and prevent crime. This partnership will help citizens to understand the challenges that confront law enforcement. Law enforcement will, in turn, receive clear direction from the community about its expectations. Thus, a common set of goals and objectives will be arrived at and implemented."

And, throughout the discussions of the advantages of accreditation to agencies, one of the few admissions of a core function of accreditation: "Strengthens defense against lawsuits and challenges." This is an "open secret" of accreditation, yet one rarely discussed in academic texts.

Conclusion

The standards on which organizational accreditation is achieved play key roles in creating the social reality of those who work within the accredited organizations. They offer rules for how people who share our organizational identity should and should not behave. They provide organizational members with easy ways to transmit such knowledge and practice. And, they can have the force of solid rules, if not laws (e.g., PREA), that produce compliance with the broader organizational governance system. As we have discussed in this section, these standards can be developed within the organizational field, or they can be imposed or coerced by the activities of other organizational sectors.

We find it curious that so little attention is paid by academic writers to professional associations and their impact on the criminal justice system. Perhaps that is because so few academic criminal justice and criminological faculty are involved in these professional associations on any regular basis. By way of disclosure, Potter has received a major recognition from one of the professional associations mentioned here. Yet, even among our peers who have been actively involved with these organizations, there seems to be little translation into the academic work they publish. We hope this discussion will spur some more rigorous work on these important organizations in the criminal justice environment.

The next section builds on our discussion of "outside" sector involvement in standards development to provide a brief overview of another "conventional" sector that helps influence CJOs—what we will term "public interest research" ("think-tanks") and advocacy organizations. The latter will also help to introduce the reader to some of our "problematic" groups.

Key words

Accreditation
Accreditation teams
Certification
Conferences
Continuing education
Dues
Government-unique standards
Licensure
Magazines
Mandatory standards
Membership dues
Membership organizations
Newsletters
Normative processes
Occupation
Peer-review
Positional organizations
Power to convene
Profession
Professional associations
Professional education
Professionalization
Quality movement
Social media
Standards
Voluntary consensus standards
Isomorphism

CHAPTER 10

Research Organizations: Types, Targets, and Ownership

Learning Objectives:

1. List and define the four types of criminal justice-focused public interest groups discussed here;
2. Identify the key differences among the four types of public interest research groups defined here;
3. Discuss the potential impact of "ownership" of public interest research groups on the outcomes of research they conduct (focus and dissemination); and,
4. Discuss the impact of public interest research groups on the formulation of criminal justice policy and legislation, as well as the implications for governance of criminal justice.

Introduction

The fact that there are so many organizations in our environment that focus on studying the CJS should be a form of validation of the importance of the criminal justice system (CJS) as a social institution. For our purposes here, we want to lump these together under the heading of "public interest" research organizations. These organizations play key roles in the development of criminal justice statutes and policy. They are rarely mentioned in texts on criminal justice. Our attempt here is to bring them into the light of understanding how these non-formal CJS organizations impact the formal CJS and CJOs. First, we offer our emerging typology of such organizations.

Types of Criminal Justice-Focused Public Interest Groups

One of the key techniques of science is to develop **typologies** of phenomenon. For our purposes here, we will offer a tentative conceptual typology of criminal justice-focused public interest groups into four categories. These are:

- Private research organizations;
- Non-university affiliated policy institutes;
- University-affiliated criminal justice/criminology institutes; and,
- Advocacy organizations, which sometimes combine research and practice.

Common to all, at least in our operational definition, is that they focus on the impact of the criminal justice system on the broader society and/or particular segments of the society or on the criminal justice system and employees themselves. Another key element of these organizations is their appeal to science and evidence (Moore, 1966). This is a first attempt at the typology, and we invite others to refine it into a true taxonomy in the future. For now, this should be considered a very descriptive and exploratory attempt.

Returning to earlier chapters many, if not most, of these organizations will be incorporated as 501(c) organizations. The third designation will generally depend on whether they have a political lobbying arm or not. This means that they will have incorporation papers in some state, boards of directors, and some form of annual report available through the agency that handles corporations in the particular state. Most will have web sites where they feature information about their mission, activities, and membership. For the purposes of this section, we are going to choose exemplars from each of the organizational types in our tentative typology listed in the previous paragraph. In many instances, we are featuring organizations the authors have worked with or managed grants and contracts with for government agencies. In that sense our offering is purely exploratory.

Private Research in the Public Interest

This category consists of non- and for-profit research organizations that have a criminal justice focus. What differentiates them from the other categories is that they have fairly clear organizational boundaries. That is, they do not have membership categories or publish subscription journals. They employ their research staff without affiliation to a university department or other organization (see next sections). In essence, they exist to serve the entity that funds them rather than a particular sector or discipline. How their research is disseminated will rely greatly on the source of the funding. Sometimes the research is considered proprietary for the funding entity. At other times, the research is published as government reports or reports to a different funding organization. In some cases, resources permitting, the research may be turned into peer-reviewed scholarship.

Exemplars:

Abt Associates—We begin in the Northeastern United States with a for-profit research organization. Abt (name of the founder) describes itself thusly:

> "Abt's mission is to improve the quality of life and economic well-being of people worldwide… We apply our energy and creativity to helping our customers—governments, businesses, and private organizations—make better decisions and deliver better products and services by providing them with the highest quality research, technical assistance, and consulting services available in the marketplace."

With regard to criminal justice specifically:

> "Abt Associates offers research expertise in criminology, criminal justice and addictions. Our teams analyze trends and emerging issues in crime, drug use and drug markets; apply pioneering methods to evaluate the effectiveness of programs to treat offenders and minimize recidivism; use advanced and Abt-original data systems designs to maximize clients' monitoring and information capabilities, and provide corrections reporting and outcome assessments. The results of our work help policymakers, practitioners and funders decide the best ways to resolve many of today's drug, crime and corrections issues."

We note that the Criminal Justice activities are housed in the "Health" portfolio at Abt (http://www.abtassociates.com/Practice-Areas/U-S-Health/Criminal-Justice.aspx). Over the years the organization has overseen the development and operations of the Arrestee Drug Monitoring Network (ADAM) for the United States Department of Justice and provided numerous evaluation studies. While at the Centers for Disease Control and Prevention (CDC) Potter worked with Abt Associates staff on a project evaluating programs to link returning prisoners living with HIV to community resources. In effect, this was one of the earliest "re-entry" projects funded by the federal government.

Washington, DC, the national capital, has probably the most disproportionate number of "public interest" organizations in the nation. At the state level, this is generally true of state-level public interest organizations in capital cities, as well. One of the most prominent in the CJS research industry is the Urban Institute, which describes itself as:

> "[F]ounded in 1968 to understand the problems facing America's cities and assess the programs of the War on Poverty, the Urban Institute brings decades of objective analysis and expertise to policy debates—in city halls and state houses, Congress and the White House, and emerging democracies around the world. Today, our research portfolio ranges from the social safety net to health and tax policies; the well-being of families and neighborhoods; and trends in work, earnings, and wealth building. Our scholars have a distinguished track record of turning evidence into solutions" (http://www.urban.org/about; accessed September 14, 2016).

Within the Urban Institute is the "Justice Policy Center" that is described thusly:

> "Our scholars conduct research and evaluations to improve justice policy and practice at the national, state, and local levels. We examine the development, implementation, and impact of policing, crime prevention, and gang disruption initiatives. As America's prisons and jails face unsustainable growth and dangerous overcrowding, we are finding ways to reduce the prison population while preserving public safety. And we are assessing whether new and emerging criminal justice technologies are effective, how they are used, and what their implications are for privacy and civil liberties" (http://www.urban.org/policy-centers/justice-policy-center/sound-strategies-combating-crime-and-promoting-public-safety; accessed September 14, 2016).

The Urban Institute's founding by President Johnson is reflected to some degree by the population of its Board of Trustees and senior staff, most of whom have been federal government executives or high-ranking researchers. The Urban Institute has played key roles in helping with the restructuring of criminal justice agencies in the New Orleans area following the damage by Hurricane Katrina (and others) in the past decade, demonstrating that it is more than just a DC-oriented impact player.

Moving to the west coast, RAND Corporation has been a major provider of criminal justice research and evaluation for several decades. Rand describes itself as a:

> "nonprofit, nonpartisan, and committed to the public interest and to making our work accessible to people throughout the world… Much

of this research is carried out on behalf of public and private grantors and clients…At RAND, we bring together the finest researchers in the world and utilize the very best analytical tools and methods to develop objective policy solutions. We deliver fact-based, actionable solutions grounded in rigorous analysis." (http://www.rand.org/about.html; accessed on September 11, 2016).

As we write this section, RAND is playing a major role in evaluating the "realignment" process of corrections in California, as well as the utilization of alternative sanctions to incarceration. Perhaps understated in their self-descriptions, the staff at RAND have played major roles in the development of the evidence-based practice movement in criminal justice discussed throughout this text.

Although we offered these three exemplars partly as an example of the geographic distribution of such organizations, most of these organizations have offices and staff in major urban hubs around the nation. There are a variety of such organizations located around the nation. Yet we know relatively little in terms of systematic knowledge about their role in the development and evaluation of criminal justice policy and practice as an organizational entity. Again, perhaps some enterprising young scholar will begin to research that dimension of influence on the formal CJS.

PUBLIC INTEREST LAW AND SWEETHEART LAW SUITS

Though not technically policy research institutes, we want to briefly address the category of public interest law organizations. Their influence on actual policy and practice in CJOs cannot be overlooked. In this brief aside, we want to focus on the particular collaborative efforts of public interest law organizations and some state- and county-level corrections organizations to bring about change. Our exemplar is the Southern Center for Human Rights (SCHR; www.schr.org, accessed September 21, 2016) in Atlanta. At the national level, the reader may wish to learn about the work of the American Civil Liberties Union National Prison Project (https://www.aclu.org/issues/prisoners-rights, accessed September 21, 2016).

When formal corrections agencies have been unable to get either the legislature or a county government to provide funding for a pressing issue—the spread of viral hepatitis, for example—the agency may turn

> to an organization such as SCHR. Over the years SCHR has entered into what are termed "sweetheart" legal actions against the formal organization seeking change. By bringing suit in either state or federal Courts against the collaborating agency, a successful judgement can be the catalyst for addressing the problem the legislative organizations has failed to do.
>
> We believe it is worth noting this example of government (executive)-private organizations aligning to force a higher-order government organizations (legislative) to bring about change. This sort of symbiotic relationship between a formal government agency and a private organization does not mean that they work hand in hand on all issues, of course. The following day the corrections department(s) and the public interest law organization are likely to be locking horns in front of another judge on another issue where they are truly in an adversarial relationship. Politics can make strange bedfellows!}

Non-University Affiliated Policy Institutes

In this category, we include organizations that focus on particular elements of criminal justice policy. For example, the Pretrial Justice Institute (PJI) focuses on pretrial justice issues; the Police Executive Research Forum (PERF) focuses on policy related to policing, and so forth. Operationally, we define this category as focusing on the operations or personnel of a particular criminal justice sector. These organizations are often affiliated with a professional association (see earlier section). In this sense, they may be viewed as a sectoral advocacy group, though they are often critical of current practices. They may employ a dedicated research staff, or they may contract work out to a variety of sources.

Exemplars:

The National Council on Crime & Delinquency (http://www.nccdglobal.org/about-us/mission-values; accessed September 18, 2016) is one of the older such organizations in the United States. The 1907 origins of the organization follow closely on the development of the original 1899 Cook County (Chicago) juvenile court with a strong emphasis on probation. They describe themselves as an organization that:

> "[P]romotes just and equitable social systems for individuals, families, and communities through research, public policy, and practice. NCCD envisions a just society in which people are safe and supported

in their communities and treated with dignity by the systems that serve them.... Research informs all the work NCCD does. We value data-driven, research-based solutions because without a foundation in data and research, solutions are just opinions about what will work. Research provides a methodology that can be replicated to get the same positive results. We are committed to the principles of quality, reliability, validity, and utility in everything we do."

NCCD now plays a key role in the Prison Rape Elimination Act (PREA) training and technical assistance arena. These are truly mandatory standards discussed in the section on Professional Associations. Here we have an example of a non-governmental organization (NGO) with great influence on the operations of jails, prisons, and probation organizations through contracts with the federal government.

Above we mentioned the Pretrial Justice Institute (PJI; http://www.pretrial.org/about/; accessed September 18, 2011). Founded in 1977 as the Pretrial Services Resource Center, the PJI has served the pretrial justice sector for four decades. They describe their organizational purpose as: "to advance safe, fair, and effective juvenile and adult pretrial justice practices and policies that honor and protect all people. We work to achieve our core purpose by moving policymakers and justice system stakeholder to adopt and implement practices and policies." In order to achieve these outcomes, they engage in "educating key stakeholders, moving stakeholders to action, working in key states to advocate for change, developing messages, stories, and media coverage in support of change, and connecting local jurisdictions to assistance." Current funding for the PJI comes from a combination of federal (Bureau of Justice Assistance) contracts and major Foundation funding (e.g., The MacArthur and Casey Foundations).

Here again we see a non-governmental organization that seeks, through research, to encourage and bring about changes in pretrial practices among formal governmental agencies and NGOs providing pretrial services. Much of the work of the organization is achieved through training and technical assistance. Again, as we noted in the section on Professional Associations, training and technical assistance are key tools for moving CJOs in the direction of "standardization" (isomorphism) and achieving a modicum of normative behavior among organizations and their members.

We also mentioned the Police Executive Research Forum (PERF; http://www.policeforum.org/, accessed September 18, 2016) in the opening paragraph of this section. PERF is another non-profit organization with a wide reach for law enforcement training and technical assistance. They describe their organization as:

> "[a]n independent research organization that focuses on critical issues in policing. Since its founding in 1976, PERF has identified best practices on fundamental issues such as reducing police use of force; developing community policing and problem-oriented policing; using technologies to deliver police services to the community; and evaluating crime reduction strategies… PERF strives to advance professionalism in policing and to improve the delivery of police services through the exercise of strong national leadership; public debate of police and criminal justice issues; and research and policy development."

PERF also provides an executive development program and an executive search for local governments wishing to do national-level searches for new police chiefs. You may remember our discussion earlier of the nature of appointed offices in the CJS. PERF individual membership also has a boundary requirement—members must hold a "four-year college degree," as well as "subscribe" to PERF's founding principles. There is a link back to the academic realm with PERF, as well. Their Research Advisory Board is comprised of luminaries in the police research literature, as well as serving and retired police executives.

PERF research and policy statements are often sent for endorsement to organizations of elected officials, such as the U.S. Conference of Mayors. Of course, this reflects the fact that appointments of Chiefs of Police across the United States is generally under the purview of city or county Mayors. Our point here is that we have another NGO that seeks to not only influence the formal CJS organizations, but organizations representing those who have responsibility for the selection and retention of PERF members. PERF members help to fund the organization, but PERF also utilizes a range of government and other funds to conduct research and technical assistance operations. The fact that PERF offers fee-based services (e.g., executive searches), provides another area of influence back on the broader political world. For us, PERF represents a NGO that provides normative, regulative, and cultural-cognitive elements for more than just the CJS.

In the attempt not to overwhelm you, the reader, with a catalog of these sorts of groups, we want to mention briefly that just about every sector of the CJS has a group similar to the three we have featured here. For example:

- The Association of Prosecuting Attorneys (http://www.apainc.org/, accessed on September 18, 2016);

- The National Association of Public Defenders (http://www.publicdefenders.us/, accessed on September 18, 2016);

- The American Judges Association (http://aja.ncsc.dni.us/, accessed on September 18, 2016).

- The National Center for State Courts (http://www.ncsc.org/, http://aja.ncsc.dni.us/, accessed on September 18, 2016).

- The American Probation and Parole Association (http://www.appa-net.org/eweb/, accessed on September 18, 2016).

You get the picture. Each of these have some branch of policy research, either internally or through linkage with another organization (e.g., the National Conference of State Legislatures, http://www.ncsl.org/; the Council of State Governments, http://www.csg.org/).

The important point is that every sector of the CJS has some affiliated organization that studies and/or develops policies related to that sector or the overall system. Understanding how these organizations exert influence on the CJS, and vice versa, seems to be an area where criminal justice (and criminological) theory are lacking. Perhaps some of our discussion will stimulate researchers to address this short-coming in looking at criminal justice theory.

University-Affiliated Criminal Justice/Criminology Institutes

Institutes and research centers are encountered frequently in university departments of Criminal Justice and Criminology programs (which may be in Sociology, Public Administration, Political Science, etc.). The exact number of such entities is difficult to state. This is partly due to the designation of "institute" versus "research center" or other name depending upon particular university rules. Some such organizations are focused on a particular element of the justice system (e.g., juvenile justice, victimization, etc.), while others chase any available funding. Likewise, some university-based research centers will focus on local or state-level issues only, while others will go after more national-level projects. Some of these institutes also provide a range of "technical assistance" programs and training in particular topics (e.g., University of Cincinnati Center for Criminal Justice Research).

Exemplars:

We begin close to our base in Florida with the Florida State University Center for Criminology and Public Policy Research (http://criminology.fsu.edu/center-for-criminology-public-policy-research/, accessed on September 18,

2016). Some version of the current Center has been at FSU since the mid-1970s. They describe their current operation as a program that "expands the influence of scholarship in the public policy arena and promotes evidence-based policy-making and practice at the state and national levels. The Center's primary goal is to support data collection and research initiatives with application to crime and justice policy that promotes social justice." The FSU Center provides an initial statement of a trend we believe can be found among most such centers: "The Center maintains relationships with several federal and state agencies as well as local-level stakeholders in the prevention, correctional education, and criminal justice communities." Relationships in this case are described in terms of research/evaluation services provided from the Center to an agency.

Since we just mentioned it, let us return to the University of Cincinnati Center for Criminal Justice Research (https://www.uc.edu/ccjr/about.html, accessed on September 18, 2016). The center is relatively new, being founded in 1996. It is not the most recent of the entrants into university-based criminal justice, however. They describe their mission as: "To improve the quality and delivery of criminal justice services, to advance knowledge on the administration of justice and on the nature of criminal behavior, and to advance research capabilities and educational mission of the School of Criminal Justice." That is, their work is oriented externally toward the CJOs in the formal system, as well as internally to themselves in terms of funding and student support.

Within the Center are two Institutes, one focused on corrections and the other on crime science. The University of Cincinnati Corrections Institute (UCCI) states its purpose as serving "both for profit and non-profit agencies, UCCI provides services for federal, state, local, and international governments as well as professional organizations to promote effective interventions for adult and juvenile offenders." For full disclosure, the authors are both associated with efforts to move the evidence-based practices developed by the UCCI into operations in Florida CJOs.

The Institute of Crime Sciences (ICS):

> "[c]ombines the knowledge and skill of both academic researchers and criminal justice practitioners to solve real world problems…The direct linking of academic theory and criminal justice practice is what sets ICS apart from other criminal justice research institutes. Other institutes merely present theory to criminal justice agencies. ICS builds long lasting, truly collaborative relationships with agencies

we work with. Working with ICS is a genuine partnership as both research and practitioners contribute their knowledge and experience on a project to produce strategies and interventions that are practical in the field."

OK, ICS has called the rest of the field out! Earlier in the text we described the elements of organizational partnerships. How would you rate this statement after having read that section?: "A partnership with ICS provides criminal justice agencies with a direct link to cutting edge research and validated best practices to tackle both the challenges agencies currently face and those challenges they will confront in the future."

Before our bias toward public colleges and universities gets called out, let us use the University of Chicago's Center for Studies in Criminal Justice as our final exemplar (http://www.uchicago.edu/research/center/center_for_studies_in_criminal_justice/, accessed on September 18, 2011). It is also one of the original criminal justice criminal justice research centers having been founded in 1965 with funding from the Ford Foundation, a private organization. They state their purpose as: "enlarging knowledge of behavior defined as criminal and with studying the operation of the agencies of criminal justice and other agencies of social control."

More recently (2008) the Chicago Crime Lab was developed at the University of Chicago (http://crimelab.uchicago.edu/page/about-us, accessed on September 18, 2016) to "use insights from basic science to help government agencies and non-profit organizations develop innovative new approaches to reducing violence, and work with them to test new innovations using randomized trials." Note the focus on "gold-standard" randomized control trials (RCTs) to "ensure that policymakers have adequate feedback about what their innovations are accomplishing so that policy approaches get better over time… Without good evidence, policymakers have no basis for allocating scarce public-sector resources across different potential uses other than hunches and politics."

We see the utilization of partnerships again in the Crime Lab's description of its services:

> "By carrying out RCTs through public-private partnerships and focusing on priority questions for government decision makers, we seek to ensure and maximize the beneficial policy impact of our work. We believe policymakers are most likely to act on new social science evidence when they are involved directly as partners in the process of innovation and knowledge-production."

As we noted earlier, we are unsure exactly how many such research centers and institutes exist at public and private colleges and universities across the United States. To add some perspective, the National Center for Education Statistics (http://nces.ed.gov/programs/coe/indicator_csa.asp, accessed September 18, 2016) stated that: "In 2014–15, there were 4,207 degree-granting institutions with first-year undergraduates, including 2,603 4-year institutions offering programs at the bachelor's or higher degree level and 1,604 2-year institutions offering associate's degrees." Even limiting ourselves to the "4-year" institutions, the potential for a college or university with a criminal justice or criminology degree program to house some form of a criminal justice/research policy center or institute is fairly large. Our apologies to our friends whose research institutes we left out of our exemplar list!

The academic sector represents one of the key areas of providing normative and cultural-cognitive elements to the criminal justice system in the United States. Likewise, it represents one of the core constituencies for the production of knowledge about the system and its effects on society. This knowledge production function also places academia in the position of being one of the primary consumers of government funding to produce such knowledge. Sometimes government allows university-based researchers to develop ideas individually ("investigator-initiated"). Other times government dictates the nature of the questions government wants answered. And, we would argue, government increasingly occupies the "regulative" function of control over the conduct of the academic research process.

Advocacy Research Organizations

In our tentative typology, we separate **advocacy research** organizations from other research organizations. This is primarily based on the focus of the organization being a category of offender or victim, including the "collateral consequence" victims. That is, advocacy research organizations will generally focus on the impact of criminal justice policies and practices on a category of persons. This is in comparison with our designation of non-university affiliated policy research institutions above, whose focus is on policy impact on criminal justice organizations.

Exemplars:

One of the very first non-university, non-government, public interest research groups Potter encountered in researching criminal justice decision-making in the late 1970s was the Vera Institute of Justice (https://www.vera.org/about, accessed September 18, 2016). In the 1960s, "Vera" was a key resource of research on bail/bond research and policy; in 2016, Vera is again tackling problems with the nation's bail/bond systems. Over the past half-century the Vera Institute has developed research and advocacy programs on a variety of criminal justice topics. They currently list immigration, sentencing, corrections, victimization, youth justice, substance use and mental health among their focus areas. Their mission statement:

> "To drive change. To urgently build and improve justice systems that ensure fairness, promote safety, and strengthen communities… Vera works in partnership with local, state, and national government officials to create change from within… We harness the power of evidence to drive effective policy and practice… We work with others who share our vision to tackle the most pressing injustices of our day—from the causes and consequences of mass incarceration, racial disparities, and the loss of public trust in law enforcement, to the unmet needs of the vulnerable, the marginalized, and those harmed by crime and violence."

You may be puzzled why we did not include Vera among the non-university affiliated and public interest groups earlier. For our classification purposes, the last selection from their mission statement above places them in the "advocacy" research category. That is, their focus is not on the CJS itself, but primarily on the impact on the vulnerable and marginalized, either by crime itself or by the CJS. Further, Vera decides which issues it will tackle based on the advocacy positions of its Board of Trustees and other partners, not necessarily on the priorities of any government of the period. Again, we offer our classification scheme as an initial model and others may wish to distribute membership categories in a different way.

Vera employs a team of research leads and assistants to carry out its research efforts. Many of the assistants are drawn from New York City-area university departments, offering an experience unavailable to many criminal justice/criminology students elsewhere. Faculty from those area colleges and universities can also cycle through Vera to conduct research and program operations. Though not directly attached to a university, Vera "leverages" the expertise of educational programs in their area to produce research-informed advocacy programs. They may also perform contract services to government agencies. Staff from Vera took over the standards development process near the end of the process for the National Prison Rape Elimination Commission, for example.

The Vera Institute also partners with a variety of other NGOs on certain projects. For example, some of their work is performed in conjunction with Human Rights Watch and other legally-oriented NGOs. Staff from a variety of NGO research and advocacy organizations in the New York City area are likely to move project to project across organizations, and Vera is no stranger to this circulation related to particular topics. Over the years, Vera has provided a range of high-impact research and advocacy products that have affected criminal justice practice not simply in the New York area, but nationally.

Advocacy research organizations may focus on a particular issue within the CJS. The Drug Policy Alliance (http://www.drugpolicy.org/, accessed on September 18, 2016), is such an organization. The DPA describes itself as "the nation's leading organization promoting drug policies that are grounded in **science, compassion, health and human rights**" (emphasis in original). The vision and mission statement of the DPA further defines their advocacy position(s):

> "The Drug Policy Alliance **envisions** a just society in which the use and regulation of drugs are grounded in science, compassion, health and human rights, in which people are no longer punished for what they put into their own bodies but only for crimes committed against others, and in which the fears, prejudices and punitive prohibitions of today are no more. Our **mission** is to advance those policies and attitudes that best reduce the harms of both drug use and drug prohibition, and to promote the sovereignty of individuals over their minds and bodies."

The DPA attributes certain qualities to their supporters:

> "Our supporters are individuals who believe the war on drugs is doing more harm than good. Together we advance policies that reduce the harms of both drug use and drug prohibition, and seek solutions that promote safety while upholding the sovereignty of individuals over their own minds and bodies. We work to ensure that our nation's drug policies no longer arrest, incarcerate, disenfranchise and otherwise harm millions—particularly young people and people of color who are disproportionately affected by the war on drugs."

Support for the DPA comes from its supporters and a host of corporations and foundations. The DPA has a very clear focus on the issue of substance use and harm reduction. In this sense, it is an outstanding exemplar of an advocacy research that focuses on an issue that has multiple outcomes.

We now turn to another "single-issue" advocacy research organization, the Families Against Mandatory Minimums (http://famm.org/about/, accessed on September 18, 2016), "a nonprofit, nonpartisan organization fighting for smart sentencing laws that protect public safety." The vision statement of FAMM is "a country where criminal sentencing is individualized, humane, and sufficient to impose fair punishment and protect public safety." Their mission is to "highlight the human costs of mandatory sentencing laws, and advocate for more efficient and effective protection of public safety."

FAMM takes the approach of highlighting empirical research and other analyses of the impact of mandatory minimum sentences for a variety of audiences. These include not only the families and individuals affected by such sentences. They also have sections that feature information for general taxpayer, law enforcement and legislative audiences. The core of FAMM's advocacy activities includes the telling of personal stories of the impact of mandatory minimum sentences on the families of those so sentenced.

One of the reviewers reminded us of the extensive use of social media by these types of organizations. Indeed, organizations such as DPA and Vera have been very active in the use of their websites for the promulgation of their work for more than a decade now. Likewise, non-governmental organizations that take different positions than the exemplars mentioned here use social media just as much. The issue of whose social media are most effective to move social policy is a question being addressed by one of our doctoral students as we write this text. Many of these organizations use their social media platforms for fund-raising activities, as well. Perhaps in our next edition we will be able to address these developments in the use of social media by CJ-affiliated organizations in a more detailed manner. For now, we want to suggest that these modes of communicating likely are affected greatly by the funding streams generated by the organizations. Again, if this spurs students to research projects, we are more than happy to play that role.

What "Public," Whose "Interests"?

There is another element of interest to CJOs regarding these public interest organizations. They exist outside the democratic process, yet have the potential to affect criminal justice policy more directly than do voters. There is nothing new about this process. C. Wright Mills (1956) noted the transition to "high-prestige" organizations dominating public policy six decades ago. In his initial formulation it was the "**military-industrial complex**," a metaphor now expanded to at least the "**prison industrial complex**" (Davis, 1998) in the world of criminal justice.

Mills' work was particularly concerned with the increasing influence of the corporate sector interacting with the political sphere. He argued that as corporate influence gained dominance the interests represented in political circles were those of the corporations, not those of the general public. The reader may recognize these as themes of recent social movements such as the "Occupy" groups. The difference between Mills' original ideas and the slogans of recent movements is that Mills did not see a conspiracy as necessary to increasing corporate domination. Rather, it was the dominance of large organizations over individuals and small groups in post-World War II society. We would argue that much of this dominance has come through the establishment and operations of many of the "public interest" groups canvassed above. Whether such groups represent the interests of the general public is both an empirical and philosophical question.

We want to suggest to the reader that the domination of "public interest" in criminal justice matters has increasingly come into the domain of these decidedly non-public organizations. Legislators receive from and increasingly turn to specific "think tank" and research organizations information designed to influence legislation and public policy. Such organizations run the perceived spectrum from "conservative" (e.g., ALEC) to "liberal" (e.g., Soros Foundation), to specifically libertarian (e.g., CATO Institute), each with their own research staff or funded researchers and dissemination outlets. We would not argue at all that universities avoid the domination of public sentiment by elites, perhaps just the opposite. It is likely that most readers would place university criminal justice research centers/institutes in the "liberal" category; but, we hope we follow the evidence…

Mills (1956) wrote that "the decline of politics genuine and public debate of alternative decisions with nationally responsible and policy-coherent parties and with autonomous organizations connecting the lower and middle levels of power with the top levels of decision" (p. 274) was one way in which corporate elites gained dominance over public interest. One way Mills suggested we could observe the dominance of public policy by corporate interests was to examine the composition of their **boards of directors**. He argued that in the 1950s one could see either the same individuals or representatives of the same set of corporations on multiple key boards of directors across corporations. These often featured retired military and politicians in the military-industrial complex.

Perhaps an enterprising young researcher will take it as a research project as to whether the world of criminal justice policy has, indeed, moved from the area of "politics genuine and public debate of alternative decisions" toward policy determined by a handful of elite non-governmental organizations providing both the solutions and research to support the solutions for criminal justice.

Likewise, it would be an interesting empirical study to determine whether the boards of directors of major criminal justice public interests groups overlap to any significant degree. This would likely require that both individuals and organizational representatives (including universities), be examined. Potter's personal experience suggests that the movement of faculty staff from government to university and/or think-tank organizations should be examined as a source of non-governmental control of criminal justice policy. Finally, in our suggestion of potential research questions, we wonder whether the funding of policy-relevant research (and technical assistance) has moved increasingly from university-affiliated faculty and research centers to organizations that fit more directly into our typology of public interest organizations.

▪ WHO OWNS CRIMINAL JUSTICE RESEARCH?

This is a good point at which to discuss research funding and ownership of research related to criminal justice organizations. In our typology of criminal justice research organizations, we note that they are funded primarily by grants, contracts, membership dues, or some combination of those funding sources. The type of funding available will depend upon the type of organization providing the funds. Here we want to outline some of the major sources and types of funding encountered in the field. Likewise, we want to discuss briefly how this might affect dissemination of the information gained from the research.

One of the primary sources of criminal justice research funding is the government sector, federal and state, in particular. At the federal level, funding is likely to fall into two primary types. The first is the "grant." In federal law, a grant is "a legal instrument of financial assistance between Federal awarding agency or pass-through entity and a non-Federal entity that, consistent with 31 U.S.C. 6302, 6304:

- Is used to enter into a relationship the principal purpose of which is to transfer anything of value from the Federal awarding agency or pass-through entity to the non-Federal entity to carry out a public purpose authorized by a law of the United States (see 31 U.S.C. 6101(3)); and not to acquire property or services for the Federal awarding agency or pass-through entity's direct benefit or use" (www.grants.gov; accessed September 13, 2016).

A primary feature of the research grant mechanism is that a government (and many non-government grant-makers) provides funds to achieve a particular outcome with minimum to no involvement on the part of the government agency beyond compliance activities. It is the responsibility of the grantee to develop all aspects of the research processss—other than the question to be answered—based on the grantee's expertise and experience.

This is in contrast to the "cooperative agreement" which provides for "substantial involvement between the Federal awarding agency or pass-through entity and the non-Federal entity in carrying out the activity contemplated by the Federal award." That is, in a cooperative agreement, a government agency may be actively involved in portions of the research design, data collection, data analysis, and/or providing results and publications. Different funding agencies will favor grants over cooperative agreements depending upon the level of involvement in the research process the agency wishes to maintain.

There is a third type of funding mechanism used by federal agencies, particularly with some of the private research providers. This is the "task order contract." According to federal law (10 U.S. Code § 2304d), a task order contract is "a contract for services that does not procure or specify a firm quantity of services (other than a minimum or maximum quantity) and that provides for the issuance of orders for the performance of tasks during the period of the contract." In practice, most agencies have a set of task order contractors who have bid for the right to have access to, mostly short-term, research tasks with competition limited to a small number of known competitors. That is, an agency will have a competition for five research organizations to bid on short-term research projects. The competitors may be eligible to bid for a set period of time before they have to compete again to be task-order providers. When the agency puts out a call for proposals, only those task order contractors may bid on the project. Selection among the proposals by federal reviewers will determine the successful bidder.

This gives the federal government flexibility to obtain research information through a variety of mechanisms. These mechanisms reflect the amount of control an agency wishes to have over the research process. Generally speaking, the results of grants and cooperative agreements are most likely to be published widely. Task order contracts are often more for the internal benefit of a government agency than for distribution to the public, though they may lay the foundation for broader research competition in the future.

Concluding Thoughts

It is our conclusion to this section that precious little attention has been paid to the roles played by groups in our typology of public interest organizations to criminal justice policy and practice. Combined with the earlier discussion of professional associations, public interest groups are hypothesized to play a key role in the development of at least the normative and regulative columns of Scott's (2008, p. 51) version of Institutional theory. Yet, as a matter of course in criminal justice theory, they receive scant attention. We would argue that at least some of the issues raised by movements such as Black Lives Matter is the return of criminal justice policy to a more public level. Whether this occurs, or whether we continue to see legislators and other policy-level actors defer to the guidance of a handful of private, corporate organizations, is another empirical matter.

Over the course of this movement from the public interest research organizations to the advocacy organizations, the reader may have noticed a shift in the way issues were expressed. There is a common theme—a focus on the delivery of justice. However, as we move from the academic, profession- and contract-supported organizations to organizations concerned with the experiences of individuals, families, and communities affected by CJ policy, the language takes on a decidedly confrontational tone at times.

As we close this section on organizational types encountered in the CJS environment, we believe we move again from organizations squarely involved in conventional, status quo operations—even if they think they are being revolutionary. In the end, some advocacy research organizations may fit into our "ressentiment" organizations, or at least provide intellectual and empirical support for some of those organizations. As we noted, our typologies are offered as starting points for refinement by those who study criminal justice organizations. We hope readers of the text may someday take up the task of refining our ideas into sharper empirically-grounded categories for criminal justice theory.

Key Words

Advocacy research
Boards of directors
Military-industrial complex
Prison-industrial complex
Public interest
Public interest legal organization
Regulative function
Research institute
Typologies
University-affiliated research institute

CHAPTER 11

Social Movement Organizations—Friend or Foe?

Learning Objectives:

1. Define the term "collective behavior" and accurately relate it to the social problems development process;
2. List, describe and explain the steps in the development of a social problem, according to Spector and Kitsuse;
3. List, describe and explain the seven steps in the process of organizational processes in the development of social movements as outlined by McAdam and Scott;
4. Define "Ressentiment" and outline why organizations that fit into our characterization might be of concern to criminal justice organizations;
5. As part of the framework of McAdam and Scott, discuss the factors associated with emerging social movements replacing previously existing organizations that have traditionally addressed the identified social problem;
6. Define "oppositional consciousness" and explain why it presents a problem to criminal justice organizations;
7. Discuss the role of non-violent (mostly) revolutionary movements in their impact on criminal justice organizations; and,
8. Using Jonestown as an example, discuss how criminal justice practice towards non-violent revolutionary movements might spur them into more radical activities that might become criminal.

Introduction

"If men define situations as real, they are real in their consequences" (Thomas & Thomas, 1928).

Nearly a century ago, W.I. Thomas and D.S. Thomas (1928) published this summary statement of one of W.I. Thomas' fundamental ideas on how groups structure an individual's perception of the environment. That is, individuals tend to look to their reference groups—in our case our employing organizations—for clues how to make sense of the world. Lauer & Handel (1977) expressed it as: "Situations must be defined for people to act in them, and definitions of situations are made on the basis of reference groups" (p. 91). As we have discussed throughout the text, organizations are quite good at creating a world view for those who are involved with the organization.

Collective Behavior, Social Problems, and Organizational Forces

Social strain may well lead to collective attempts to resolve the imbalances that produce the strain, especially trying to attain overemphasized societal outcomes such as wealth and power. More often, these groups may be seeking a more fundamental societal value such as equal treatment before the law (and by representatives of the CJS). Individuals who find themselves perceiving their worlds in similar manners are likely to encounter each other, especially when they live in close proximity. Properly motivated, they are likely to begin to explore mutual solutions to their real or perceived situation.

Sociologists call this mutual approach "**collective behavior**." Smelser (1962) wrote that "collective behavior is a *compressed* way of attacking problems created by strain. It compresses several levels of the components of action into a single belief, from which *specific operative solutions* are expected to flow" (p. 71; italics in original). In Smelser's formulation this is the unorganized beginning of a process that may end in the institutionalization of the solution to perceived or actual social strain. As we move from less organized activities to more organized activities, we move from collective behavior to social movement, and perhaps even institutionalization.

> "*Troubles* occur within the character of the individual and within the range of his immediate relations with others;… *Issues* have to do with matters that transcend these local environments of the individual and the range of his inner life" (Mills, 1959, p. 8; italics in original).

"**Social problems theory**" also informs how a particular issue can rise from the concerns of a small group to a national problem. You guessed it—organizations play a key role in this process. To avoid the scourge of "self-plagiarism," we will refer the reader to our fuller discussions of this process (Akers, et al., 2013) and acknowledge we are summarizing the works of people like Herbert Blumer, Spector & Kitsuse, and a host of other Sociologists known as "social constructionists" as we combine social problems, social movements, and organizational theory generally with our "values" approach. Briefly, social problems were defined by Spector and Kitsuse (1973) as "the activities of groups making assertions of grievances and claims to organizations, agencies, and institutions about some putative conditions" (p. 146). They call these complainant groups "claims-makers."

The first stage in this process is for at least one group to define a given situation or behavior as problematic. They must then convince other groups that the situation or behavior is truly problematic. If an alleged problem is local and not shared in other communities, this is likely to remain a local issue. However, if this alleged problem is experienced in other communities and if the groups experiencing the problem can be linked, we have the beginnings of broader collective action. The involvement of celebrities in assisting the claimant groups to bring the issue to broad public knowledge is an important part of this process. The key point is that for a problem experienced by one group to become a "social problem," it must become perceived as a problem by at least powerful segments of the broader society.

The second stage involves the recognition of the "claims-making group," by some official agency or institution of the group—not necessarily the problem yet, but the group. We would suggest that having a formal organizational structure is a key element of this recognition. Now that the group is recognized, some form of official investigation may occur. This investigation will likely lead to proposals for reform, perhaps even result in some official organization to address the problem. We would also note that such official organizations often employ members of the formerly claims-making organization to be involved in developing the official solutions.

Stage three of the social problems construction approach involves the eventual perception by members of the original claims-making group(s) that the solutions to the problem have not actually accomplished the desired outcomes. Confidence in the official process and agencies or policies designed to alleviate the problem is lost or weakened substantially. This change leads to the fourth stage of the process. Here, the original claims-making group(s) rejects the official solutions and seeks to achieve either new or alternative approaches to solving the problem. Often this means essentially that the original problem becomes highlighted and whole process begins again.

The role of claims-making groups and potential social movements that emerge from them should not be overlooked by those in CJOs. If we think of claims-making groups as "ressentiment" groups in terms of values, we can see why such groups may be either helpful or problematic for CJOs. If these groups organize to produce social movements that move larger portions of our society toward conventional goals by using conventional means/strategies, they are actually beneficial for CJOs. On the other hand, if they begin to employ unconventional means/strategies, especially criminal means, CJOs will encounter more problems in the environment. If such claims-making groups begin to challenge the conventional social goals and employ criminal means, we are shading over into rebellious groups. We will address those elsewhere.

The social constructionists paid relatively little attention to the nature of the organization of claims-making groups and organizational theorists paid even less attention to social movements, until the early 2000s, at least. McAdam and Scott (2005) provide a brief overview of how these two previously separate academic specialties have begun to merge. They outline a seven-step framework that merges similarities between the two fields of study and seeks to bridge the differences. Of course, this will require further research. The reader should recognize some of these from our discussions of institutional theory and parts of ecological theories presented earlier, as well as some of the social constructionist ideas above.

The first element of the framework (McAdam & Scott, 2005, p. 17) goes back to the idea of an organizational field. This brings the ideas of "**institutional actors**" into focus. These are the organizations existing in the field that provide power to influence the environment and provide the "**institutional logics**" or "organizing principles" to get other organizational entities to act on the identified problem. A key question from our discussion earlier is whether new organizational actors will emerge, or whether some level of established organization is required to move problem definition, recognition, and reaction to the problem forward. New groups could bring with them a new form of organizing principles that might conflict with the existing institutional logics. This leads to the second element of the framework.

For analytic purposes, the second element requires that a time frame be established and that at least three "classes" of organizational actors be identified. The first is to identify the "dominants," or the organizations that currently tend to control the activities and discussion about the problem. The second is to identify the "challenger" organizations (and individuals in some instances) who want to change the way in which the problem is currently defined and approached by the dominants. Finally, "**governance units**" comprise the third class of organizational actor. These may be formal government agencies or non-governmental organizations. McAdam and Scott recommend that analysts conduct something similar to what we will describe elsewhere as a "SWOT" analysis to identify the strengths and weaknesses of the governance units, as these may play a key role in how challengers move into dominance roles.

The third element of the organizational processes of social movements framework is the wider social environment. These include "external actors," who influence the direction the movement takes, but whose initial influence may not be immediately recognized. The second set of groups in this element is "external governance" units. This includes more formal government organizations. Their importance lies in their ability to control access to a particular arena in which legal actions, for example, may be taken. Likewise, access to funding opportunities has come to play a leading role in developing some social movements.

The fourth element involves more emphasis on the "institutional logics" element mentioned above. Here we have a more direct link back to our use of Merton's structural strain approach. Institutional logics are fundamentally the values and beliefs about the means-ends relationships held by organizations (McAdam & Scott, 2005, p. 18). They may be the "primary" logics of a field—those that legitimate the actions of the dominant actors. Or, they may be "secondary"—the ideas associated with the challengers to the dominants. Secondary groups are associated in this scheme with "emerging" and "suppressed" organizations. Consistent with the definitional elements of social constructionist approaches, dominant and challenger organizations may view the same situation quite differently. The congruence between their logics will say a great deal about how quickly a challenger organization's alleged problem is accepted as a "real" problem by the dominant organizations.

The fifth element (nothing to do with the movie), focuses on the stability of the organizational field. McAdam and Scott (2005) note the tendency of organizational fields to move toward stability, but through a more dialectical process. That is, "destabilizing events or processes"—often the result of events outside the organizational field—bring challenger organizations into the field. This leads to the sixth element of "reactive mobilization" and three types of "**mobilizing mechanisms**." The first mechanism is perceptions that the challenger organizations pose either a threat or an opportunity (back to that SWOT analysis). The second is "social appropriation"—a process by which one group takes the perspective of another to become the primary organizational player in the field. Finally, if a challenger group has managed to get their logic appropriated by a more dominant group, can they use that logic to further change the field? This is termed "new actors and innovative action" in their framework; some might see it as subversive.

The seventh element of the organizational processes of social movements framework is really an outcome. That is, the degree of difference on the first six elements will predict the level of conflict within the organizational field. The more closely the values and views of the emerging organizations align with those of the established dominant organizations, the less conflict likely; if the values and views are highly different, the more likely there will be conflict. One of the key questions becomes whether it is higher conflict within the organizational field that moves the organizations toward achieving their desired social outcomes.

Campbell (2005) notes the importance of "**political opportunity structures**" for emerging social movements. These social political conditions help to either derail or assist emerging movements, sometimes moving them in a particular direction over another. Formal political institutions (think Courts in our case, as well as policing) can play a key role in attempting to suppress a movement or they can offer safe harbor through which grievances can be brought into public view. Such opportunity structures become part of the organizational strategy. Eventually they may shape the organizational structure and the ultimate success or failure of the movement. Here again we see the influence of other powerful organizations in the emerging movement's environment. Table 11.1 provides a brief overview of the major elements of the social constructionist and the organizational approaches to the definition of social problems.

Combining Case Studies

In their integration of social movements and organization theory McAdam and Scott (2005) use the "rights revolution" as a case study. This case study provides an example on which we can build to illustrate the utility of understanding ressentiment social movements using the various tools in this section. The case study focuses on the race issue in rights, especially the issues related to African Americans. One of the elements they highlight, in addition to domestic changes in legal interpretation of rights following World War II, is the international embarrassment caused by the United States' treatment of African Americans. They argue this assisted civil rights organizations in their efforts to organize and challenge the dominant groups, as well as the ways in which the dominant groups sought to resist the challengers and changes. They outline the number of new organizations that emerged to challenge the status quo (e.g., Southern Leadership Conference [SLC], Student Non-violent Coordinating Committee [SNCC]), sometimes joining and sometimes challenging the existing rights groups (e.g., National Association for the Advancement of Colored People

TABLE 11.1: STAGES OF THE SOCIAL CONSTRUCTION OF A SOCIAL PROBLEM (SPECTOR & KITSUSE, 1973) AND ELEMENTS OF SOCIAL ORGANIZATIONS INVOLVED (MCADAM & SCOTT, 2005)

Spector & Kitsuse—Social Construction	McAdam & Scott—Organization
Group defines a situation or behavior as problematic.	Powerful organizations provide "institutional logics" to move other organizations to action on the newly identified "problem."
"Claims" that the problem exists are recognized by other powerful social groups.	"Dominant" and "challenger" organizations in the problem definition are established.
Claims lead to implementation of some form of formal intervention (law, policy, regulation, etc.)	"External" organizations are brought into the problem to provide access to funds, legal action, etc.
Original "claims-making" groups decide official programs set up to address the problem are inadequate	The relative power between dominant and challenger groups leads to outcome on whether the new "problem" is worthy of social action.
New problem cycle begins...	Some event occurs to bring the challenger group to re-stabilize the organizational field.
	"[n]ew actors and innovative action" emerge as a result of interactions between the dominant and challenger organizations.
	Organizational stability is restored in the organizational field, generally with movement toward some new social outcome.

[NAACP], Congress of Racial Equality [CORE]). There were more openly challenging groups to emerge, as well. These include the original Black Panthers and some elements of the Nation of Islam.

Relations between police and African Americans were often an element of the civil rights movements. The importance of the riots sometimes associated with civil rights disputes in the formulation of the President's Commission on Law Enforcement and the Administration of Justice in 1967 cannot be understated. Some of the recommendations from the Commission were part of what McAdam and Scott refer to as the "institutionalization of the rights revolution." That is, returning to Spector and Kitsuse, the government created procedures, laws, regulations, and even agencies to ameliorate the damages claimed by the claims-making groups. And, for a while, things were fine..., right?

Returning to McAdam and Scott, the more "radical" black power movement groups faded into the background as the more moderate rights groups (e.g., NAACP, SLC) gained dominance in the rights revolution organizational field. We might also note that the racial equality movement provided the basic movement template for the women's movement, the gay rights movement, and as we write this draft, the transgender rights movement. In a sense, these other rights movements drew attention away from racial rights movements, as attention to social issues is an environmental resource that may not be unlimited. It is also possible that some people took the enactment of a variety of civil rights legislation and the establishment of government agencies such as the Equal Employment Opportunities Commission as the end of the struggle. This is consistent with Blumer's and Spector's and Kitsuse's social problems creation cycle.

It took the events of Ferguson, Missouri in 2015 to re-energize some of the attention to police-African American community relations. The emergence of the "Black Lives Matter" (BLM) groups around the nation now brings us back to the role of organizational theory in criminal justice. We would argue that BLM is an example of a **ressentiment group**. The groups around the nation share a common perception of reality of the devaluation of African American lives by the CJS. For us the question is whether BLM will engage in the structuration that moves it from a loose social collectivity to a social movement an on to an institutionalized status. As time progresses, we will observe what sorts of accommodations government agencies make to the movement and how those adjustments are received by the complainant groups. We will also observe whether BLM moves into a prominent position in the organizational field of rights groups. Whether BLM is absorbed (merger) into another established rights group, or whether it displaces another organization in that field will also be something we can observe. How CJOs can work with BLM is another area for observation, as well as the outcomes of those interactions. Finally, consistent with constructionist social problems theory, we will look to observe how long the official accommodations continue to satisfy the complainant groups before a new round of claims-making begins.

We have more confidence in predicting that BLM will be transformed into an established rights organization than we do that another nascent social movement—Occupy Wall Street—will re-emerge and become a successful ressentiment movement. Why? Because the Occupy group downplayed the key elements of organization that seem to be keys to the success and longevity of a social movement (see later section). Want to place bets?

Concluding Thoughts on Ressentiment and Organization

We hope this brief trip through a century of Sociology helps the reader understand why the use of Merton's "ressentiment" belongs in a text on CJOs. Social movements born out of a collective sense of oppression have the potential to bring both positive social change and "destabilizing events or processes" to society. Predicting how they will fall may be a tricky feat.

For leaders in the CJ organizational field, we hope it points out that there are intervention points at which they can utilize and/or influence the social movements to achieve outcomes beneficial to the aggrieved group and the larger community. There is no formula for this implied. We would caution that such attempts must be undertaken with an eye to mutual benefit. Otherwise, when the claims-making groups recognize the attempt to appropriate or co-opt their efforts, the original situation may be made worse.

If, on the other hand, ressentiment goes unsatisfied (empirically or in perception), we may see the abandonment of both conventional goals and means. This leads us to a brief section on rebellious groups and organizations as they related to CJOs. If, as we have argued so far, the resulting organizations still pursue conventional or slightly altered goals through predominately conventional means, the likelihood is higher that the organizations will turn into social movements that benefit or at least do not harm society.

Rebellious Organizations

> "You say you want a revolution
> Well, you know
> We all want to change the world"
>
> (Lennon-McCartney, 1968)

One of the reasons we do not discuss Merton's "rebellion" adaptation in most criminal justice courses is because of the "+/-" indicators in standard tables of adaptations. It is our hope that by separating out "rebellion" from "ressentiment" we can further differentiate types of organizations in the CJO environment. For our purposes here the key is whether or not the types of organizations growing out of individuals organizing to vent their frustration with social strain reject both conventional goals (ends) and means (ways of achieving ends). Revolutionary groups replace the goals of the dominant society with another set of goals and seek to achieve the new goals through means that are also unconventional. We often think of these revolutionary groups as militaristic in their outlook and behavior, even while they may be spouting a vision of peace. This has been especially true of late 20th and early 21st Century political revolutionary organizations. Yet, revolutionary organizations do not have to use violence or criminal activities (e.g., bank robbing, kidnapping, and extortion) in their attempts to move societies toward new goals. We will outline briefly some different types of revolutionary organizations in the remainder of this section.

Resources and Revolutions

This is a good place to bring in another approach that may predict whether or not a particular movement will tend toward ressentiment or revolution. Groch (1994), utilized resource mobilization theory to examine the development of "oppositional consciousness" among the disabled. Her work concentrated on the settings and conditions in which this form of awareness develops. Groch contrasted "collective identity" with "oppositional consciousness." Following Gurin, Miller, and Gurin (1980), **collective identity** is "the awareness of having ideas, feelings, and interests similar to others who share the same stratum characteristics" (p. 30). That is, one knows there are others who have the same or similar experiences in one's environments. **Oppositional consciousness** is defined by Morris (1992), as a "set of insurgent ideas and beliefs constructed and developed by an oppressed group for the purpose of guiding its struggle to undermine, reform, or overthrow a system of domination" (p. 363).

Oppositional consciousness requires collective identity; but, collective identity does not have to transform into oppositional consciousness. One of the key factors in the transformation to oppositional consciousness is the existence of organized communication channels. In Groch's (1994) research, formal organizations provided the means for the sorts of communications that resulted in collective action. It was also required to gauge the successes or setbacks experienced by the movement. Following the logic of writers mentioned throughout the previous section, Groch argued that the "ability of activists to secure and mobilize necessary resources (i.e., members, preexisting networks, funds, and a repertoire of strategies and tactics)" was more important to the development of oppositional social movements than simply a breakdown of society. By utilizing ideas from resource dependency (mobilization) theory, presented earlier, we are better prepared to predict which types of social movements and affiliated organizations are likely to take a non-conventional approach to action.

Keep in mind that this was written before the advent of what we now term "social media." How social media has changed the need for formal organization is an empirical question. However, we would note that social media are controlled to a great extent by conventional organizations. The relationship among CJOs, corporate organizations that control the access to the media, and oppositional groups is one ripe for further research.

We note in the chapter on criminal organizations that some writers believe that criminal organizations are devoid of "ideology." That is, their criminal activities are not based on the idea that such activities are necessary to achieve some new social ideal—they use criminal means to achieve conventionally-prescribed goals, especially wealth and power. Revolutionary groups have used criminal activities to finance revolutions since at least the Bolshevik (Russian Communist) revolution. Bank robbery has often been a favorite tool of revolutionary groups ("it's where they keep the money!"), including groups some members of our families may consider heroic rather than villainous. These behaviors were justified (at least initially) to finance the various revolutionary movements.

Political Utopians, Religious Utopians, and Terrorists

In the late Twentieth Century, a variety of "pro-communist" and anti-captialist revolutionary groups in Europe and the Americas utilized a variety of criminal methods to finance their efforts. Kidnapping and bank robbing were especially prominent in the media (e.g., Patty Hearst and Aldo Moro), sometimes ending in either ransom or murder (see http://web.stanford.edu/group/mappingmilitants/cgi-bin/ for a "mapping" of similar groups to the present; accessed on August 20, 2016). For much of the period from just after World War II until late in the Twentieth Century political revolutionary groups were motivated by either pro- or anti-Communist rationales for their activities. The use of criminal activities was justified as a necessary "evil" in the attempt to bring about a new social order.

By the late Twentieth Century new motivations began to emerge in the ends and justifications of revolutionary groups. Communism went into decline and its use as a justification for revolution waned, but hasn't disappeared. As colonialism shifted form and previously dominant nations lost influence, religious-based and anti-secularization movements began to emerge around the world. The anti-secularization goals are often accompanied by anti-globalization and anti-industrialization themes. Likewise, some of these revolutionary movements employ a range of criminal activities to finance their operations. These include activities such as drug, weapons, and human smuggling. Much like the political movements of the previous few decades, these behaviors are often seen as necessary to move to the ideal social end that will replace the current society's goals. Of course, as soon as that new ideal social situation is achieved, new modes of behavior will be put into place, especially governing the behaviors of those who resisted the change. This may be an appropriate place to listen to The Who sing "Won't Get Fooled Again" (Townshend, 1971).

So far we have discussed revolutionary groups that employ violence and other criminal activities as part of their attempts to change the social world. Many of these groups also engage in activities designed to bring populations into submission through violence and other forms of terroristic behaviors. These activities are likely to merge with those of non-political criminal organizations and bring them into conflict with CJOs. The example of the FARC (Revolutionary Armed Forces of Columbia—People's Army) and cocaine traffickers in Columbia provides an example of this sort of relationship. A political movement in a nation provides supplies of an illegal substance to a criminal organization that transports and distributes the product to other nations in order to finance the movement and provide profits to the criminals. The FARC, like most similar armed revolutionary movements, are labeled terrorists.

The corruption, complicity, and cooperation of governments in that process (among others) provides a link back to one of the major harms caused by criminal organizations outlined in the coming chapter. Combine that with perceptions that a government might allow those drugs to be targeted toward a certain ethnic group in a nation to repress that group, and we move back into the ressentiment area. Of course, we may be wandering dangerously close to conspiracy theory rather than social theory—but it makes a good read! For a more empirical examination of these ideas, we refer the reader to the works of William Chambliss (1989) on government involvement in criminal activity and similar movements referenced elsewhere.

Theodore Roszak (1969) is credited with coining the term "**counter culture**" to refer to a period of time in which a generation rejects the dominant societal goals and means to achieve them of the elder generation. Roszak's work focused on the rejection of the perceived dominance of industrial society and the alienation youth felt from the corporate and technocratic (technical elite) values of that society—i.e., western civilization of the 1950s and 1960s. This was required reading for some of us educated in the 1970s. We want to reference Roszak's work here because it offered examples of how social movements and organizations could reject both the preferred goals of the dominant society and advocate for alternate means of achieving new goals that did not involve violence. Of course, some of those alternate means of achieving new goals involved the utilization of substances that might not have been illegal at the time, but became illegal soon after the movement began. The "counter culture" of the 1960s and early 1970s began as a "deviant," but not necessarily criminal, movement. Because it did challenge the status quo/hegemony of the time, some of the means to the new ends were criminalized by the dominant organizations of the time. Beyond these pressures, we would argue that most of those who experimented with the counter culture were fundamentally enmeshed in the network of conventional values and behaviors, to which they eventually returned as adults.

Of course, the "counter-cultural revolution" of the 1960s and 1970s was not the first in American history. In many ways the early religious organizations of Colonial America were examples of groups looking to achieve different socially-valued outcomes than the dominant European societies from which they emigrated. The variety of 19th Century utopian communities, especially the communal experiments (http://www.ushistory.org/us/26b.asp; accessed August 20, 2016), represented another set of counter-cultural organizations. We would add the early Church of Jesus Christ of Latter-day Saints ("Mormons," "LDS") to this list of utopian groups whose behaviors were either criminalized or punished for their deviance from the status quo. These groups often had values and behaviors that placed them at odds with the dominant society. While they may or may not have been criminal behaviors, the degree to which they acquiesced to the dominant society predicts why we still see some of them in operation, and others are simply historical footnotes. Others, such as some adherents of a more "fundamentalist" LDS sect, continue to challenge the dominant morals and laws of the United States with regards to sexual practices.

Utopian movements in the late Twentieth and early Twenty-first Centuries have featured more counter-cultural organizations. We have observed in several of these organizations the use of criminal activities internal to members and external to the broader culture. The "Jonestown" communal tragedy that Jim Jones brought on his followers is an extreme example of the use of violence internally and externally. The instances of the use of biological agents to attempt to influence the residents of Antelope, Oregon, by a group of followers of the Bhagwan Shri Rajneesh represent another attempt by an organization to develop a community organized around principles counter to the dominant American society. There is a host of exemplars of separatist spiritual and philosophical movements around the world whose stated values and means to achieve those values are at odds with their dominant cultures and legal systems. They do not all become involved in criminal activities, though some may.

The key point to be made here is that revolutionary movements need not involve violence, criminal activity or terrorism. When we think of revolutionary movements, we need to understand that some may be deviant, and that may bring them into conflict with the legal system. Whether it is the criminal justice or civil justice systems where the conflict is settled is often a result of the reactions to the perceived deviance posed by the group to powerful organizations in the environment. The CJS is sometimes an independent player in this process; at other times, the CJS inherits the decisions of higher-order civil organizations such as legislative bodies.

A contemporary exemplar of a non-violent revolutionary utopian movement and CJOs can be found in the "Occupy Wall Street" (Occupy) movement that began in 2011 and lasted until …, well, it depends. Occupy still describes itself alternatively as a "leaderless resistance movement," yet also having "leaders of a leaderless (and leader-full) movement" (http://occupywallst.org/; accessed August 21, 2016). Occupy claimed to have spread from New York City to more than 100 other cities in the United States and more than 1,500 cities around the globe. Occupy appeared to go into a period of hibernation after brief appearances at the major political conventions of the 2012 election cycle in the United States. It appears from the Occupy website that the 2016 run for the Democratic presidential nomination by Bernie Sanders galvanized at least some portion of the movement. His loss to Hillary Clinton appeared to spark an effort at organized protest at the 2016 Democratic National Convention that was absorbed along with other protests. Indeed, the tactics of the "Arab Spring" movements are credited as inspiring the approach taken by Occupy, and protests and demonstrations are chief among those tactics. However, on July 8, 2016, such protests were called into question by the one "leader" of the "leaderless movement," Micah White following the "murder of five police officers in Dallas." He continued: "You knew your protest marches weren't working." Coincidentally, Dr. White had published a book titled *The End of Protest* in early 2016 (White, 2016).

We would argue that the primary reason Occupy has failed to maintain its momentum is the lack of an organizational structure to guide its strategy. Occupy appears to utilize the organization of others, such as the Sanders campaign. The problem with such a strategy is that when those other organizations' desired ends are attained or quashed, the objectives of the Occupy movement are, at best absorbed; at worst, they go back into hibernation.

Several journalistic sources (e.g., Schmidt & Moynihan, 2012), often citing data from the Partnership for Civil Justice Fund (http://www.justiceonline.org/), have documented how federal and local policing agencies have employed the same tactics against Occupy that are normally reserved for terrorist and criminal organizations. Even though the movement has been remarkably peaceful and poorly organized, we are led to believe that law enforcement agencies have taken it quite seriously. We will await peer-reviewed studies of how Occupy was policed to define the reality, of course.

FORMATION OF PROBLEMATIC SOCIAL MOVEMENTS: A METEOROLOGICAL METAPHOR

As we near completion of the first draft of this text, sitting in the central Florida region, we are reminded that it is hurricane season. If it was late February in the Northern Territory or northern Queensland, it would be tropical cyclone season. It strikes us that the formation of a tropical system is a good metaphor to use for the formation of a social movement that proves to be a problem for criminal justice organizations (CJOs).

In the Caribbean Sea and Gulf of Mexico areas our tropical systems can develop locally. Such storms are often short-lived, as they lose the fuel of the warm waters of these two bodies of water as they move onto land, which is relatively close by. That does not mean they are not powerful on occasion, however.

On the Atlantic side and up the eastern coast of North America, the systems often start as "open waves" off the coast of Africa. It is that "open" feature that is analogous to what we elsewhere term "collective identity." That is, the path of the collection of thunderstorms is much like those who know they share certain experiences as others "like them," and an identity may begin to form. If the identity begins to draw individuals more closely, much like the decreasing air pressure associated with a tropical depression, an identity may begin to form.

Like the tropical system, the identity group may not yet have a name. If the barometric (air) pressure drops, and there appears to be an "organized" circulation in the complex of thunderstorms moving over water (generally), we are on our way to a tropical storm, which will be named. Of course, one of the by-products of this dropping pressure and organized circulation is wind intensity. Up to one-minute sustained winds of 38 miles per hour (MPH), we are still in tropical wave and depression categories. From 40 to 74 MPH we are in tropical storm territory.

Much like the transition from tropical depression to storm, an identity group can begin to develop the characteristics of a core organizational center that sets strategy. The more that core group can generate a social identity for the organization, as opposed to just the leadership, we move into the tropical storm area—we now have a name. Tropical storms can have both beneficial and harmful effects. We often say in Florida dry seasons that we need a good tropical storm to bring us back to sufficient rain in our swamps and lakes. However, when both of the authors moved to central Florida in 2008, a slow-moving tropical storm dropped so much rain that many coastal areas flooded and there was a great deal of damage done. Texas and Louisiana have likewise had devastation caused by tropical storms, mostly due to rain and flooding damage.

Likewise, our ressentiment organizations can bring about great positive social outcomes, as well as potential social damage. So long as organizations retain their focus on conventional social outcomes for aggrieved groups and employ conventional means to achieve those outcomes, we may get some uncomfortable transitions, but the end product will be positive for the overall society. Just like enduring the stronger winds and heavier rains of the tropical storm, these ressentiment organizations may do a little harm to existing structures, but they will improve the environment once they have achieved their ends. Of course, it is the achievement part we have argued elsewhere may never fully be finished.

When the organization of a tropical cyclone results in a closed "eye wall," and the wind speeds reach 75 MPH, we have a hurricane. This is where our notion of "oppositional consciousness" comes into focus. One feature of an organization is a boundary wall between those who are "in" the organization and those who are not. Like the eye wall of a hurricane, the oppositional organization will develop a core of strategy and tactics separated from the surrounding social world. The oppositional organization is set on destruction, from symbolic to physical. Hurricanes are not consciously harmful, they simply are. Like the tropical storm, they can be beneficial under the right circumstances, such as breaking a drought. Oppositional organizations are consciously destructive. The difference between the two is that the oppositional organization intends to bring about change through destruction; the hurricane simply does what it does.

This metaphor also calls to mind our attempts to predict tropical system developments and manage their impacts. Many of the same data collection and statistical analysis techniques used to generate the "spaghetti maps" you see on weather reports for tropical system movement are the same we use to explain the trajectory of social movement organizations in the social environment. We in the social sciences tend to do our modeling after the event of the organizational movement. It is much easier to "fit" one's model than trying to do it prospectively as the weather services attempt.

Conclusion

We have separated ressentiment and revolutionary organizations out from other environmental factors because we believe both present similar challenges to criminal justice organizations. Yet, at the same time, they present differences from each other and sometimes within categories, which should help dictate strategy toward dealing with them. A key point we want to make here is that the way criminal justice deals with an organization still in the ressentiment category can make the difference between whether it is likely to move into a revolutionary and/or criminal enterprise. As we have noted, several political movements over the past couple of centuries have featured criminal activities as part of their development. Learning how to identify groups at the different stages of formation, and how to deal with them appropriately, may play a role in decreasing organized criminal activity. At least, that is our hope in making these distinctions. In the next chapter, we will deal with organizations that are engaged in criminal activity.

Key Words

Claims-making (groups)
Collective behavior
Collective identity
Counter-cultural revolution
Counter-culture
Governance units
Institutional actors
Institutional logics
Issues

Mobilizing mechanisms
Oppositional Consciousness
Political opportunity structures
Rebellious groups
Ressentiment groups
Social problems theory
Troubles
Utopian groups

| CHAPTER 12

Criminal Organizations

Learning Objectives:

1. Apply the various legal definitions of criminal enterprise and organized crime used in the United States;
2. Outline and apply the legal definition of transnational crime employed by the United Nations;
3. Compare the scope and specificity of the differing legal definitions and implications for controlling criminal organizations;
4. Compare and contrast the components of criminal organizations/organized crime employed by criminologists and discuss which typology is strongest;
5. Discuss whether criminal organizations face the same issues as conventional organizations and, if not, where they differ from conventional organizations;
6. Explain how individuals in similar social settings learn to adapt in similar ways using Social Learning/Differential Association theory; and,
7. Outline von Lampe's two levels of criminal organization presented here and relate them to corruption of conventional government and non-governmental organizations.

Introduction

Textbooks on organized crime, criminal organizations, and transnational criminal organizations are common in the criminal justice field. Along with such texts are others that focus on specific types of crimes in which these organizations engage, including human trafficking/modern slavery, money laundering, and all manner of smuggling. Yet, curiously, very few of these texts deal with criminal organizations as organizations through the use of organizational theory.

In this chapter we want to explore the legal and academic approaches to defining notions of criminal organization and organized crime. We will also attempt to use the values approach outlined in Chapter 8 to provide some insight into criminal organizations as organizations. Finally, we will examine the benefit of examining criminal justice organization to criminal organization interactions to reduce corruption and prevent certain crimes. In the end, we want to suggest that studying the interactions of these two sectors in organizational terms may provide a better path to understanding and controlling criminal organizations.

The Law Says

Keeping with the idea that the criminal law defines criminal activities and the proper government responses to those activities, let us take a look at how United States federal law defines "criminal organization." Well, it doesn't. We do find two related ideas in federal law, the "criminal enterprise" and "organized crime."

The **Racketeer Influenced and Corrupt Organizations (RICO)** statute, or Title 18 of the United States Code, Section 1961(4), defines an enterprise as "any individual, partnership, corporation, association, or other legal entity, and any union or group of individuals associated in fact although not a legal entity." The **Continuing Criminal Enterprise statute**, or Title 21 of the United States Code, Section 848(c)(2), defines a criminal enterprise as any group of six or more people, where one of the six occupies a position of organizer, a supervisory position, or any other position of management with respect to the other five, and which generates substantial income or resources, and is engaged in a continuing series of violations of subchapters I and II of Chapter 13 of Title 21 of the United States Code. That division of labor will become important for us later in this section.

The FBI defines a **criminal enterprise** as a group of individuals with an identified hierarchy, or comparable structure, engaged in significant criminal activity (https://www.fbi.gov/investigate/organized-crime; accessed 8/11/2016). These organizations often engage in multiple criminal activities and have extensive supporting networks. The terms Organized Crime and Criminal Enterprise are similar and often used synonymously. However, various federal criminal statutes specifically define the elements of an enterprise that need to be proven in order to convict individuals or groups of individuals under those statutes (see above).

The FBI defines **"organized crime"** as any group having some manner of a formalized structure and whose primary objective is to obtain money through illegal activities. Such groups maintain their position through the use of actual or threatened violence, corrupt public officials, graft, or extortion, and generally have a significant impact on the people in their locales, region, or the country as a whole. The concept of "significant racketeering activities" is defined by the FBI as those predicate criminal acts that are chargeable under the Racketeer Influenced and Corrupt Organizations statute. These are found in Title 18 of the United States Code, Section 1961 (1). The reader is encouraged to review Finklea's (2010) summary of definitions and activities prepared for the United States Congress for more detail.

So far our legal definitions have focused on the United States. We know, however, that like "The Big Money" in the Rush song (1985), criminal organizations go around the world. This leads us to the role of **transnational organized crime**:

> Transnational organized crime refers to those self-perpetuating associations of individuals who operate transnationally for the purpose of obtaining power, influence, monetary and/or commercial gains, wholly or in part by illegal means, while protecting their activities through a pattern of corruption and/or violence, or while protecting their illegal activities through a transnational organizational structure and the exploitation of transnational commerce or communication mechanisms. There is no single structure under which transnational organized criminals operate; they vary from hierarchies to clans, networks, and cells, and may evolve to other structures (http://www.justice.gov/criminal/ocgs/org-crime/docs/08-30-11-toc-strategy.pdf; accessed 8/11/2016).

Transnational criminal organizations, which may or may not morph into or out of revolutionary and terrorist organizations, represent a very complex issue for governments. These may be out of the jurisdiction of most non-federal criminal justice organizations (CJOs) in the United States, even though the local jurisdictions may bear disproportionate burden of such activities (e.g., human trafficking/slavery).

The United Nations Convention against Transnational Organized Crime (https://www.unodc.org/documents/treaties/UNTOC/Publications/TOC%20Convention/TOCebook-e.pdf, accessed 8/11/2016) provides key definitions for defining transnational criminal organizations:

- **"Organized criminal group"** shall mean a structured group of three or more persons, existing for a period of time and acting in concert with the aim of committing one or more serious crimes or offences established in accordance with this Convention, in order to obtain, directly or indirectly, a financial or other material benefit;" (p.5)

- **"Structured group"** shall mean a group that is not randomly formed for the immediate commission of an offence and that does not need to have formally defined roles for its members, continuity of its membership or a developed structure;" and,

- **"Proceeds of crime"** shall mean any property derived from or obtained, directly or indirectly, through the commission of an offence;"

The elements of "structure," continuity, and that the activities are carried out in more than one nation help to provide a legal definition of such crimes. While there are no specific definitions of a criminal organization, there are aspects of the activities, structure, and benefits on which we can build.

Why is a definition of "organized crime" or "criminal organization" relevant? We will point toward the chapter on organizational planning and analysis (Section 4), where understanding the relationships among objectives, activities, and inputs is explored. For now, we will rely on Finckenauer's (2005, p. 68) analysis:

> "[h]ow the problem of organized crime is defined goes a long way toward determining how laws are framed, how investigations and prosecutions are conducted, how research studies are done, and, increasingly, how mutual legal assistance across national borders is or is not rendered. What they perceive organized crime to be, and how seriously they regard it, also determine the degree of the public's support for policies and resources to combat it. In general then, to the extent that there are substantial differences in opinions and views of what exactly organized crime is, to that extent each of the aforementioned practices, from law enforcement to research, is made more complicated."

With that, we turn to how academics have approached this problem from an organizational perspective.

Academics Say…

The issues surrounding the term "organized crime" has become something of a dispute in Criminal Justice and Criminology academic circles. Hagan (2006) provides a summary of his own and the works of Albanese (2005) and Finckenauer (2005) in attempting to define these terms. Hagan's (2006, p. 128) summary of traits of organized crime among the authors was that it:

- "Represented a continuing, organized hierarchy";
- "Profited from illegal activities";
- Used violence and threats"; and,
- Represented corruption and immunity."

Some of the other characteristics of organized crime identified by the Albanese, Finckenauer, and Hagan include being a monopoly (supplier), have **restricted membership**, are non-ideological, have a **code of secrecy**, involve extensive planning, and often have specializations in terms of products or services they provide. Hagan, in a note, makes the observation that "many writers" simply fail to provide an explicit definition of organized crime when they employ the term.

Hagan proposes a two-tiered continuum of factors that distinguish between non-organized and organized crime. The primary tier includes the **ideological** and **longevity** of the group. He appears to suggest that the less ideological and the longer the group has been around, the more likely they are to be organized. Likewise, the more they rely on threats and actual violence, the more they provide illegal services and products, and the more they enjoy the fruits of **corruption** and **intimidation**, the more likely they are to be organized crime.

Finckenauer (2005) noted that the issue of ideology had become murkier in the early Twenty-First Century because of the involvement of ideologically-driven organizations deemed terrorist that also engaged in criminal activities. Finckenauer (2005, p. 66) also argued that hierarchies had been replaced by "more amorphous, free floating, and flatter" organizational structures than their previous hierarchies, though some of those hierarchies persist in some organizations. This sounds very much like the "**flattening**" of major corporate organizations in the latter part of the Twentieth Century and into the current century. Using the term "continuity" to mean self-perpetuation beyond any individual member (i.e., a charismatic leader), Finckenauer reflected what we have referred to as sustainability elsewhere—the organization continues despite personnel changes.

Finckenauer maintains the use of **violence** and threats of violence as central to the character of criminal organizations. He does allow that such organizations may be involved in legitimate enterprises as well as illegal dealings. Sometimes these are to "launder" proceeds of the illegal activities through legitimate fronts. Likewise, the corruption of government, especially CJS officials, remains a necessary portion of the criminal organizations' activities. One of the messages in Fickenauer's (2005, pp. 75–76) analysis of criminal organizations is that it is not enough to focus on either the activities of an organization and/or the structure of the organization. He focuses on whether the nature of the criminal acts requires group activity, groups have some continuity, and group members identify themselves as a criminal organization. He boils these down into four characteristics that again vary across a continuum:

- **Criminal sophistication**—basically, is the nature of the criminal activity opportunistic or does it require a degree of structured planning and;

- **Organizational structure**—do the activities of the group require a clearly defined division of labor which is maintained over time;

- **Self-identification**—do the participants in the criminal behaviors identify as members of the organization through the use of identifying symbols, including speech (remember "collective identity" in Chapter 11?); and,

- **Authority of reputation**—does the reputation of the group actually "instill fear" and "intimidate others" to the extent the group has power over the others?

The higher groups "score" on these four dimensions, the more likely they are to be criminal organizations rather than simply organized criminals. The latter are generally one-off or limited in duration, have little division of labor, and are not really known to themselves or others as an organization.

Finckenaur (2005, pp. 78–79) also focuses on the various levels of "**harm**" caused by criminal organizations. Intimidation often leads to emotional and physical harm. These harms can also lead to harms against the civic process, such as an unwillingness of conventional persons to perform criminal justice-related occupations. Likewise, members of the public may not wish to fulfill civic duties such as serving on juries or acting as election monitors for fear of harm. The greatest level of harm involves the corruption aspect of the criminal justice (and civil) process of system actors. This type of systemic harm can be achieved only by an organization in Finckenauer's analysis. We tend to agree with him.

So, after this brief trip through the difficulty in defining criminal organizations, we are left with the question: How are criminal organizations different from other "conventional" organizations? In many ways, we believe there is little difference between the two. Finckenaur's four dimensions suggest that criminal organizations struggle with many of the same issues as conventional organizations. We want to now explore the use of criminological theories (well, sociological) that we believe has been ignored in examining criminal organizations. In the end, what is valued by criminal versus conventional organizations may not be the issue; how they get there definitely is.

Relations with Other Organizations—A Values Approach

In the section on networked governance (Chapter 8) and Chapter 13 on organizational planning, we noted that the values expressed by formal organizations are often a way of determining what non-governmental/community-based organizations (NGOs/CBOs) make suitable partners. Here, again, we want to suggest that criminal organizations can be partly differentiated from other organizations in terms of the values they espouse. The basic idea behind structural strain is that there is an imbalance between the socially acceptable goals and the distribution of opportunity to use conventional means to achieve those goals. We generally concentrate on wealth and power as the socially acceptable goals, and then look at the ways in which certain groups' ability to utilize conventional means is blocked.

For our purposes, we want to focus on three of the five modes as they apply to criminal organizations, revolutionary organizations, and conforming organizations. Most formal organizations are going to express both their goals and the means for attaining those goals in "conventional" terms. The organization and its members are pursuing socially acceptable ends (goals) using socially acceptable means. Some individuals and groups operating under the umbrella of the conventional organization may indeed act in non-conventional ways. From "dirty tricks" squads in political organizations to industrial espionage to illegal dumping of chemicals, we have many examples of deviance within conventional organizations (Simon, 1996). However, for the most part, these conforming organizations pursue conventional social goals through conventional means.

As noted in Chapter 8, the mode of adaptation we focus on mostly in criminal justice is "innovation." To review, **innovation** occurs when we have the intersection of:

- a cultural emphasis on success and mobility, the blockage of access to the prescribed means to achieve success and mobility for a portion of the society, and;

- individuals who have not been fully socialized into accepting the means-ends linkage in the society.

Because the source of the strain between goals and means is blocked at a societal level, groups of people experience the blockage. Merton wrote of individual adaptations, but it is not a stretch to believe that individuals in groups might form organizations to address these strains. Those organizations will vary in the degree of formality. That is, some will remain loosely coupled associations, while some may become state-recognized organizations, such as non-profit groups. Some of those organizations may well promote "innovative" solutions to the problem ("criminal organizations"). Others will seek to utilize the conventional political processes to obtain desired outcomes ("social movements"). Certainly, we see organized rebellious groups from time to time. We also see organizations with their roots in the "ressentiment" condition. Whether the adaptations those organizations take will be along the accepted social behavioral path, or down the deviant path, can be observed empirically.

Mixing theoretical traditions, when groups of individuals experiencing this strain and innovative adaptation come together, we have the conditions for **differential association** and **social learning** (Akers, 1998). In the original formulation, Sutherland (1947) focused on group-level transmission of the legitimation and transmission of justifications for engaging in deviant behaviors. Through these groups, individuals were trained in not only how to do criminal acts, but how to justify them to self and others. In the end, criminal behavior is learned, just as is any social behavior. Whether organizations formed out of shared definitions favorable to criminal behavior are fundamentally different from organizations formed out of shared conventional definitions is a matter for empirical research. We would argue it is the ways favored to achieve the socially-defined goals that matters, not how the means are learned.

Miller (1958) likewise located the source of much adolescent gang behavior to the role of lower class culture and delinquent behavior. He located the source of conflict as being between lower class adherence to unique codes of conduct (norms and values) which were in conflict with middle and upper class codes of conduct. These conflicting norms and values were part of the identity of lower-class youths.

Merton (1967) also argued that the social strain that led to his "innovation" mode of adaptation were unique to the social structure of the United States during the Twentieth Century. Whether such strain could occur in societies with strong class and/or caste systems, where social mobility was unlikely, was left as an open question. In that sense, Merton's ideas were very limited in explaining criminal activity. It was truly an example of "American Exceptionalism." However, rebellion/ressentiment could exist elsewhere even with constrained social mobility.

In our section on the rise of organizations, we noted that one of the profound changes in the Industrial Revolution was the decay of traditional forms of authority. This would include the decay of colonialism world-wide. We want to suggest that, as colonialism declined, material and intellectual culture changed. Especially as communications have allowed almost instantaneous knowledge of events to most of the world, perceptions of who can obtain the goals of wealth and power have also changed. Groups who were previously at the bottom of the social ladder can now see others in similar positions who have obtained these goals. They may note how these others have organized to provide some service or product to a market in order to obtain socially desired goals. Sometimes the means employed are less than legal. While there may be no official charter for the organization or a formal organizational chart, to achieve success these groups must form some aspect of organization. These are the groups we think of as traditional criminal organizations.

We would also like to offer the **"Willie Sutton" hypothesis** to suggest that one of the reasons we see so many of these criminal organizations operating in industrialized nations is because that is "where the money is." Societies with relatively high levels of discretionary spending represent the markets for a variety of goods. Some of those goods might be legally produced to begin, but are illegal or scarce in the target market. Some of the goods are illegal to begin, and illegal in the target market. Illegal substances are our usual go-to example here. However, human trafficking/slavery—labor or sex—fall into this category, as well. Because the demand for these products exists in these more affluent societies, criminal organizations from around the world seek to sell their products and services in those markets.

To summarize, when groups of people experience the blockage of opportunities to achieve social goals that have become more highly valued than using the socially-prescribed ways of obtaining them, it is likely that some form of organization will develop to help at least some of those group members to achieve the highly-valued goals. These may be criminal organizations, rebellious and/or revolutionary organizations, or some form of mass political movements. We may even see morphing from one to another or aspects of two types of organizations combined over time. In order to obtain the highly valued social goals by alternative means, criminal organizations will exploit those demand markets where money and power are available. This brings such organizations into conflict with criminal justice organizations.

Criminal organizations face most of the same challenges as faced by conventional organizations. Where conventional organizations (mostly) accept the restraints of civil and criminal law as givens, criminal organizations do not. Overall, we are unlikely to see leadership of conventional organizations threatening or using violence and intimidation to keep their employees in line; such forms of "compliance" are not uncommon in criminal organizations. We want to argue that what separates criminal organizations from conventional organizations is the pursuit of socially-defined goals, especially money and power, without regard for the legality of the means used to pursue those goals. This may sometimes involve consciously utilizing violence, intimidation, and corruption rather than conventional means to achieve their goals.

Organized Crime and Governments—Routine Activities?

Building on the corruption aspect of the definitions of criminal organizations outlined earlier, von Lampe (2011b) has attempted to apply the ideas from **routine activities theory** (Cohen & Felson, 1979; Cornish & Clarke, 2002) to "organized crime," and especially transnational crime (von Lampe, 2011a). To refresh the reader's memory, routine activities predict criminal activity when we have the presence of a motivated offender, a suitable target (victim), and a lack of capable guardianship to protect the target. von Lampe's "**offenders as problem-solvers**" brings him back to one of the "functions" of deviant modes of adaptation from Merton, we would argue. However, there are other key elements of his analysis we want to highlight here.

von Lampe (2011b) notes that organized crimes have a "broader time horizon and geographical scope" than crimes committed by individuals or transitory groups. This sort of time horizon is similar to those of most formal organizations, we would note. He returns to the notion of a somewhat complex division of labor by the involvement of expertise and time taken to engage in organized crime. He also notes the importance of the convergence of offenders in particular settings. This is much like organizational planning meetings. As we see with conventional organizations, these are increasingly likely to be held via electronic means, no longer requiring the summit of bad guys depicted in many movies. His description of "foraging" reminds us of corporate market research. In many ways, von Lampe is describing the activities associated with any organizations whose survival is not guaranteed—unlike, a stable government.

The areas we want to focus on here build on the works of Cornish and Clarke (2002) mentioned earlier. It has to do with the **social harms** of corruption of government—particularly criminal justice organizations—and conventional organizations for the protection and profit of criminal organizations. Some of these ideas have made their way into United States government thinking on transnational criminal organizations. These revolve around the involvement of conventional actors as:

> "**Facilitators**"—"semi-legitimate players such as accountants, attorneys, notaries, bankers, and real estate brokers, who cross both the licit and illicit worlds and provide services to legitimate customers, criminals, and terrorists alike.... The range of licit-illicit relationships is broad. At one end, criminals draw on the public reputations of licit actors to maintain facades of propriety for their operations. At the other end are "specialists" with skills or resources who have been completely subsumed into the criminal networks" (http://www.justice.gov/criminal/ocgs/org-crime/docs/08-30-11-toc-strategy.pdf).

While the focus here is on individual roles, the problem of their involvement with criminal organizations shows itself at the organizational levels.

In relation to Europe, von Lampe (2008) provided a typology of "manifestations of organized crime" (pp. 14–15) that ranges across "subcultural," "mainstream," and "elite" embeddedness in societies. His fourth and fifth types of relationships are of importance to this presentation. The fourth type consists of criminal networks among members of power elites. At this level, governments themselves are involved in "conventional criminal activities." Of course, Chambliss (1978) was among the earliest to write about government involvement in criminal activities. Unfortunately, it is nothing new since at least the early colonial periods. von Lampe emphasizes that criminal activities described in his fourth typology level are generally for the enrichment, monetary or power-wise, of the elites themselves.

The fifth level of von Lampe's typology involves the networking of political elites and criminal organizations. He argues that this requires a "**congruence of interests**" between the two groups, which may shift in balance from time to time. His statement: "Political leaders, for example, may be willing to use violent groups in furtherance of their own power interests, while in exchange grant these criminal groups immunity from prosecution in other illegal activities" (von Lampe, 2008, p. 15), is an extreme end of this typology. However, there have been persistent rumors of the involvement of United States government officials and criminal organizations over the years, ranging from attempted and completed assassinations to distribution of drugs to specific communities. We hope this is an extremely rare instance. For our readers seeking to be leaders in the criminal justice system and allied organizations, it is an aspect of criminal organizations that needs to be guarded against on a constant basis. Otherwise, it represents an insidious threat to the perceived legitimacy and subsequent authority of the criminal justice system, in addition to issues we will now discuss in terms of social movements and criminal justice.

This fifth level takes us back to von Lampe's (2011b) critique of applying situational crime prevention approaches from routine activities theory to criminal organizations. That is, criminal organizations sometimes have the ability to make **capable guardians** incapable through corruption. He (von Lampe, 2011b, p. 158) argues that "in societies in transition and in developing countries, weak, corrupted and contested state authority will most likely have a defining influence on crime opportunities" by limiting capable guardianship. In our scheme outlined earlier, this brings us back to the issues of rebellious and ressentiment groups and movement. If such groups contribute to a lack of social cohesion, they will likely allow criminal organizations—if they are not among them—to flourish.

Criminal Organizations and Criminal Justice Organizations: A Summary

Definitions are important, as Finckenauer has argued. The focus on harms caused by criminal organizations is important. These include the direct harms caused to members of the community through the various activities these organizations carry out. They also include the damages done to the larger society through the corruption of those we rely on to provide our "capable guardianship." This is especially true when this involves the overlap of criminal organizational interests with those of the wealthy and powerful.

In the end, criminal justice organizations must deal with criminal organizations as part of their social environment. On the one hand, preventing and limiting the direct harm caused to members of the community may appear to be the most pressing activity confronting criminal justice agencies. On the other hand, ensuring that criminal organizations do not corrupt criminal justice organizations to the point that social support for the legitimacy and authority of criminal justice agents is impaired seems equally pressing. Pick your poison?

Conclusion

This chapter has presented what we believe is a more organizational approach to criminal organizations than generally encountered in criminal justice and criminology texts. Viewing the criminal organizations as organizations interacting with other organizational entities in the environment allows us to focus on the similarities they share with other organizations. Likewise, we can focus on those areas where they differ from more conventional organizations, such as in their use of violence. While CJOs are authorized to use violence, that use is legally constrained. The use of violence by criminal organizations, on the other hand, is constrained only by the actions of CJOs. Such differences provide us with "pressure points" where we may begin to disrupt the operations of criminal organizations. However, as pointed out just above, we see how criminal organizations can likewise infiltrate CJOs and weaken the very organizational sector that seeks to control criminal activity.

In the remaining chapters of the text, we now turn to some of the ways in which we use organizational design and intervention techniques to better plan organizational action for CJOs. Finally, we will examine the nature of changing technology on how CJOs operate in the environment.

Key Words

(Non) Ideological
Authority of reputation
Capable guardianships
Code of secrecy
Congruence of interests
Continuing Criminal Enterprises
Corruption
Criminal enterprise
Criminal organizations
Criminal sophistication
Differential Association
Facilitators
Flattened organization
Harm
Innovation
Intimidation

Longevity
Offenders as problem-solvers
Organizational structure
Organized crime
Proceeds of crime
Racketeer Influenced Criminal
    Organization (RICO)
Restrictive membership
Routine activities
Self-identification
Social harm
Social Learning
Structured group
Transnational organized crime
Violence
Willie Sutton hypothesis

CHAPTER 13

Organizational Change: The Logic of Planning, Implementing, Outcomes, and Feedback

Learning Objectives:
1. Describe and differentiate organizational "change" and "planned change."
2. Describe organizational planning and relate it to decision-making.
3. Differentiate organizational problem solving and organizational planning.
4. Identify and describe key elements of the criminal justice planning process according to Hudzik and Cordner (1983).
5. Describe and differentiate policy analysis and planning.
6. Describe the following: strategic planning, tactical planning, GAP analysis, and SWOT analysis; relate strategic planning to tactical planning, GAP analysis, and SWOT analysis.
7. Differentiate the missions and values of CJOs and CBOs and discuss how differences may create conflict.
8. Define and distinguish goals from objectives; describe SMART objectives.
9. Define, describe, and apply logic modeling.
10. Relate strategic planning, tactical planning, GAP analysis, SWOT analysis, missions, values, goals, SMART objectives, and logic modeling to developing an organizational plan for change.
11. Describe readiness for change, program fidelity, and various continuous quality approaches; relate them to implementing plans for organizational change.
12. Relate logic modeling and program fidelity to evidence-based programs.
13. Explore how organizational change efforts can be developed, implemented, and maintained in a networked CJ and non-CJ program setting.

Introduction

Although Max Weber warned us of the perils of the "iron cage of rationality" a century ago, **rational** approaches to organizational change still seem to hold the most promise for keeping organizations on track. There are organizations that can engage in more creative, non-rational and non-linear ways of conducting their business. For most organizations, however, the links among desired outcomes, organizational structures, strategies, technologies, etc., still need to be expressed rationally.

For organizations in the criminal justice system (CJS) and affiliated organizations, the **outcomes** desired and the ways of achieving them need to be even clearer than they are at present. This will sometimes require that criminal justice organizations (CJOs) help translate the demands of external audiences/stakeholders into rational, **observable**, **measurable**, and **meaningful** statements. Internally, this rational approach should be a **standard of practice**. This has become increasingly true as the era of **organizational accountability** takes root. In this chapter, we want to explore the process of **organizational planning** as it relates to **organizational change** within CJOs, monitoring activities of the CJO to ensure that stated goals are being achieved via prescribed means, and using such information to anticipate and plan the need for further organizational change.

Change versus Planned Change: "You Can Let It Happen; or, You Can Make It Happen"

Organizations change—just like everything else. We touched on forces that cause change and ways in which we can document change in CJOs and affiliated organizations in earlier chapters. Here we want to explore techniques CJOs (and affiliated organizations) can use to control at least some aspects of the changes required of them. The statement in the section title—you can let it happen; or, you can make it happen—provides a summary of the difference between "change" and "planned change."

Change is any difference between the way things are at Time 1 and how they are at Time 2; Time 2 being later than Time 1. Change happens for a variety of reasons, some under our control and others not under our control. **Planned change**, on the other hand, is driven by a "purposeful decision" to bring about what we believe are improvements in the organization. Whether or not this process is something that requires professional assistance has been a matter of debate since the late 1950s (e.g., Lippitt, Watson, & Westly, 1958). What is important here is that planned change starts with a "vision" of where an organization wants to be at some point in the future and develops a plan for getting there. We employ this same logic in the design of research studies, interestingly enough.

Planned organizational change is also characterized as a "conscious, deliberate, and collaborative effort" (Bennis, Benne & Chin, 1976) aimed at improving an organization's operations to make them better achieve desired goals and objectives. A key component of this process is the application of valid knowledge and information to the process. We touch on the issues of valid, useful data in Chapter 14. Likewise, and particularly as CJOs are tasked with addressing increasingly complex issues such as health issues, the "collaborative efforts" are becoming more important. We address these issues in the sections on inter-organizational relationships (IORs) in Chapter 5. In the next sections, we want to explore what planning takes, and how it is done.

What Is Organizational Planning?

Because one of the themes of this text is organizational decision-making, it seems appropriate to locate decision-making in relation to planning:

> "**Planning** can best be understood as what is done before making a decision or taking action. It is a process of preparation: information is gathered, alternatives are considered, and the likely effects of alternatives are estimated. Two additional characteristics set planning apart from other analytic strategies: in planning, the future is given explicit consideration, and comprehensiveness, or at least coordination, is sought among sets of interrelated decisions or actions. Without the kind of preparation provided through planning, decisions and actions are taken without regard to their long-term effects or to their effect on related decisions or actions" (Hudzik & Cordner, 1983, p. 34).

Hudzik & Cordner further link planning to decision-making by noting that planning seeks to broaden the amount of available information to be considered by decision-makers; decision-making then reduces the range of information through the choice of alternatives. In short, organizational planning focuses on the future (i.e., **future-oriented**) and considers multiple information sources and perspectives. Otherwise, decision-making is mostly based on "snap judgements" and impulse.

Solving Organizational Problems and Doing Organizational Planning: A Matter of Perspective?

We want to begin this section with a discussion of organizational problem-solving contrasted with organizational planning. The key difference between the two, as pointed out by Hudzik and Cordner (1983), is the matter of a **time perspective**. For our purposes, **problem-solving** is a set of activities focused on a solution to a current situation. Planning is a set of activities focused on the future. Kaufman and Stone (1983) note that planning involves the future; otherwise, the action could just "be done." Problem-solving may well morph into a planning process, and is certainly a part of the planning process. Organizations must solve problems to survive. The real question is whether the organization lurches from problem to problem; or, does the organization plan toward a future in a way that identifies problems, solutions to those problems, and provides a process for trying to define what the organization should be doing in the future. Problem-solving is focused on the problem; planning is about future problems, solutions, and the nature of the organization.

Hudzik and Cordner (1983) outlined key elements of the criminal justice planning process. The first of these focused on the need for "**prediction** and **control**." They note that while neither is easy to accomplish, attempting to accomplish them lies at the heart of the planning process (and most of social science approaches to criminal justice). We noted earlier that sometimes CJOs have to help their stakeholders understand the nature of the expectations that can be addressed by using the criminal justice sector as a social tool. Hudzik and Cordner (1983) noted that when the constraints on CJOs are poorly understood by stakeholders the expectations of CJOs become unrealistic. Further, when the unrealistic is not achieved, it is the CJO that is judged to be a failure. Because CJOs operate in a very public sphere, such "failures" are amplified. The nature of media coverage of criminal justice also tends to focus on the "crisis-prone" nature of our sector, rather than on the efforts taken to predict future problems and control them. We touched on these issues in Chapter 11.

The second element of criminal justice planning outlined by Hudzik and Cordner (1983) focuses on "goals." **Goals** can be either "normative" or "instrumental" (or "functional") in the planning process. It has been our experience that when CJOs engage in the planning process, it is almost always an **instrumental** process. That is, there is relatively little attention paid to whether the outcome ("ends") to be achieved is desired by the community; we tend to assume it is. The **normative** element of goals and planning are generally overshadowed by whether or not the "means" to achieve the goal(s) will be successful. Hudzik and Cordner point out that CJOs are often "handed" their goals, or have them imposed, by other organizational entities (from legislatures and Courts to social movements), so the ability to decide the normative is not there in the first place. It falls to the CJO to devise the instrumental plan to achieve the imposed goal(s).

Returning to the fact that crime as a social problem is a core feature of criminal justice, "**defining problems**" is another focus of the planning process, according to Hudzik and Cordner. They note that a problem or problems can refer either to addressing a situation that exists (the "unsettled question"), or from a "gap'—the difference between where we are now and where we want to be. Crime is legally/socially defined, so criminal justice is essentially a problem-solving operation. As part of a planning process, CJOs can help to define the nature of the crime problem, including the causes, magnitude, and impact of behaviors defined as criminal. CJOs may develop monitoring systems that help to anticipate (sentinel) or detect (surveillance, in public health terms) crime problems.

Finally, once the nature and scope of the problem have been defined, the CJO can develop and recommend procedures and policies for addressing the problem. This leads to the segment of the process Hudzik and Cordner (1983) discussed as developing alternatives and analyzing the consequences of organizational action. They argued that a key role of planning is to "identify and to weight alternative courses of action, and perhaps to select what seems the best course of action." They raise the question of how "best" is to be defined and determined, which takes us back to the issue of values, or the normative aspect of planning. The cost associated with the optimal solution to the crime problem may in the long run prove to be higher than acceptable. We might look at the current debates over "mass incarceration" as an example. While this has probably contributed to the reduction in crime observed, it has come with an unsustainable direct fiscal price, as well as the less direct costs of "collateral consequences." Sometimes we settle for less effective crime control policies, but policies and practices that have a more socially acceptable cost.

We can summarize this discussion by pointing out that planning involves making choices about how to achieve the goals—the outcomes chosen/desired by an organization—in the future. Problem-solving, while potentially part of the planning process, is more present- to short-term oriented. Prediction is future-oriented, as is achieving goals (and objectives). Our emphasis in this text is on organizational planning, subsuming organizational problem-solving. In the next section, we will turn to what constitutes planning, and then provide some examples of approaches and tools for that planning process.

Hudzik and Cordner also differentiate between planning and policy analysis. Like planning, **policy analysis** seeks to provide a broad consideration of alternatives to the decision-maker. However, the scope of the activities considered by policy analysis tends to focus on a single policy or decision-point. **Planning** is a broader and more comprehensive form of analysis. Policy analysis is generally focused on the effects of the policy, either currently in effect or proposed. Policy analysis is also not specifically focused on the future, while planning is.

Strategic Planning: Really, Do We Have To?

We have now covered the key elements of organizational planning and how they relate to other types of analysis. In the next sections, we want to explore some ways of developing an organizational plan for change. We will then discuss some issues with regard to implementing the plans. We want to end this section with a brief discussion of a type of organizational planning that has earned something of a dubious reputation over time—strategic planning. OK, now that the eyes have rolled, let us take a look at why strategic planning is important to CJOs.

As Hudzik and Cordner (1983) point out, strategic planning should allow CJOs to focus on their core mission(s), yet anticipate and plan to meet new challenges. **Strategic planning** is based on a knowledge of the organization's basic/core mission(s), an understanding of where the organization needs to be at some point in the future, and an analysis of constraints within the organization that might pose a challenge for obtaining the desired future position. Strategic planning assumes that some change in the organization is needed to achieve the desired future. Hudzik and Cordner subsume "tactical planning" under strategic planning. **Tactical planning** addresses the necessary changes in management control and allocation of resources within the organization to achieve the outcomes (sound like Resource Management Theory?).

Part of the criticism and distrust of the term "strategic planning" comes from the fact that it has become ritualized. If the planning process becomes something every new manager does, regardless of when it was last done; or, we do it every year at this time, etc., it is hard to reinforce the value of the process. When the strategic planning process is not allowed to mature and evidence of its success or failure allowed to be empirically assessed, trust in the process is voided. In organizations like the CJS, where missions are often set officially by other organizations, or informally by developments in the social world, some question the value of this approach. Lest you decide it is not of value, let us provide some guidance from the United States Office of Personnel Management (accessed July, 2016):

> Changing and significantly increasing demands for programs, products, and services and greater demands for accountability and good governance are several of the many reasons public organizations have turned to strategic planning and strategic human capital planning. Strategic planning is a disciplined effort to produce fundamental decisions and actions that shape and guide what an organization is, what it does, and why it does it. The Government Performance and Results Act of 1993 (Public Law 103–62) legislated that Federal agencies should develop year strategic plans and now, almost all Federal agencies have a strategic plan of some sort. The Modernization Act of 2010 (Public Law 111–352) has expanded the law to require agencies also develop annual performance plans and identify performance improvement officers. Strategic planning should not stop with a formal plan. Creating effective and results-oriented organizations requires linking the strategic plan and annual performance plan goals to the PM [personnel management] program so that organizational outcomes are tied to individual accountability (https://www.opm.gov/services-for-agencies/performance-management/organizational-performance-management/).

Here we have an example of linking the strategic plan to what we earlier described as the tactical plan, at least in terms of having the proper personnel or training personnel to achieve the organizationally-desired outcome.

Strategic planning can be most simply described by what is often called a "**GAP analysis**." This generally begins with the idea that the organization in question needs to be changed to meet some required or desired performance objective. Note that word "objective," as we will be returning to it. In many ways, most organizational planning is really a backward-to-forward process. We begin with the outcomes (objectives) we wish to achieve. Then, we perform some assessment of where the organization is at present. The difference between where we are now and where we wish to be is the 'gap." We then begin to develop a plan/strategy to move to the desired new position. Simple enough, right? Well… Go backwards to move forward.

When an organization thinks about moving in a new direction, they may also employ what is known as a "**SWOT analysis**." Over the past decade, we have used this approach with multiple correctional agencies seeking to develop re-entry programs. SWOT stands for strengths, weaknesses, opportunities, and threats. After deciding where the organization wants to be with a new program or service (sometimes using a GAP analysis), the first step is to figure out what "strengths" the organization brings to the process. For example, if release planning starts inside the correctional facility, the organization may have a strength in the ability to structure the process and planning for the soon to be released person. However, if the organization does not have individuals with proper training to develop release plans, this is a "weakness."

"Opportunities" in CJOs are generally about providing a new or revised service to the community. For corporate and non-government organizations (NGOs) such opportunities are often some form of new market or product niche to be exploited. Taking re-entry as an example, there are opportunities to serve the community through reduced offending, victimization, and cost-savings from future incarceration, along with the multiple "collateral consequences" that have been identified. Likewise, for the correctional system, there are the outcomes of reduced populations and costs. Unlike the NGO world, these opportunities are often not directly related to the CJO, but often are more indirect, but still important. One of the key questions to be answered at this point is whether the CJO has a real opportunity in developing this service or program. Unfortunately, we have seen too many CJOs and affiliated CBO partners who viewed the "opportunity" mainly in terms of some short-term funding opportunity, rather than in developing the service to the community aspect.

Finally, "threats" refer to both internal and external factors that might blunt the success of the new effort. We mentioned earlier that personnel in the CJO might not be trained properly to deliver the service needed. Thus, the cost of training and personnel becomes a potential threat. If the decision is made that an outside service provider should be utilized, a potential threat is that no such provider is available in the jurisdiction. Community attitudes toward the new service or program must also be considered as either a strength or a weakness. This is true even if the service or program has been legislatively mandated.

Taken together, and often presented visually in a two by two table, the organizational decision must be made whether the opportunities and strengths outweigh the weaknesses and threats. In NGOs, this is often a very rational decision-making process. In CJOs, where either legislation or some pressure toward isomorphism (prestige, in our experience), compels the development of new services or programs, decision-making is less clear-cut or almost irrational. Regardless, the SWOT analysis helps organizations begin to flesh-out what it will take to fill the GAP to develop a successful organizational service or program. Increasingly this will involve NGO partners. The next section discusses some of the issues inherent in working with NGOs, and sometimes other CJOs.

Missions, Visions, and Values: Why Can't We All Just Get Along?

We have introduced the idea of using CJO mission statements to observe how the different segments of the "system" express their mission(s) publicly and internally. The idea of the mission is very important in organizational planning. **Mission statements** are sometimes separate from, and sometimes contain, "vision" statements. The **vision statement** generally conveys the type of organization it will be in the future, if the elements of the strategic plan are achieved. The mission statement explains why the organization exists. Again, for those in the formal government CJOs, the mission is often provided by a legislative body. The vision for how that gets carried out may be more open to modification by the organization. Allied organizations may change their mission and vision much more readily than the formal CJOs. This is one reason we find that there are times when more community- and faith-based organizations (CBOs) are involved in the CJS as they find their mission and vision statements congruent with the desired objectives of the CJOs.

We should add also the notion of a "values" statement here. **Values statements** tell us how the organization will behave and what the organization believes in. While the legislative process may provide the values and mission statement equivalents for the formal CJOs, CBOs and for-profit allied organizations set their own. This can lead to friction when the mission of a CJO and an allied organization conflict and they find a need to work together.

As an example, Potter was involved in a collaboration between a state prison system and a health CBO. The objective of the project was to provide sexually-transmitted infection prevention education to prisoners in a state facility. The health CBO staff were instructed that condoms were considered contraband and could not be introduced into the prison. After some negotiation, the CBO staff was allowed to bring in one condom for demonstration purposes. We are sure you have seen the banana or cucumber "fitting" demonstration at some point. Crisis averted, right? No, the CBO staffers brought in more than one condom per session and distributed them to some of the attendees. In the minds of the CBO staff, providing condoms to prisoners to prevent disease transmission was more important than obeying the state prison system's rules on contraband. After several of the staff were banned from state prisons (but, happily, not arrested), a behavioral contract was developed that all CBO staff that entered the prison were required to sign, and abide by the results if they violated the contract.

To the extent possible, part of the planning process should be a clear discussion of what the CJO (host) values and is required to do by law. Likewise, any agency that volunteers to participate or is sought out as a contract partner should lay those same cards on the table at the beginning. Understanding the overlaps and frictions between CJOs and the allied organizations with which they collaborate is an essential early step in the planning process. At least, that has been our experience to date.

Goals and Objectives—The Difference Is Important for Organizational Planning

So far we have not really distinguished organizational goals from objectives. **Goals** are generally considered to be general statements of what an organization wants to achieve or go (see the mission statement above). Goals are not specific. **Objectives**, on the other hand: "Specify an observable performance standard that lets everyone know exactly what is to be accomplished and the specific criteria to be used to determine if the required results have been achieved" (Kaufman & Stone, 1983). By "objective" we mean specific and measurable.

We generally encourage organizations to develop "SMART objectives." **SMART** stands for specific, measurable, achievable, relevant, and time-based (phased, sensitive). Think of "specific" as something that allows you to know that an outcome has been achieved. This is something that can be observed and agreed upon by multiple viewers, not just one person's opinion (remember "validity" in methods?). We often try to use some observable change expressed in terms of a percentage or frequency that increases or decreases, depending on whether we want to increase or decrease something. Specific is closely tied to "measurable." That is, in order to demonstrate that the specific change we seek has happened, we use measurements to track the change and direction. In short, how do you know whether you have succeeded, whether the project is done, unless you have specific measures and a way to collect them? Only then can you say that you have achieved the objectives and outcomes you set out to achieve.

A good objective is also achievable. Why set objectives you cannot achieve? OK, so sometimes unachievable goals (note the difference between a goal and objective) are imposed on CJOs. But, when we can specify the objectives associated with a goal, we can often demonstrate that, while the overall goal may be unachievable, specific outcomes associated with the goal can be. Another product associated with SMART objectives is the relevance of the outcome to the organization. Again, we point back to the mission statement to help guide our thinking on whether or not the outcome affects the organization. If it does not, perhaps the outcome is not as important to our organization as it is to others. Finally, a good objective is time-based. We want to accomplish the outcome within some reasonable period of time. Goals may be open-ended, objectives are time-sensitive.

The relationship between goals and objectives is reflective of the relationships among mission, vision, and values statements. Goals more closely mirror those statements, often without regard to outcomes and time frames. Objectives, on the other hand, are more operational in nature. They specify the outcomes we wish to achieve over a given period of time, and how we will know we have achieved them. In the next section, we want to provide a summary of one technique that allows us to move the organization toward specifying and achieving objective outcomes.

Logic Modeling as a Planning Tool

So, you've identified an opportunity (grant)—or had one thrust upon you (mandate)—done your GAP and SWOT analyses, and decided to pursue the opportunity. It is now time to figure out how to get the job done. You know where you want your organization to go (outcomes or objectives). You know where your organization is. It is time to figure out how to get there. In this section, we want to provide a brief overview of logic modeling, a planning process we have found works well with CJOs, their government partners, and the NGOs whose participation may be necessary. This is an overview only.

Whether we are talking about developing a program to change a client's behavior or changing the way we do things in an organization, we must begin with a **theory of change**. In short, why do we think what we are thinking about doing will actually lead to the change we want to bring about? Sometimes these are very straightforward—we have a theory that says if we do A, then B will happen. Other times, we have a vague idea, or what Argyris and Schon (1978) called a "theory in use" that is guiding us. One of the things about a logic model is that it makes us be very specific about why we think what we want to do will bring about the outcomes we want. Be warned, this can be a very confronting process. We often find our cherished assumptions about human and organizational nature challenged.

Earlier we wrote that often you have to look backward to go forward in organizational planning. Logic modeling is a process where we encourage you to do exactly that: Start with the outcomes (i.e., objectives) you wish to achieve. This may not be as easy as it seems because logic modeling requires that you are very specific and objective in defining the outcome you wish to achieve. Part of the development of a good logic model involves developing a system of data collection about the specific change (and associated factors) that allow us to determine whether or not we have actually accomplished our outcome.

At its base, a logic model is a graphic description of the relationship between what you plan to do and the intended effects of those actions (**means → ends**). It is quintessentially rational. The model is a series of "**if-then**" statements that lay out the relationship(s) between (among) the activities to be done and the outcomes that should be accomplished if those things are done correctly. The "if-then" statements move from inputs through outputs to outcomes (Inputs → Outputs → Outcomes). We will define each of these terms in reverse order. We will then put them together in an example. Please keep in mind that this is an overview of the logic modeling process.

We generally begin with the **outcomes** an organization wishes to accomplish by changing something. That something may be implementing a new program, or it may be a change in the organizational structure to achieve some new way of responding to the environment. This is where we want to go back to our SMART objectives. We want to be specific about how we will know the change has been accomplished (specific, measurable) and over what period of time. Some outcomes may be short-term, others more mid-term, and some long-term. How those time frames are measured often depends upon the nature of the change desired and the size of the organization involved. In the end, the objectives are the measurable changes you want to observe if your theory of change actually produces the change you intend. How do you know it worked?!

Outputs are the activities required to achieve the outcomes. These are often subdivided into the activities and the populations to whom they will be applied. Outputs are often measurable, and this can sometimes confuse the process. These "products" of the activities of organizational change are necessary to achieve the final outcomes intended; but, the products are not the outcomes, only a step on the way to achieving the outcomes.

The theory of change mentioned above becomes very important here. For example, if we are talking about developing an inmate re-entry program, our activities would be directed to the inmates preparing for release into the community, at a minimum. The activities would include the evidence-based practices (EBPs) associated with successful re-entry, such as criminogenic risk assessment, cognitive-behavioral restructuring, and life-skills (employment, education, etc.). These activities might produce the outputs of "X% of inmates held for 30 days receive criminogenic risk assessment," and "Y% of all inmates scoring medium-high to high risk receive a discharge plan." While these are measurable, they are still activities needed to achieve the final outcome of, in this case, z% decrease in prisoners returning to prison.

Another output along the way to our successful re-entry outcome might be the development of a specialized re-entry unit in the organization. This would require that organizational members and contractors receive specific training in the EBPs that are associated with our intended successful outcome(s). Thus, outputs such as "Z staff will be trained to conduct criminogenic risk assessments" will help in the establishment of the re-entry unit. The unit itself is still an activity along the path toward achieving the outcome of reduced recidivism of the inmates who go through the program. Even then, the program itself is an output, leading to the desired outcome of reduced recidivism. Some people tend to see the means as ends in themselves. This was a problem noted by Hudzik and Cordner (1983) before the wide-spread use of logic modeling.

Inputs are the resources required to deliver the activities to the target audience(s) (outputs) in order to achieve the desired outcome(s). These generally consist of personnel (staff, contractors, volunteers, etc.), the target audience, money, time, and technology, as it was broadly defined in the section on organizational structure. In the criminogenic risk assessment mentioned above, the organization may choose to go with an EB risk assessment that is proprietary, and thus requires both money to train staff and money to purchase the utilization of the assessment instrument. One of the items often left out of logic models is the target audience—who generally show up only in the outputs section. But, without the target audience as an input, why bother to go further?

Based on the example of the inmate re-entry program, we have developed a basic logic model (see Figure 13.1). This format was taken from the University of Wisconsin's Extension Service (http://fyi.uwex.edu/programdevelopment/logic-models/bibliography/). We like this format because it invites the planners to be specific about what is needed, what we are going to do to whom, and what will be produced over specific time frames. There are other formats available (see Knowlton & Phillips, 2013). We encourage readers to explore the format that works best for the process used in organizational planning efforts.

Another feature of the logic model template we are using is a space for listing "assumptions" and "external factors." Whether or not they are included in the final logic model presentation, these are important factors to consider. We noted earlier that confronting the **assumptions** that underlie our choices for organizational change can be confronting. This is the spot

234 CRIMINAL JUSTICE ORGANIZATIONS

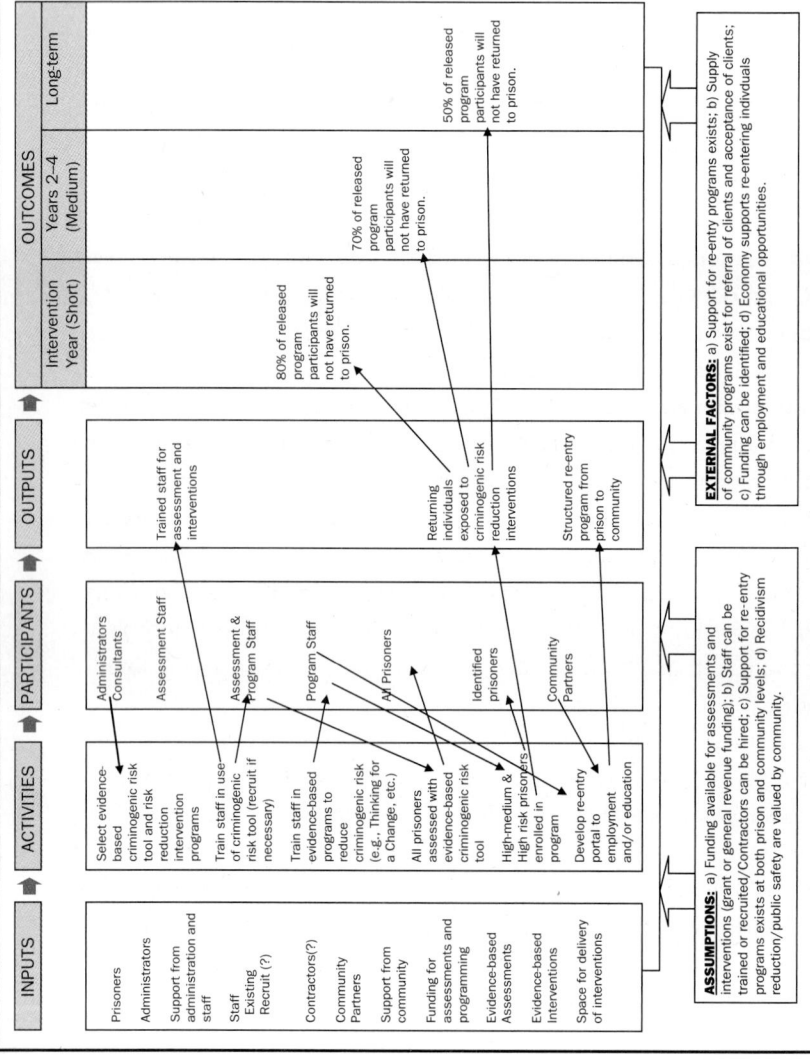

Figure 13.1: LOGIC MODEL Example Worksheet (A simple prisoner re-entry program)

where the assumptions that you believe call for and support the change proposed are fully laid out. If those assumptions are not consistent with the logic model, then perhaps the assumptions need to be revisited. Likewise, if a change is affected by the **external environment**, this is the place to specify what factors are necessary to make the change effective. If, for example, the assumption is that there will always be federal grant dollars available to fund the program, the federal budget must be included as an external factor. Changes in community attitudes toward some of the activities of the CJS is another external factor. And, if you work in an agency that can be affected by election or appointment, change in administration may be another external factor to consider.

This has been a very brief introduction to logic modeling as a technique for managing organizational change and planning. We have found that it is a powerful process for assisting CJOs in thinking through why and how they want to make changes in their organizations. We have seen agencies decide that they could not achieve their desired outcomes with the resources available to them, including other organizations in the community. We have seen others form effective networks of relationships with other organizations in the community to achieve desired community outcomes. Sometimes, putting things in stark "if-then" statements and looking at strengths, weaknesses, opportunities, and threats (SWOT) at the same time provides that reality check needed. Of course, if the change is imposed by the power of the purse or administrator whim, none of this really matters.

Readiness for Change—Not Just for Inmates Anymore

Now that you've conducted your GAP and SWOT analyses and developed your logic model, it is time to implement the changes. To this point, we have assumed that the organizational change being planned is either required or a matter of consensus within the organization. If this is not the case, then one of the first orders of business is to assess the organization's **readiness for change** (Clardy, 1997). Harrison (2005) notes that intentional change of the type we have been discussing (contrasted with incremental change) is most likely to encounter resistance. Harrison (2005, p. 50) suggests the use of outside consultants to determine at least four things:

- Does the organization have the resources necessary to implement the proposed change?
- Can changes within the organization bring about the change?

- Will the dominant culture of the organization allow the change to occur (does "culture eat strategy for breakfast")?
- Will the environment facilitate or hinder the change?

In the logic model example (Figure 13.1), we noted a decision point where either existing or new staff would be required to develop our hypothetical re-entry program. If existing staff are resistant to change, one of two approaches may be taken. The first is to employ training to bring the resistant staff into agreement with the objectives and operations associated with the program. We also noted that one of the short-term objectives would be to train all of the staff in the philosophy and practices that underlie the new program or group in order to address some of the cultural issues. If that fails or is considered unlikely to be successful, the organization may decide to bring in new staff who are "on board" with the program.

Readiness for change issues take on more importance as we talk about more "voluntary" changes. A move from a patrol car-based to a foot patrol-oriented policing strategy provides one example; likewise, from a more "traditional" policing to a "problem-oriented" approach. Moving from an incapacitation model of corrections to a re-entry-focused model provides a corrections example consistent with our logic model. When change is involuntary, such as a Court Monitor's order or a change in funding priorities, readiness for change is still important. It may, however, bring about other "remedies" such as removing elements of the organization that do not fall in line with the mandated change.

Fidelity and Continuous Quality Approaches

So, we have arrived at implementation of our change. Here we return to an issue associated with all evidence-based programs/practices (EBPs)—fidelity. Taxman and Belenko (2012, p. 220) state:

> "**Implementation** and **program fidelity** go hand-in-hand. Without knowing whether an EBP has been implemented in a way that retains the integrity of the evidence-based intervention, there is no guarantee that an EBP will deliver and achieve a similar degree of effectiveness in either a new setting or with a different population…. Achieving and maintaining fidelity in real world settings can be quite difficult."

Taxman and Belenko (2012, p. 286) provide a list of "inner setting factors" for implementation that address many of the ideas we have covered so far in this chapter. We would add that fidelity applies not only to the implementation of EBPs, but to any program of planned change in an organization.

The "quality" movement in the US is often traced back to Philip Crosby's (1979) book, *Quality Is Free*. From his statements that effectively say "do it right the first time and you won't have to do it again," several approaches to **quality assurance**, **management**, and **improvement** have developed. Fidelity is measured against specific elements of an EBP; quality assurance (QA) is the process of assessing compliance with necessary standards. The Health Resources Services Administration (http://www.hrsa.aquilentprojects.com/healthit/toolbox/HealthITAdoptiontoolbox/QualityImprovement/whatarediffbtwqinqa.html; accessed August 2, 2016) provides a comparison of QA with "quality improvement" (QI) approaches (see Table 13.1) in the health fields. QA approaches are often described as reactive and surveillance-like (in CJ, not public health, terms). QI approaches, however, are viewed as more geared toward improvement.

We suggest that QA approaches may be most applicable to the intervention and fidelity processes. Ensuring that the program being adopted is implemented with fidelity in the first place allows the organization to determine whether or not the theory of change and EBPs are accomplishing the objectives (outcomes) desired. If not, the QI process may be implemented to find where the program assumptions and practices are ineffective and seek

TABLE 13.1: COMPARISON OF QUALITY ASSURANCE AND QUALITY IMPROVEMENT MODELS

	Quality Assurance	Quality Improvement
Motivation	Measuring compliance with standards	Continuously improving processes to meet standards
Means	Inspection	Prevention
Attitude	Required, defensive	Chosen, proactive
Focus	Outliers: *"bad apples"* Individuals	Processes Systems
Scope	Medical provider	Patient care
Responsibility	Few	All

Source: Health Resources Services Administration on Quality Approaches http://www.hrsa.aquilentprojects.com/healthit/toolbox/HealthITAdoptiontoolbox/QualityImprovement/whatarediffbtwqinqa.html

ways to replace them and achieve the desired outcomes. Because conditions change around and within the organization, the QI process may become a continuous quality improvement (CQI) process, sometimes known as "**total quality management**."

Quality processes involve all of the elements of organizational research we have discussed in the text: defining problems with processes, analyzing data to identify the problems, developing solutions based on the analysis, and evaluating the effectiveness of the solutions; rinse and repeat as necessary. It should not be surprising to the reader that an "implementation science" specialty has arisen in academic circles (http://implementationscience.biomed central.com/; accessed August 3, 2016). Like many of the developments in evaluation and performance management over the past thirty years, much of this is geared toward the health fields. However, the principles apply just as much to the CJS. We find that many prison systems have CQI groups in their medical units to review and improve the delivery of health care. The logic of such groups is very much like those of "after-action" review groups in other segments of the CJS, except that the quality improvement groups meet regularly to review procedures and problems.

Putting It Together

There is an old saying that what drives change in CJOs are lawsuits—and the Court orders and settlements that flow from them. Sadly, in many instances this is true. At other times, legislative changes will drive change either through changes in statute or redirecting funding to bring about change. More locally, of course, are elections of Sheriffs, State/District Attorneys (prosecutors), Public Defenders, and Judges. For local police agencies, as well as the statistical handful of non-Sheriff-operated jails, appointments of new administrators can drive change. This means that the outcomes or objectives of organizational change are sometimes handed to CJOs, rather than such outcomes being a matter of choice by the CJO. Not always, of course.

Regardless of the source of the outcomes to be achieved, the planning process to achieve them can follow the same process outlined here. It truly is a "go backwards to get forwards" process. Know where you want to go and how it will be measured, and working backwards toward what it will take to achieve the outcome will become clearer. We do not promise the effort will be easy, but it does make the implementation and quality enhancement that follows much easier.

This has been a brief overview of one approach to organizational planning. We want to end with a cautionary note. What we have provided here are the basic tools of organizational planning, implementation, and maintenance. When you enter the field, there will be those who treat these tools as ends in themselves. Logic modeling is a prime example. For some it is more about the shape of boxes in a logic model flow-chart that is more important than the if-then relationships they describe. Remember, these are tools, not fetishes! There are for-profit corporations who package these essential tools under proprietary names and sell their services to you, and many of us academics are involved in that market. One of the decisions you may have to make early in the planning process is whether or not to bring in an outsider, such as an academic or corporate planning facilitator.

What we hope you gain from this chapter is the basic knowledge to know what you are being offered matches your need. Likewise, we want you to be able to judge whether the quality of the process being offered is truly high enough to fulfill your need. In short, knowing the basics of social science research will assist you in organizational planning, implementation, and maintenance just as much as they will help you decide whether the theories of change being used are sound.

Key Words

Assumptions
Change
Continuous quality improvement
Control
Decision-making
Defining problems
External factors
Future-orientation
GAP analysis
Goals
If-then statements
Implementation
Inputs
Instrumental
Logic model
Meaningful
Means-ends statements

Measurable
Mission statements
Normative
Objective
Observable
Organizational accountability
Organizational change
Organizational planning
Organizational problem-solving
Outcomes
Outputs
Planned change
Policy analysis
Prediction
Program fidelity
Quality assurance
Quality improvement

Quality management
Rational
Readiness for change
SMART objectives
Standard of practice
Strategic planning
SWOT analysis

Tactical planning
Theory of change
Time perspective
Total quality management
Values statements
Vision statements

Criminal Justice Informatics, Data, and Decision-Making

Learning Objectives:
1. Describe informatics and how it relates to criminal justice organizations.
2. Describe how information creates a system.
3. Identify, describe, and distinguish the six types of information systems according to Satzinger and associates (2002) and relate them to Ioimo's (2006) list of information and technological systems.
4. Describe how CJO information captured at the Transaction Processing Systems level can be used to make decisions for the agency.
5. Describe the types of problems associated with planning and implementing records management systems within an organization, and distinguish these issues from data shared across CJOs.
6. Outline and describe the information system steps used in crime analysis according to Dunworth (2006).
7. Describe and analyze the 10 categorical functions of computers in local police as compared to sheriffs' offices in 2000 and 2007.
8. Discuss issues related to data accuracy and how data can be used by CJOs and researchers.
9. Describe the day in the life of a datum in an arrest.
10. Explore the national-level BJS databases listed in Appendix 14.1 and describe CJOs according to those data.

Introduction

In 2015 an article in *The Sheriff's Star* titled "The 21st Century Florida Sheriff" (Shoar & Dunagan, 2015) listed three areas where the authors believe future leaders of law enforcement must develop special knowledge and skills. We suggest that leaders of all CJOs need this skill set. The three are:
1. Accountability and transparency;

2. Training and education; and
3. Technology and social media

Our focus here is on technology and information ("informatics") and their utilization in the protection of communities ("social informatics"). As Shoar & Dunagan (2015, p. 17) note:

> Technology available to sheriffs is rapidly multiplying, and sheriffs are continually adopting model policies and best practices for deploying this new technology. However, new technology always presents new challenges, and may carry unanticipated consequences, identifying the downside as well as the benefits of new technology, and how it is deployed will ultimately be the responsibility of each elected sheriff… What is important is that the rationale for these decisions be communicated to the communities that will be affected.

Each of the three areas above is inter-related. They relate to the internal strategies and the external environments discussed throughout this text. We hope here to introduce students of criminal justice organizations to some principles of informatics, how they relate to your work, and how information is collected and utilized for organizational decision-making.

A Brief History of Criminal Justice Informatics

Information has been with us for the entire history of criminal justice systems. For those readers born after the mid-1990s, the idea of a world without personal computers, perhaps even "smart phones," may seem far-fetched. Those of us of older years remember when information once existed mostly on paper forms held in file folders in filing cabinets or desk drawers, (we still have those in our offices for certain legal purposes). Attorneys and other professionals didn't know how to type, and would handwrite or dictate information for secretaries. Almost all information exchanges occurred by paper or voice until the fax machine arrived, and then it was still basically a paper form transmitted by telephone—which was all "land-line." Carbon copies were replaced by the revolutionary copy machine.

The elder author's (Potter) dissertation was among the first typed on a "word processing machine" with 7.5 inch "diskettes" at the University of Florida in 1982. Typing a manuscript onto a disc which allowed one to alter entire paragraphs prior to printing was a leap forward, as compared to manuscripts typed on an IBM Selectric typewriter with a single backspace correction feature. Most of my friends still had to use erasers or some liquid cover-up painted on like nail polish to make corrections as they typed. Only the largest criminal justice agencies and state and federal systems had computers, and much of that information was input from punch cards (See example in Figure 14.1).

The situation in most criminal justice organizations (CJOs) was similar. In the early 1980s, only **mainframe computers** or mini-computers were available to organizations. Potter's first job at a state agency required the use of a mainframe computer at the state court system to run statistical analysis software. They were one of the few agencies with that capacity at the time. Final production of documents was done on a word processing machine by a secretary (when did you last meet one of those?); personal/desktop computers were rare. It was a time when mainframe computers were the size of a car (mini-computers the size of a refrigerator), and personal computers were not intuitive. They ran on DOS program commands, as Microsoft Windows hadn't yet become an institutionalized office staple. Tablets still had paper... you get the picture.

By the mid- to late 1980s, personal computers were becoming much less expensive, in relative terms, and more frequently a part of CJO offices. Still, without the internet, all across machine communications were carried out on local area networks (LANs), and the cost of such hardware systems was prohibitive to most organizations. Even then, it was rare for two organizations' information technology (IT) systems to talk with each other without specialty software and telephone (still land-lines) hook-ups. Software packages were also more easily developed to perform primary tasks for CJO and others, such as case tracking, income and expenditure, and so forth. Developers began to produce specialty packages for CJOs, some of which continue today as

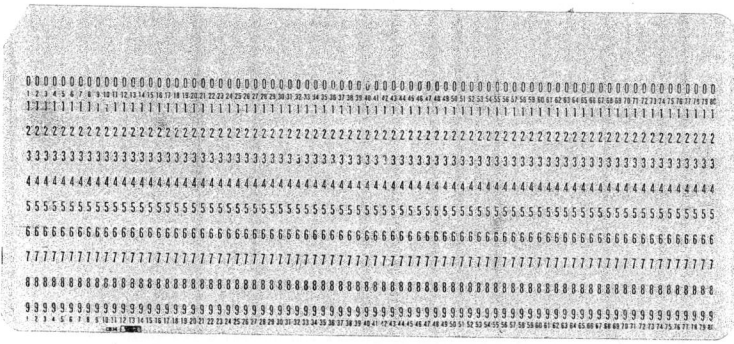

Figure 14.1: Punch Card Example

"**legacy**" **systems**. Yet, we paid relatively little attention to the relationships among organizational theory, information technology, and agency operations in the field of criminal justice.

Things began to change dramatically in the 1990s with the broad availability of the internet, decreasing costs for computer hardware and many software products, and a workforce more familiar with using computers than in the previous 20 year period. New applications that provided greater utility to CJOs and affiliated organizations began to appear at reasonable prices. Academic Criminal Justice programs began to prepare students to utilize these new technologies by the early 2000 period, and criminals began to utilize the new technologies frequently at about the same time. Since then, computer applications for CJOs have proliferated, and computer forensics and cybercrime have become staples in academic programs. Yet, as we will explore below, we still rarely teach or read much about criminal justice informatics, especially as it relates to various CJO functions, structures, and authorities.

What Informatics Is and How It Relates to Criminal Justice Organizations

The term "**informatics**" rarely occurs in conjunction with "criminal justice" in most texts. Yet, we discuss certain types of data we collect, and sometimes how it is collected, in many of our courses. We tend to use the term "analysis" more regularly, usually in relation to certain types of functions, such as intelligence analyst. Both data collection and analysis practices can be subsumed under the term "informatics," as shown in these definitions:

> Information science, the study of the processing, management, and retrieval of information (Oxford Dictionary)

> Informatics, a broad academic field encompassing human-computer interaction, information science, information technology, algorithms, areas of mathematics (especially mathematical logic and category theory), and social sciences that are involved. (taken from Mikhailov, Chernyl, & Gilyarevskii, 1966).

Another definition provided by Wan (2006, p. 333) is:

> [a]n interdisciplinary science employing information on science, information technology and statistics. Informatics research is a general term for the process of data warehousing, data mining, data analysis, and simulation with an interface with computer and information system technologies.

Curiously, just about every other social science linked to a field of practice has its own informatics field, such as health care informatics, nursing informatics, etc. Wan (2006, p. 334) describes the uses of informatics in criminal justice thusly: "crime informatics performs data matching to identify offenders and monitor changes in the distribution of pharmaceutical drug diversion and uses geographic information system (GIS) software to map 'hot spots' of crime or bioterrorism." We believe this is a good starting point, but one that requires development as we think of CJOs as decision-making entities.

In our field, actors within criminal justice organizations have regular interactions with computers, inputting a wide range of information. Some of that information gets utilized on a regular basis while other portions go into storage and may or may not ever be utilized. Unlike many other sectors, we also have a range of legislation and court decisions that require that certain types of data be stored and accessible for a specified period of time. As we begin to move into the almost continuous video recording of staff interactions with citizens, the issues of data storage are moving to the fore as we think about the cost of such data storage, retrieval, and protection. "**Data mining**" approaches (Wan, 2006) may be utilized increasingly by some agencies to unlock potential patterns in those stored data. As new techniques for analyzing stored visual and audio data are developed, it is likely we will see more data mining by CJOs.

Some Basic Ideas

Some may reduce the notion of informatics to basically the "**information systems**" that operate in the variety of criminal justice organizations (e.g., Ioimo, 2016). However, Satzinger, Jackson and Burd (2002) discuss information systems as integral to the decision-making process in just about every modern business organization. They write that the technology behind the information systems itself is not the key element. Rather, it is the people who make sense of the data and the technology—they term them **systems analysts**—that brings the power of the information system to bear. We could not agree more. Understanding how data are collected, corrected, stored, analyzed, and utilized remains an under-developed area in criminal justice organizations.

Satzinger, et al. (2002, p. 6) define a **system** as "a collection of interrelated components that function together to achieve some outcome." Sound familiar? An "information system is a collection of interrelated components that collect, process, store, and provide as output the information needed to complete a business task." Using their definitions, the total criminal justice system (CJS) comprises a "**supersystem**." Each of the components that make up the CJS is a "subsystem." As we have noted elsewhere, each of these subsystems has its own "business task" to achieve, as well as contributing something to the outcome of the supersystem.

Likewise, each of these **subsystems** is likely to have its own, often unique, information system. The ability to share data across these subsystems requires that "system boundaries" between the organizations be bridged. Within each of those information subsystems lies the "**automation boundary**" where work done by hand gets turned into automated information (Satzinger, et al. 2002, p. 8). For example, think about those forms you have to complete every new insurance year when you go for a physician's appointment. You fill them out by hand, give them to the office staff, and they then scan them into a computer file. Not that long ago, every report completed in the criminal justice system, from an incident report to court filings, was first completed "by hand" and then either physically filed away. Now any such documents can be scanned into accessible computer files.

Increasingly we see organizations seek to reduce the automation boundary by moving more and more information to direct digital (keyboard or pointing device) input rather than manual, though human error still works its way into the process. Here are two examples from our local experience. The first involves an in-vehicle system that allows street-level officers to input information required for booking at the county jail before they arrive at the jail. This allows the officers to remain at the jail for only a brief time before returning to the street. Likewise, it gives the booking section at the jail information about individuals being transported before they arrive at the sally port. The second is more visual, allowing officers to log into court proceedings and deliver their testimony remotely, but with full visual. This allows for cross-examination, if necessary. Of course, these sorts of innovations may require new procedural rules in the other segments of the CJS involved.

An Overview Of Information Systems

Satzinger, et al. (2002, pp. 8–9) list six types of information systems encountered in most business environments:

1. **Transaction processing systems** (TPS) capture and record information about the transactions that affect the organization.

2. **Management information systems** (MIS) are systems that take information captured by transaction processing systems and produce reports that management needs for planning and controlling the business.

3. **Executive information systems** (EIS) provide information for executives to use for monitoring the competitive environment and for strategic planning.

4. **Decision support systems** (DSS) allow a user to explore the impact of available options or decisions. These may also be called "what if" analyses.

5. **Communication support systems** allow employees to communicate with each other and with customers and suppliers. All of the technologies most of us take for granted, especially social media and internet communications, are included in this category.

6. **Office support systems** help employees create and share documents,... [and] help maintain information about work schedules and meetings.

Ioimo (2016) provides a similar list of information and technological systems in the CJS:

- 9-1-1 services;
- Computer-aided dispatch systems;
- Police record management systems;
- Police workgroup applications (e.g., GIS, fingerprint, case management, etc.);
- Mobile computing (e.g., in-vehicle, smartphones, tablets, etc.);
- Crime analysis and mapping
- Corrections information technology;
- Prosecutor information management systems; and,
- Court management information systems;

The overlaps between the systems outlined by Satzinger, et al. (2002) and Ioimo (2016) are fairly clear. Each of the information management systems can subsume functions of CJ technology.

Every encounter between a criminal justice system worker and citizens or among system workers has the possibility of generating information. Incident reports from police and/or correctional officers usually generate some written record that can be entered into an agency information system. As noted above, the increasing use of body camera devices to record officers' encounters with the public will generate an abundance of data that must be stored for potential analysis. These are all TPS in the Satzinger, et al. (2002) list.

In the world of criminal justice organizations, we would probably call these "**records management systems**" or RMS (Dunsworth, 2000, p. 380): "An RMS is the informational heart of any police department's operations. It provides for the storage, retrieval, retention, manipulation, archiving, and viewing of information, records, documents, and files about every aspect of police business." Ioimo (2016) has expanded Dunworth's characterization to include corrections, Courts, prosecution and public defender agencies and their subsystems. This is not to suggest that any one CJS sector utilizes their data systems better than another in any systematic nature. Given the diversity of CJOs, we would predict that the utilization of RMS is quite variable, though likely to cluster by the type and size of agencies involved.

As well, it is likely that one RMS serves the Executive and Decision Support Systems purposes in most CJOs. That is, the information captured at the Transaction Processing Systems level is input into the overall RMS, and executive and decision support data are drawn primarily from that management information system, or MIS. In the case of Compstat, New York police used real-time crime data and crime-mapping technology as a management tool for commanders to make pro-active decisions on the effectiveness of tactics, deployment of personnel and resources, and organizational learning (O'Connell & Straub, 2007). As Dunworth (2000) pointed out, once the core RMS is in place, it can then be used to facilitate a range of outcomes. He concluded:

> These capabilities create significant new potential for police departments: to conduct advanced crime analysis; to ground strategic and tactical decisionmaking *(sic)* on sound information; to deploy resources on a proactive rather than simply a reactive basis; and to execute many other functions that either were impossible to perform under earlier systems or were performed under conditions of extreme uncertainty (Dunworth, 2000, p. 380).

He also noted the problems associated with planning and implementing these RMS. These include the (seemingly) inevitable cost over-runs and slipping delivery dates. Perhaps more importantly, the tendency not to hire and adequately train staff, and the costs associated with properly trained staff. Another of the issues forecast by Dunworth (2000, p. 382) that has become real is the problem of having sensitive information "hacked." Aside from those concerns, however, Dunworth rightly predicted that RMS and the subsystems that rely on them would become indispensable for CJOs. Ioimo (2016) offers a much more detailed discussion of the various standards in place to counteract these problems than we have space for in this text.

Criminal justice organizations (CJOs) are chock-full of management information systems (MIS/RMS), and vendors offering to replace, re-develop, and build new MIS are a constant presence at trade shows (e.g., http://www.informationbuilders.com/solutions/integrated-jsfc). For jails and prisons, the health MIS—medical/health electronic record—is becoming an increasingly valuable tool as mandated health care costs increasingly consume a larger portion of incarceration budgets. Office and communication support systems tend to be separated from the overall MIS and provided by third-party commercial vendors. Ioimo (2016) provides a summary of some issues involved in developing CJ MIS systems, especially when dealing with outside vendors. In sum, MIS represent big business interactions with organizations outside of the CJS, as well as increasingly important elements of management, planning, and decision-making for CJOs.

Many of the issues outlined above are primarily within-organizational issues. When it comes to the issues of **data sharing** across CJOs, things become even more complicated. Dunworth (2000, p. 398) provided a list of impediments of adopting integrated justice information systems:

- Persistence of entrenched information processing systems and data at local agencies.
- Difficulty of coordinating interagency projects.
- Limited understanding of technological issues and capabilities.
- Need for systems to be private and secure.
- Fundamental interagency differences in recording/reporting systems.
- Shortage of information technology professionals.

In the end, Dunworth notes that while there are major headaches, **integrated justice information systems** are well worth the resources expended to develop them. Ioimo (2016, pp. 31–41) provides a more technical overview of national and regional developments in CJ information sharing since the early 2000s.

Dunworth (2006, p. 9) provides an abbreviated outline of one major use of such information systems in the area of crime analysis. These may appear familiar to the reader as the basic steps in applied science problem solving common to criminal justice and public health (Potter & Krider, 2000):

- **Data collection**—such as arrest reports, calls for service, etc. As noted, much of this data collection is now computer-assisted, with direct entry into a system. This means that errors are ideally reduced by not having to translate from paper forms to electronic files;

- **Data collation**—information collected is saved into data base programs that allow a variety of analyses. Dunworth notes that such data still require "completeness, reliability, and timeliness" in order to be of value to the agency;

- **Analysis**—quality data allow a range of analytic techniques to be employed. For readers who have completed a data analysis course, those techniques you learned can be applied to these data using a variety of analytic software packages. It is likely most agencies will have Excel or a similar package for analysis purposes. As one moves up the analytic software sophistication, mapping and other predictive analytic techniques can be found in some agencies. The quality of the analyses depends on the quality of the data collection and collation—"garbage in, garbage out," as the old saying goes.

- **Dissemination**—as Dunworth notes, information is prepared for internal and external audiences. It is difficult for some academics to understand that many data analyses are never meant for public dissemination. For people in agencies, there are topics and questions that are required for internal planning, but are not to be shared with those outside the organization. It is always a good idea to know the lines between such data and their dissemination.

- **Feedback**—Dunworth (2005) restricts his presentation to feedback from the agency. In this case, information satisfaction surveys to determine how internal actors utilize the data provided and how helpful they find it. We will return to this topic below to expand it.

While Dunworth (2006, pp. 15–20) does address other components of the CJS, his primary analyses are among the policing sector. Ioimo (2016), as noted earlier, provides a more systemic overview of CJS MIS technologies and standards.

At this point it may be instructive to look at what the data available at a national level tell us about how at least one component of the CJS uses computers. Table 14.1 data taken from a nationally-representative sample of state and local law enforcement agencies, the Law Enforcement Management and Administrative Services (LEMAS) survey, regarding the utilization of

TABLE 14.1: FUNCTIONS OF COMPUTERS IN LOCAL POLICE AND SHERIFFS' OFFICES—2007 (PERCENTAGES)

Computer Functions	Local Police Departments		Sheriffs' Offices	
	2000	2007	2000	2007
Records Management	60%	79%	63%	81%
Crime Investigation	44%	60%	48%	66%
Personnel Records	40%	53%	46%	58%
Information Sharing	28%	50%	33%	53%
Dispatch	32%	49%	47%	69%
Automated Booking	18%	32%	60%	66%
Fleet Management	16%	27%	22%	36%
Resource Allocation	10%	20%	11%	23%
Crime Analysis	30%	38%	27%	36%
Crime Mapping	15%	27%	13%	29%

Sources: Burch, A. M. (2012). *Sheriffs' Offices, 2007—Statistical Tables* (NCJ 238558). Bureau of Justice Statistics; Hickman, M. J., & Reaves, B. A. (2003). *Sheriffs' Offices 2000* (NCJ 196534). Bureau of Justice Statistics, Law Enforcement Management and Administrative Statistics; Hickman, M. J., & Reaves, B. A. (2003). *Local Police Departments 2000* (NCJ 196002). Bureau of Justice Statistics, Law Enforcement Management and Administrative Statistics; Reaves, B. A. (2010). *Local Police Departments, 2007* (NCJ 231174). Bureau of Justice Statistics, Law Enforcement Management and Administrative Statistics.

computers in law enforcement agencies in 2000 and 2007. These are currently the most up to date results from the LEMAS survey available. Here we present results on 10 categories of use, from dispatch to booking to sharing with other agencies. Of special interest is how much or little change occurred in the use of various technologies by LEOs over a seven-year period.

Over half (or nearly) of all departments utilize computers in records management, crime investigations, personnel records, information sharing, and dispatching. More than half of Sheriffs' Offices also use computers to conduct booking (because jails are mostly operated by Sheriffs' Offices). Less than half of these agencies were using computers to conduct fleet management, resource allocation, crime analysis and crime mapping in 2007. With the exception of fleet management, dispatch and booking, the percentages of police departments and SOs were relatively small.

The changes in the utilization of computers for these functions over the seven year period are quite interesting. In all categories, the employment of computers increased. The smallest increase was observed in the area of "crime analysis" (8% for PDs and 9% for SOs), and the largest in the area of "information sharing" (22% for PDs and 20% for SOs). Again, this probably reflects the developments in information sharing after the events of September 11, 2001. In most areas where the two types of LEOs are alike in function, the percentage changes are relatively similar.

It is enough to note from these data that the utilization of computers in the world of law enforcement agencies, and probably other sectors of the criminal justice system, continues to grow toward them being involved in almost all aspects of the field. Many readers will be familiar with the principles of "Moore's Law," (http://www.mooreslaw.org/; accessed 10/12/15) that the processing power of computers would roughly double every two years. In looking at the data from LEMAS, while not doubling, we can see that computer utilization is moving toward "saturation." Understanding their role in data collection, analysis, and decision-making has become an absolute necessity for leaders at all levels and all sectors of the system.

Using the Data

Dunworth (2000, 2006) describes a fairly standard process of data collection, analysis, and utilization in most organizations. We argue these extend to all of the agencies in the formal criminal justice system, and many/most of those agencies that deal with the CJS. The quality of the data collected and utilized in CJO decision-making is subject to the same issues as in any other field, though the outcomes of faulty data may be more impactful. The old GIGO idea ("garbage in—garbage out") dates back at least to the late 1950s/early 1960s among computer programmers. The crux of the idea is that if you put inaccurate data into your computing system, the analyses based on those data will be wrong. Data quality and accuracy become core issues for organizational decision-making that utilizes recorded data. This is true at the local level all the way to utilization of data by those far removed from the data collection—such as academics.

Returning to personal history, when Potter began his work history (i.e., late 1970s), data forms were completed by hand at the local level. Those forms then were generally shipped to the relevant state agency—for local police it might have occurred at the agency level—where they were input into a state-level database. In the early days, that required people using a "card punch" machine to produce an input card. Those cards were then run though a "card reader" and the data transferred to a data tape that could be run through a mainframe or min-computer and stored for analysis. By the early 1980s such data were input directly to the computer database from a terminal, but still required the interim data entry specialist. As noted earlier, we now do most of this directly from computer-assisted programs that allow us to enter data "in real time" to the database. It would take too much space to discuss how we keep data "clean" now versus the card-punch days. The quality of the data, as noted earlier, remains a key issue for any use in feedback to the agency.

Dunworth raises the utilization of data internally as "feedback." This is at the heart of many "quality improvement" organizational efforts. Every CJO relies on its information systems to describe what it accomplishes to the public. Each agency will utilize its information systems to assess progress against internal and external "benchmarks" and to develop management responses to areas where it is falling short of targets (performance management). Increasingly, we will see the utilization of visual and audio data collected in real time to make personnel training decisions and retention decisions, especially in police and corrections sectors. And, on occasion, academic and other researchers may utilize such information to describe, analyze, and make recommendations about developments in criminal justice practice and theory.

Once you assure the quality of your data, you have to assure the quality of your analyses and analysts to produce information of value to the justice system and citizens. For those who aspire to lead CJOs, developing an understanding of information systems is no longer something to be completely delegated to a specialist. It is now an integral part of organizational leadership.

■ A DAY IN THE LIFE OF A DATUM

Let us consider the life of a datum, one piece of data (which are plural). For our purposes let us take that simple event—an arrest. When a LEO makes the decision to arrest someone (say, as opposed to issue a notice to appear), a whole set of paperwork is set in motion. The agency for which the LEO operates has developed a form for capturing information about the incident, the persons involved, and especially, the person(s) arrested. These forms may have to comply with a state statute, so they may be relatively standard across all LE agencies in that state. Those forms will be (ideally) set up for direct entry into a computerized system that captures the information for the LE agency.

Again, depending upon the state, certain information captured on those forms must be reported to a state-wide law enforcement agency. In Florida this is the Florida Department of Law Enforcement; in Georgia, the Georgia Bureau of Investigation, each state has some equivalent "peak" law enforcement agency. If you are lucky, a state-wide computerized program will select the information needed for the state's purposes. Here you can begin to see the value of standard data definitions, common coding schemes, etc. Again, these do not always exist. From these standard data elements, the state agency can then compile annual reports that allow us to know how many arrests, characteristics of the alleged offender(s), victim(s) and types of crimes we had in a given time period.

Now, in an ideal world, every state-level "peak" law enforcement agency would then make sure that their data systems were synchronized with the "peak" law enforcement agency in the United States—the Federal Bureau of Investigation. Yes, we know that is open for debate, but they do maintain the Uniform Crime Report, so that is why they are important here. Once the state reports to the federal agency, we can then produce an annual report on crime in America, curiously titled *Crime in America*. When you read the disclaimers on the annual report, you will quickly see that not all states follow the FBI's wishes with regards to data (Florida has been among the most egregious about following directions). There is always something wonky about how one little datum can get so screwed up on the way up the chain. Not that we are unique. Even with only about nine reporting entities, the differences in the ways crimes were reported in Australia were just as interesting as the 55 or more reporting sources here in the United States.

But, let us say you are the datum "age of the arrestee." You would be recorded, accurately or not, by the arresting officer, become part of an electronic record of the arrest, get sent on to Tallahassee for recording and reporting by the FDLE. Then, the FDLE would send you on to the FBI for more categorization and reporting. If you were recorded incorrectly at any point along the way, it doesn't matter. The final report is official, real. Our decisions made as the result of faulty data do matter.

Wrap-up

The Office of Justice Programs (OJP) of the United States Department of Justice, especially the Bureau of Justice Statistics (BJS) maintains multiple data systems and data sets around organizational aspects of the criminal and juvenile justice systems. Many of these data systems operate in a manner similar to the Uniform Crime Reports, though they may be collected on a much less frequent basis. This set of information should become a core part of your criminal justice knowledge. Most of these data are going to be at least two years behind the years in which they were collected. It takes that long to clean the data and get them through the various "clearance" processes used to make sure they are the best data available about criminal justice issues. As the note above about our experiences with one local agency suggests, having quality data on which to base data-driven decisions requires a deal of work on the part of those who prepare it for processing.

In sum, for now at least, our purpose is to make sure you have an initial grasp on the best sources of the most recently available data on the criminal justice system, its constituent organizations, and the cases and individuals they process. Working from the street up to state and federal agencies, information flows into data sets that can be accessed for decision-making purposes. Part of our task in this text is to begin to employ those data in understanding how the organizations themselves influence the data available, as well as how the data help to guide the re-structuring of the organizations themselves. Like any good system, feedback is important.

Key Words

Automation boundary
Data analysis
Data collation
Data collection
Data mining
Data sharing
Decision support systems
Dissemination
Executive information systems
Feedback
GIGO
Informatics
Information
Information systems
Integrated justice information systems
Legacy systems
Mainframe computers
Management information systems
Moore's Law
Office support systems
Records management systems
Subsystems
Supersystem
System
Systems analysts
Transaction processing systems

Appendix 14.1

Bureau of Justice Statistics Data Collections on Criminal Justice Organizations

This chapter has provided an overview of a variety of information management systems and technologies commonly encountered in modern organizations, including criminal justice organizations. This appendix focuses on national-level data collections available for use by practitioners and researchers.

The Bureau of Justice Statistics (BJS) operates as the primary data collection, analysis, and repository for information about criminals, victims, criminal justice agencies, and a variety of information about those for the United States. Given the relatively small size of the Bureau, their productivity is amazing. Here we want to provide an overview of the types of data they collect so that readers will have a good idea where to begin searching for data on criminal justice organizations and issues in the United States. Remember, it takes around two years from the end of a data collection period—say, the end of the year—and the time official government reports are issued. That is, data collected at the end of 2016 are not likely to be published before sometime in 2018. This is the same in criminal justice as it is for health and education data collections. Thus, even by the time a new textbook is published, their data are likely three or more years behind the publication date. For that reason, students and faculty should always consult the BJS data collections for the most up to date official data on these topics.

Corrections Organizations

CENSUS OF STATE PAROLE SUPERVISING AGENCIES

(http://www.bjs.gov/content/pub/pdf/cspsa06.pdf)

The 2006 Census of State Parole Supervising Agencies collected data from parole supervising organizations about the organizational structure of the agencies, staffing, supervision levels of offenders, and whether the parole agency had a role in considering prisoners for release, setting the conditions of supervision, and conducting parole revocation hearings. This collection was conducted one time in 2006. The census was sent to 68 respondents, including 50 central state reporters, the California Youth Authority, and the District of Columbia. Sixteen local Minnesota Community Corrections Act agencies were asked to provide information on staffing and supervision not available from the state.

CENSUS OF STATE AND FEDERAL ADULT CORRECTIONAL FACILITIES

(http://www.bjs.gov/content/pub/pdf/csfcf05.pdf)

Conducted approximately every five to seven years, the Census of State and Federal Adult Correctional Facilities provides detailed information on the types of inmates housed, facility age and type, building plans, security level, court orders, programs, facility operations and security conditions, confinement space, and staff characteristics.

INVENTORY OF STATE AND FEDERAL CORRECTIONS INFORMATION SYSTEMS

(http://www.bjs.gov/content/pub/pdf/sfcisq.pdf)

Collected basic information on state and federal offender-based corrections information systems including a description of the capabilities of the information systems for producing data extracts, linking records, and exchanging information electronically. This was a one time collection conducted in 1998. The inventory was conducted by the Urban Institute with sponsorship from BJS, the National Institute of Justice (NIJ), and the Corrections Program Office (CPO), and with assistance from the State-Federal Committee of the Association of State Corrections Administrators (ASCA).

Court-affiliated Organizations

THE CENSUS OF PUBLIC DEFENDER OFFICES

(http://www.bjs.gov/index.cfm?ty=dcdetail&iid=401)

The Census of Public Defender Offices (CPDO) involves the collection of data from all state- and county-funded public defender offices across the country, including offices that are publicly funded but privately operated and offices that handle capital cases only. These public defender offices handle the largest proportion of indigent defense cases of the three major indigent defense delivery systems: public defender offices, assigned counsel systems, and contract attorney systems. A variety of data elements are collected in this census, including office expenditures, number and types of cases handled, staffing, funding sources, use of technology, training opportunities, and the adherence to standards and guidelines by the offices. The CPDO serves as an important source of information on the overall conditions of public defender offices and the changes that have occurred in these offices since the late 1990s. It allows for comparison of offices situated within different funding and administrative structures.

NATIONAL CENSUS OF STATE COURT PROSECUTORS

(http://www.bjs.gov/index.cfm?ty=dcdetail&iid=265)

The data obtained from the National Census of State Court Prosecutors (NCSP) provide a complete picture of prosecutorial activities nationwide as well as a variety of administrative and legal issues facing prosecutors who handle felony cases in state courts. The 2007 NCSP data collection was a census, rather than a survey, and included 2,330 prosecutors' offices. Prior to the 2007 census, the most recent census of state prosecutors had been conducted in 2001. Probability samples of state prosecutors were surveyed in 1990, 1992, 1994, 1996, and 2005.

CENSUS OF STATE COURT ORGANIZATION

(http://www.bjs.gov/index.cfm?ty=dcdetail&iid=284)

This collection serves as the primary source for detailed information on the structure and framework of state courts. The series collects information on the overall number of courts and judges in the nation's state courts; the selection and service requirements of judges; the governance, funding and administration of the judicial branch; the jurisdiction, staffing, and procedures associated with the nation's appellate courts; the administration, procedures, and specialized jurisdiction of state trial courts; the composition and workings of state juries; the sentencing context; and the overall structure of appellate and trial courts in each state. These data were last collected by the National Center for State Courts (NCSC) in 2011.

NATIONAL SURVEY OF INDIGENT DEFENSE SYSTEMS

(http://www.bjs.gov/index.cfm?ty=dcdetail&iid=285)

Conducted during 1999–2000, this survey represented the first systematic study of indigent criminal defense services by BJS since the 1980s. The study collected indigent criminal defense data at the trial level for 1) the 100 most populous counties in the United States, 2) 197 counties outside of the 100 most populous counties, and 3) states that entirely funded criminal indigent defense services. Information obtained includes the number of program staff, program expenditures, and types of cases received by indigent criminal defense programs.

Law Enforcement

CENSUS OF LAW ENFORCEMENT TRAINING ACADEMIES

(http://www.bjs.gov/index.cfm?ty=dcdetail&iid=280)

Collects data on the number and types of staff employed at training facilities, budgets, sources of funds, number of officers trained, and policies and practices. In addition to basic organizational data, the survey collects information on training curriculum issues critical to current law enforcement policy development.

CENSUS OF MEDICAL EXAMINER AND CORONER OFFICES

(http://www.bjs.gov/index.cfm?ty=dcdetail&iid=281)

Provides data on the personnel, budgets, and workload of medical examiner and coroner offices by type of office and size of jurisdiction. The census gathers information on the number of unidentified human decedents handled by these offices, record-keeping practices, and use of national databases for unidentified remains.

CENSUS OF PUBLICLY FUNDED FORENSIC CRIME LABORATORIES

(http://www.bjs.gov/index.cfm?ty=dcdetail&iid=244)

Provides a comprehensive look at the forensic services provided by federal, state, and local crime labs across the nation and the resources devoted to completing the work. The Census of Publicly Funded Forensic Crime Laboratories collects data on staff, budgets, and workloads within publicly operated labs. The census also provides information on lab accreditations, proficiency tests, and other quality assurances.

CENSUS OF STATE AND LOCAL LAW ENFORCEMENT AGENCIES

(http://www.bjs.gov/index.cfm?ty=dcdetail&iid=249)

Provides data on all state and local law enforcement agencies operating nationwide. Data collected include the number of sworn and civilian personnel by state and type of agency, and functions performed by each agency.

LAW ENFORCEMENT MANAGEMENT AND ADMINISTRATION STATISTICS—LEMAS

(http://www.bjs.gov/index.cfm?ty=dcdetail&iid=248)

Conducted periodically since 1987, LEMAS collects data from over 3,000 general purpose state and local law enforcement agencies, including all those that employ 100 or more sworn officers and a nationally representative sample of smaller agencies. Data obtained include agency responsibilities, operating expenditures, job functions of sworn and civilian employees, officer salaries and special pay, demographic characteristics of officers, weapons and armor policies, education and training requirements, computers and information systems, vehicles, special units, and community policing activities.

NATIONAL SURVEY OF DNA CRIME LABORATORIES

(http://www.bjs.gov/index.cfm?ty=dcdetail&iid=279)

Provides national data on publicly operated forensic crime laboratories that perform DNA analyses. Data are collected on personnel, budgets, workloads, equipment, procedures, policies, and data processing. BJS first surveyed forensic crime laboratories in 1998, focusing solely on agencies that performed DNA analysis. The National Institute of Justice (NIJ) funded the 1998 study as part of a DNA Laboratory Improvement Program.

SURVEY OF CAMPUS LAW ENFORCEMENT AGENCIES

(http://www.bjs.gov/index.cfm?ty=dcdetail&iid=247)

Provides data describing campus law enforcement agencies serving U.S. 4-year universities or colleges with 2,500 or more students. Also surveyed were 2-year institutions with 2,500 or more students and a sample of 4-year institutions with 1,000 to 2,499 students. Data were collected on personnel, functions, expenditures and pay, operations, equipment, computers and information systems, community policing activities, specialized units, and emergency preparedness activities.

General Organizational Information

JUSTICE EXPENDITURE AND EMPLOYMENT DATA

(http://www.bjs.gov/index.cfm?ty=tp&tid=5#data_collections)

Every year since 1980, BJS has extracted justice expenditure and employment data from the Census Bureau's Annual Government Finance Survey and Annual Survey of Public Employment. BJS publishes these data in the Justice Expenditure and Employment Extracts series, which presents estimates of government expenditures and employment for the following justice categories: police protection, all legal and judicial functions (including prosecution, courts, and public defense), and corrections. This series includes national, federal, and state-level estimates, as well as data for large local governments (counties with populations of 500,000 or more and cities with populations of 300,000 or more). The unit of analysis in the Justice Expenditure and Employment Extracts series is the government. For example, the corrections employment reported for a particular state represents the total of all correctional personnel employed by that state, regardless of which prison, probation office, or other corrections agency employs them. BJS also periodically collects more detailed justice expenditure data through the Justice Assistance Data Survey. These data are used to help calculate formula grants.

CRIMINAL JUSTICE DATA IMPROVEMENT PROGRAM

(http://www.bjs.gov/index.cfm?ty=tp&tid=4#data_collections)

The Criminal Justice Data Improvement Program works to fulfill BJS's mission of improving the criminal record-keeping of States and local governments while improving the ability of States and localities to produce statistics on crime and the administration of justice.

This list does not include data collections that focus on characteristics of criminals. These would include data on characteristics of jail inmates and prisoners, for example. It also does not include the information on data from the National Crime Victims Survey. Such information can be located at http://www.bjs.gov/index.cfm?ty=dca (accessed September 26, 2016).

No excuses for using old data now!

CHAPTER 15

Returning to the Key Questions about Criminal Justice Organizations

Learning Objectives:

1. Discuss why criminal justice organizations are different from or the same as other types of organizations;
2. Identify and discuss at least two issues unique to criminal justice organizational decision-making;
3. Discuss the conflicts and constraints related to the ability to change;
4. Discuss whether the expansion of interorganizational relationships between criminal justice organizations and other types of organizations widens the net of formal social control; and,
5. Explain how organizations contribute to the "social reality" of individuals and why this matters to leaders in CJOs.

Strange Days, Indeed (Thanks to John Lennon)

We are living in interesting times for the organizations that comprise the criminal justice system (CJS), those who act on behalf of those organizations, and the organizations with which the CJS must interact. Perhaps it is the end of a self-described "progressive" administration in the Executive Branch, but the past year or so (as we write this in early 2017) has had several "watershed" moments. Early in 2016 were the changes in how the federal Executive branch (White House and the Sentencing Commission) handles those convicted of drug crimes without accompanying violent convictions. As noted earlier in the text, the Federal Bureau of Prisons (Executive branch) announced their intention to cease using private corrections providers, with other Executive branch agencies in Homeland Security stating they will review similar procedures. And, in October 2016, the International Association of Chiefs of Police (IACP) apologized for having played oppressive roles toward certain communities in the past.

As we put the final touches on the text, it is nearly time to inaugurate a new President, who does not describe himself as a "progressive." Already we are reading of plans to not only re-think the idea of cutting ties with private corrections providers, but perhaps even expanding the utilization of such contractors in the federal government. As you might have noticed in an earlier chapter, one of the major players in the for-profit corrections arena, Corrections Corporation of America, has "re-branded" itself as CoreCivic. It now offers "solutions" to a broader range of government entities than just corrections. A series of shootings by police officers and shootings of police officers (including one graduate of the department in which we teach), has changed the discussion that began with the Black Lives Matter movement.

The great American philosopher (and not a bad baseball player!), Yogi Berra, is credited with saying: "Prediction is hard; especially when it is about the future." The 2016 election cycle has certainly made this relevant to the world of criminal justice. In this last section we want to revisit some of the major themes of the text and make a few predictions about the future for criminal justice organizations. This will be oriented toward the practicalities we think will be faced by the future leaders of criminal justice organizations. We will also try to locate these in terms of criminal justice theory.

Same or Different?

In this text we have wrestled with a central question of whether criminal justice organizations (CJOs) are the same as or different from other types of organizations. Now that you have read this far, the answer is clearly—yes. Criminal justice organizations are the same as other types of organizations in many cases; yet, as outlined in the first section of the text, they are clearly unique among organizations in the social environment.

Potter's (2007) "Hughistic" that "all jails are alike and no two are the same" can be generalized within CJ sectors and across the criminal justice system (CJS). That means that within each sector of the CJS, all of the agencies/organizations involved have similar elements of their missions. However, given differences in size, location, environmental demands, resources—all of the issues discussed in the first few chapters of this text—it is unlikely any two randomly selected organizations will be exactly the same.

Further, because most formal organizations share certain characteristics, we can treat CJOs much like other types of organizations for planning and operational purposes. For example, we can apply most of the planning tools employed by other organizations to CJOs. It continues to surprise the authors that so many in both the "real" and academic worlds seem to think that CJOs do not need to implement the same levels of continuous staff development as private industry does when new programs and approaches—especially evidence-based practices—are implemented. The only other environment where we have encountered this sort of "one and done," and "make it happen" attitude without proper implementation training is higher education. Too often we see CJS leadership imitate what they see in the private sector ("isomorphism"), but without the levels of investment made by those private sector organizations in the people (or technology) to carry them out effectively.

On other dimensions we believe that CJOs are fundamentally different from other types of organizations. While we have only touched on it in this text, the monopoly on the authorized use of force (some say violence) on behalf of the State makes the CJS and CJOs unique, even among other government sectors. The role of force is as important a topic to the applied world of criminal justice as it is to academics. Use of force is perhaps even more important to the applied world at the moment than issues of corruption, at least in the popular media. How this concern over the use of force is impacting CJOs and the street-level workers in policing and corrections will continue to be a hot topic for seminars and articles for the foreseeable future.

Liability and responsibility are tied up in these discussions of use of force, of course. These are issues that again exist at the organizational and individual levels, as well as the institutional level. While probably not expressly written in any statute, "the public" assumes that the public safety function of the CJS means that the CJOs are "responsible" for the outcomes associated with those under its supervision. Here again we see a difference between non-CJOs that have defined outcomes and products. It is difficult to state exactly what "justice" is. How long should "rehabilitation" last—the standard one-year post- jail or three-year post-prison evaluation period, or forever after? Whose definition of "successful" is to dominate? Like those private organizations that produce defined products, we see an emerging "product liability" legal doctrine developing with regard to CJS decisions. Once such doctrines become more stable, it will be interesting to note how CJOs adjust to them.

Because we work in the areas of "**vulnerable populations**," such as mentally ill, substance users, co-morbid/occurring, and re-entry, we have the opportunity to take part in discussions of the role of CJOs in dealing with these complex social problems. In the end, although there is a great deal of dissatisfaction from non-CJOs about how CJOs do certain things, most agree that only the CJOs have the authority, personnel, and facilities to deal with these groups at sensitive moments. Returning to our chapter on interorganizational relations (IORs), this passing of responsibility to CJOs occurs for a variety of reasons. Not all of these reasons are due to the nature of the problem, simply the current structure of resources and authority.

We tend to think of the criminal justice system (CJS) as something relatively stable during our life time. We hope that some of what we have reviewed in earlier chapters makes you aware that these are organizations are:

a. subject to many of the same societal forces as any other organizational type;

b. subject to unique societal forces not experienced by other organizational types; and,

c. immune from some societal forces with which other organizational types must deal.

In short, CJ organizations are the same as and unique from other organizational forms. They are often very complex organizations themselves. Once you add in all of the different groups we described in earlier chapters, they become even more complex in their internal and interorganizational relationships. These are some of the reasons we enjoy studying and teaching about them. We hope we have passed some of that interest on to you.

Decision-Making

The "vulnerable populations" allow us to return to the decision-making theme of the text. Sitting in a "staffing" for a drug or veteran's treatment court (VTC), one can see the range of professionals involved in the provision of care and accountability for the clients involved in the court. What is revealed is the lack of information that can be contained in one centralized information system to assist the Court in decision-making. Focusing on a VTC, for example, one might observe the Court Administrator bringing in one laptop with court data, the probation officer with another laptop with criminal information data, the Veterans Administration (VA) justice specialist with access to the VA data (including health), the community-based social/behavioral health provider with their laptop for their data; you get the picture. All of this information must be collated in one meeting verbally because it cannot be loaded into one system. This is partly because of a variety of federal data protection programs. It is also because many organizations are wary about sharing their data and systems with other organizations. Yet, for the Judge to make a representative decision on behalf of the Court, all of that data must come together to inform the decision. In our experience to date that decision is generally a consensus decision, not an individual decision.

Within the formal CJS, we observed the outcome of failure to share information for decision-making in the September 11, 2001 attacks. Preliminary work by students has demonstrated that re-structuring of the federal domestic intelligence information sharing process has not necessarily resulted in a seamless transition at all levels. Fusion centers were created to facilitate the sharing and analysis of CJS and other data at multiple levels. Yet, as Nate VanNess has demonstrated in his doctoral prospectus, the extent to which law enforcement organizations provide information to, or utilize information from, fusion centers is not well-established.

While our chapter on informatics touches on these inter- and intra-organizational issues in the area of decision-making for CJOs, we recommend readers consult some of the texts we have referenced for fuller information. Far too often we hear from CJO representatives who tell us their information systems are useless. When we ask them what planning process they utilized to select the vendor, the answers are disturbing. Apart from the "legacy system" extension answer ("well, it's the upgraded version of what we've been using for years—and still isn't any better"), we hear stories that come dangerously close to ethical violations.

Standards developed by government and voluntary professional associations can go only so far in avoiding "snake oil" sales and outright corruption in the information systems procurement process for CJOs. It will take a generation of leaders who have a clear understanding of how informatics fit into their organizational decision-making procedures and some familiarity with hardware and software products to guide the increasing reliance of CJOs on such products. These leaders will need to be aware also of the range of legal and ethical issues associated with the increasing use of information about private individuals and other organizations in CJO decision-making. In short, CJO leaders will need to be as aware of informatics as any other aspect of their organizational operations, perhaps even more than some other areas.

Bringing standards back in reminds us that the accountability movement requires that leaders in the CJS need to understand the basics of performance measurement and management, especially in terms of developing indicators of performance (McDavid, Huse & Hawthorn, 2013). Whether the indicator measures for complying with standards are developed externally or left up to the organization to develop, this is a core skill leaders need to develop. Beyond that, recognizing the components of a program and developing schemes for collecting and utilizing data to evaluate the effectiveness of those programs is an increasingly important knowledge and skill set for leaders. Linking all of those to information systems that can serve multiple needs within a CJO and its accrediting associations or state agencies will become even more important as we develop organizations. We hope that our brief introduction to these ideas and tools in Chapters 13 and 14 assists in moving students toward developing those knowledge and skill sets.

Ability to Change

Another theme of this text has been the ways in which organizations go about changing. Criminal justice organizations (CJOs) do change, even though it may be somewhat slow relative to other types of organizations. To some degree this is a result of the legal environment in which CJOs operate. This was detailed in the first few chapters of the text. This renders CJOs particularly sensitive to the demands of legislators and the Courts. We have tried to introduce readers to the ways in which social movements (our "ressentiment" groups) work to change the laws that govern CJOs or change the Courts interpretations of the Constitution and legislation with regard to criminal justice behavior. Here we would use the history of marijuana law interacting with social justice movements to bring about a wave of change, even in the face of resistance from a variety of groups opposed to change. By the time this text is published, we may well see more states changing their laws based on popular vote and/or legislative action. How this type of change will reverberate through arrest policies, drug court diversion programs, sentencing, and other treatment options will be an empirically interesting question for both practitioners and researchers.

This is core to the development of criminal justice theory. Why does society decide to give the responsibility and attendant liability to certain organizational forms rather than others? Are they simply extensions of the authority conferred on behalf of the State? Under what circumstances might society move to transfer certain authorities to another set of organizations or institution? Returning to vulnerable populations such as the mentally ill, substance dependent, and co-occurring (both mental health and substance dependent) persons, we do see challenges ahead to CJOs in terms of whether they should be handling such persons who have not committed serious crimes (however those are going to be defined).

Frazier, Sung, Gideon and Alfaro (2015), using the term "**transcarceration**," explore the impact of moving such populations out of prisons into community treatment services, assuming a "hydraulic" system with no leakage to other social institutions. They note the issues of ensuring adequate treatment provision (but not workforce development), outreach to clients and organizations, networking of referral and receiving organizations, and, of course, funding. Missing from their discussion is the impact on organizations that would "lose" these clients.

If organizational survival is as, or more, important than the function the organization provides, then there may be a tendency for the organization perceiving the threat of loss to resist the change, as suggested in the idea of **goal displacement** (Scott, 2008). More popularly, this is captured in the notions of "**mission creep**" and loss. Organizations, including CJOs, are not necessarily passive actors when such institutional level changes are discussed. Again, we have tried to outline some of the roles played by a variety of organizations in the environment in changing and protecting the status quo of CJOs in the social control environment. We believe this will be especially true as we move into an era where higher knowledge and skills are required to accomplish the social goals of CJOs relative to other organizations in the environment.

Ultimately, one of the major constraints on any governmental organization (most organizations, really) is the control of their budgets by the political entity that sets the budget. At the local police agency level, that might be the town or city council; for Sheriffs (and county-level jails), the County government; for states, the Legislature, and; for federal CJOs, the Congress. The ability to change is often linked to cost. As we have noted in the feature on "sweetheart lawsuits," costs can be measured in more ways than direct budgets. While few CJOs might think in terms of "opportunity costs" lost, most will recognize not making changes can incur costs, whether the result of a consent decree or other external action. The idea of these sorts of costs are also present in the Chapter 5 on interorganizational relations (IORs). Calculating the cost of change, or the lack of change, is something every CJO must do.

"It takes a long time to turn an aircraft carrier" has been a favorite response amongst (especially) government organizational leaders when they try to explain why their organizations are so slow to change. There are so many articles in the academic and applied literature that take the "change is hard!" approach to CJO change that it almost seems hopeless to hope for change. We would argue that the majority of these articles are focused on the "natural" or within-organization levels of analysis, usually expressed in terms of "organizational culture." We would also note that few cover more than one segment of the CJS at a time, and likely use a non-representative sample of CJOs within that sector.

In the end, we hope we have demonstrated how changes in other sectors of the CJS can affect other sectors; for example, think how policing activities regarding substance use might affect corrections and specialty courts. Likewise, actions brought by organizations outside of the CJS, such as lawsuits and social movements, can also bring about change in CJOs. All of these pressures can change a CJO just as quickly as a tsunami might turn an aircraft carrier. While there are special constraints on how quickly some aspects of CJOs can change, there are other facilitators of change that are rarely discussed because we tend to focus on the attempts at change within specific organizations. Perhaps it is the benefit of two writers with a collective 60 years of experience with the CJS and multiple levels of that experience that we can see how much change has occurred in CJOs over the years. Things are definitely different than when we started in the field. We hope one outcome of reading this text is that CJ leaders will begin to think more organizationally about how to affect change in not only one's own organization, but all of the CJOs within and across sectors.

Tangled Webs or Effective Networks?

We have not utilized a great deal of metaphorical analysis (see Morgan, 2006) in this text, but we think webs and networks are appropriate as we wrap things up. We hope that the reader has seen just how many different organizational relationships CJOs have in the larger social environment. What we hope to help the reader avoid is that experience of walking into a spider's web; having the initial shock of the stickiness, trying to wipe the web off one's face, hands, and clothing, and feeling overwhelmed. We would argue that without an organizational sense, that is how many new leaders feel when they realize just how many different organizations they must deal with. Trying to disentangle the strands of the web once they have been merged is not an easy task.

This is where we hope switching to a network image makes the process make better sense. Networks exist within and external to all CJOs. Being able to map them will assist leaders to determine what role each network segment plays in the construction and maintenance of an effective CJO. We have referenced the seminal work of Goldsmith & Egger (2004) throughout the text. But, network analysis and its application to the world of criminals has been with us since at least the early 1990s. We would say that its roots are to be found in the works of the first wave of Chicago School sociology and criminology, early in the 1900s.

We want to summarize the importance of networks in the world of CJOs by asking whether the use of contracting-out for services by agencies of official social control represents a further example of "widening the net" of criminal justice oversight (AKA, "**net-widening**")? Or, as some of our colleagues in those organizations that fulfill the contracts from the CJOs have said, are we "bringing others in" who can modify the behaviors of those CJOs? For the past two decades we have had around four million individuals under some form of CJO control in the community through pre-trial, probation or parole supervision. In many cases, these people are being "supervised" or "treated" by a non-CJO organization. Yet, they are subject to further criminal justice processing if they do not comply with the programs in which they are "enrolled." While the ability to invoke further criminal justice processing or penalties does not lie with the non-CJ organizations, it may be the non-CJO agency that makes the decision that will trigger the return to the CJS and/or penalties. We covered a particularly egregious example of how a non-CJO agency could "penalize" clients in our earlier discussion of private probation problems in Georgia. We would argue this is an example of widening the net of criminal justice control.

At the same time, we work with organizations that bring in programs to the CJS that would not likely be there if not for the external organizations. In some instances, this is a clear attempt to keep people out of the CJS who do not belong there. Our experience with **Crisis Intervention Teams (CIT)** provides a good example. In our area, the coalition that provides the "Memphis model" of CIT is led by non-CJO staff. The coalition is comprised of probably more mental health provider organizations than CJOs. The trainings offered focus on separating the behaviors attributed to mental health and referral to proper treatment alternatives than on subduing individuals whose bizarre behavior brings them to the attention of law enforcement. We believe this offers an excellent example of the "intrusion" of non-CJOs into the criminal justice process without necessarily widening the net of official social control.

We offer these examples because we do not believe that there is yet consistent empirical evidence to determine whether the interactions of CJOs and non-CJOs in the community tips more in one direction than the other. Our initial hypothesis would be that such interactions tip more in the direction of net-widening. Perhaps that is something an enterprising young scholar would like to pursue as a research agenda. Given our focus here, we want to sensitize future leaders in the CJS and affiliated organizations to the dilemmas to be faced when merging the punishment, regulatory, and therapeutic functions. There is, of course, a value judgement to be made when thinking about the expansion of official social control into the community through non-CJOs. Like almost everything in the world of CJOs and practice, values do creep back in. We offer no solution, only awareness in this issue.

Creating Reality

As we come to the close of this text, we want to address a topic we have not developed to a great degree in the text. Organizations are primary contributors to the social creation of reality (Berger & Luckmann, 1966). Criminal justice organizations (CJOs) are no less players in the process of creating **social reality** than any other organizational type (Quinney, 1970). They are perhaps even greater players than many other organizational types. CJOs create realities for those who work within them (a natural systems approach), as well as creating reality for those outside of them. In many instances, CJOs compete with the media, especially the formal media, to create a reality about crime and disorder in a given area and/or nation-wide. For example, think about the ways in which crime statistics are used by CJOs, Chambers of Commerce, realtor organizations, and the media in a given community. Just about any criminal justice/criminology methods text is going to devote an early chapter to the "reality" of criminal justice statistics and their misuse. Crime matters; the reality of crime matters.

From a natural systems approach, the within-organization reality created by CJOs can be viewed as an important component of the identity of members of the organization. This is far too complex a process to be lumped into "organizational culture," unless one truly understands the nature of organizational reality. We prefer to think of these in terms of how an organizational reality creates a "**social world**" for members of the focal organization, and perhaps those from organizations outside of the focal organization who interact with the focal organization. Simply put, the organizations with which we interact most frequently and intensely will provide us with a framework for interpreting the reality of the social world we inhabit. We see this in the social world of the employees of CJOs (e.g., "thin blue line," etc.), as well as in the social world of those subject to the control of the CJOs (e.g., "inmate culture").

We have touched briefly on the influence of "institutional theory" in this text. Within institutional theory there are different strands. We have, for example, written about the early institutional theorists such as Parsons, as well as the "new institutionalists" such as Scott, DiMaggio and Powell, and others. We believe some of the other concepts such as "collective identity," "oppositional consciousness," and "culture" fit into these discussions, as well. In wrapping up this text, we hope that the future leaders reading it will pay close attention to how this process of reality development within organizations and among organizations affects how criminal justice gets done. Perhaps we will need to develop that further in the next edition? For now, please appreciate that not everyone shares the same notions of social reality, and that very often the version of social reality they hold is strongly influenced by the organizational affiliations they hold.

Conclusion

This text is our attempt to fill a gap we perceive in the criminal justice educational process. We wanted to, at a minimum, address the following areas:

1. The importance of studying CJOs as organizations, not individuals and within-organizational groups;

2. The importance of interorganizational behavior and relationships within the CJS and among CJOs and the variety of other organizational types with which they interact in the broader social environment; and,

3. The importance of information, information systems, and the utilization of information (data) for quality organizational planning and decision-making in the CJS.

We hope that we have conveyed to you the importance of viewing CJOs and the other organizations they encounter in the social world at the organizational interaction level. We believe this is a level of organizational behavior often overlooked in the world of academic criminal justice and applied education.

Further, we believe that this level of knowledge is a necessity for those who would provide leadership to the CJS. Likewise, for those who will lead other organizations that interact with the CJS, understanding interorganizational relationships is equally important. Humans tend to achieve great things through organization and organizations (verb and noun). Developing a clear understanding of how to harness organizational process and planning will be a valuable knowledge and skill set regardless of which sector you might find yourself in.

Finally, we want to thank those who have stuck with us through this text. It is our hope that you will find the knowledge and skills touched on—and we have to say we could only touch on them—interesting. As you move forward in your development as a leader in the CJS and associated organizations, we believe you will find this to be an excellent resource for starting your more specialized learning process with regards to organizational leadership. If we can get you just excited enough to want to pursue further skills and knowledge about organizations, then we will feel like our effort has been worthwhile. Thank you for your time. We welcome any feedback you would like to provide as we look for ways to improve the text in the future. All the best in your endeavors.

Key Words

Crisis intervention teams (CIT)
Goal displacement
Isomorphism
Mission creep
Monopoly use of force

Net-widening
Social reality
Social world
Transcarceration
Vulnerable populations

References

Akers, R. L. (1998). *Social learning and social structure: A general theory of crime and deviance.* Boston: Northeastern University Press.

Akers, T. A., Potter, R. H., & Hill, C. V. (2013). *Epidemiological criminology: A public health approach to crime and violence.* San Francisco: Jossey-Bass/Wiley.

Albanese, J. (2005). *Organized crime in our times.* Cincinnati: Anderson/Lexis Nexis.

Aldrich, H. E., & Pfeffer, J. (1976). Environments of organizations. *Annual Review of Sociology, 2,* 79–105.

Alexander, E. R. (1995). *How organizations act together: Interorganizational coordination in theory and practice.* Luxembourg: Gordon and Breach Publishers.

Alter, C. (1990). An exploratory study of conflict and coordination in interorganizational service delivery systems. *Academy of Management Journal, 33*(3), 478–502.

Anno, B. (1991). *Prison health care: Guidelines for the management of an adequate delivery system.* Chicago: National Commission on Correctional Health Care.

Argyris, C., & Schon, D. (1978). *Organizational learning: A theory of action approach.* Reading, MA: Addison Wesley.

Bachman, R., & Schutt, R. K. (2015). *Fundamentals of research in criminology and criminal justice* (3rd ed.). Thousand Oaks, CA: Sage Publications.

Backer, T. E. (2005). *Blueprint for building evidence-based community partnerships in corrections.* Encino, CA: Human Interaction Research Institute.

Banks, D., Dutch, N., & Wang, K. (2008). Collaborative efforts to improve system response to families who are experiencing child maltreatment and domestic violence. *Journal of Interpersonal Violence, 23*(7), 876–902.

Bassford, B. (2008). The role of faith-based/government partnerships in prisoner reentry. *SPNA Review, 4*(1), 2–20.

Baum, J. A., & Shipilov, A. V. (2006). 1.2 Ecological approaches to organizations. In S. Clegg, C. Hardy, T. Lawrence, & W. Nord (Eds.), *The Sage handbook of organization studies*, (2nd ed., pp. 55–110). Thousand Oaks, CA: Sage Publishing.

Beatty, J. F., & Samuelson, S. S. (1996). *Business law: For a new century.* Boston: Little, Brown and Company.

Belenko, S. (2006). Assessing released inmates for substance-abuse-related service needs. *Crime & Delinquency, 52*(1), 94–113.

Bennis, W. G., Benne, K. D., & Chin, R. (1976). *The planning of change in America.* Austin, TX: Holt Rinehart & Winston.

Berger, P. (1963). *Invitation to sociology. A humanistic perspective.* New York: Anchor.

Berger, P. L., & Luckmann, T. (1966). *The social construction of reality: A treatise in the Sociology of knowledge.* Garden City, NY: Doubleday & Company.

Berman, M., & Lowery, W. (2015, March 4). The 12 key highlights from the COJ's scathing Ferguson report. *The Washington Post.* Retrieved from https://www.washingtonpost.com/news/post-nation/wp/2015/03/04/the-12-key-highlights-from-the-dojs-scathing-ferguson-report/?utm_term=.cc62df97192e

Blau, P. M. (1965). The comparative study of organizations. *Industrial and Labor Relations Review, 18*(3), 323–338.

Blumer, H. (1971). Social problems as collective behavior. *Social Problems*, 18(3), 298–306.

Bottoms, A., & Tankebe, J. (2013). Beyond procedural justice: A dialogic approach to legitimacy in criminal justice. *Journal of Criminal Law and Criminology, 102*(1), 119–170.

Boulding, K. E. (1956). General systems theory-the skeleton of science. *Management Science, 2*(3), 197–208.

Branham, L. S. (2013). *The law and policy of sentencing and corrections* (9th ed.). St. Paul, MN: West Publishing.

Brewer, T. W., Jefferis, E., Butcher, F., & Wiles, T. D. (2007). A case study of the Northern Ohio Violent Fugitive Task Force. *Criminal Justice Policy Review, 18*(2), 200–220.

Burch, A. M. (2016). *Sheriffs' office personnel, 1993–2013*. Washington, DC: Bureau of Justice Statistics.

Byrne, J. M., Taxman, F. S., & Young, D. W. (2002). *Emerging roles and responsibilities in the reentry partnership initiative: New ways of doing business*. College Park, MD: Bureau of Governmental Research, University of Maryland.

Campbell, J. L. (2005). Where do we stand? Common mechanisms in organizations and social movement research. In G. Davis, D. McAdam, W. Scott & M. Zald (Eds.), *Social movements and organization theory*. New York: Cambridge University Press.

Carroll, G. R. (1984). Organizational ecology. *Annual Review of Sociology, 10*, 71–93.

Chambliss, W. (1978). *On the take: From petty crooks to presidents*. Bloomington & Indianapolis: Indiana University Press.

Chambliss, W. (1989). State organized crime. *Criminology, 27*(2), 183–208.

Chen, H. (1990). *Theory-driven evaluations*. Newbury Park, CA: Sage Publications.

Clardy, A. (1997). *Studying your workforce: Applied research methods and tools for the training and development practitioner*. Thousand Oaks, CA: Sage Publications.

Clemmer, D. (1940). *The prison community*. Boston: Christopher Publishing House.

Cohen, L. E., &. Felson, M. (1979). Social change and crime rate trends: A routine activity approach. *American Sociological Review, 44*, 588–608.

Congress. (n.d.). *Constitution annotated*. Retrieved from https://www.congress.gov/constitution-annotated

Cornish, D. B., & Clarke, R. V. (2002). Analyzing organized crimes. In A. Piquero & S. Tibbetts (Eds.), *Rational choice and criminal behavior: Recent research and future challenges* (pp. 41–62). New York: Routledge.

Council of State Governments, (2007). *Increasing collaboration between corrections and mental health organizations: Orange County case study*. New York: Author.

Crank, J. P. (2003). *Imagining justice*. Cincinnati, OH: Anderson Publishing.

Crank, J. P., & Langworthy, R. H. (1992). An institutional perspective of policing. *The Journal of Criminal Law & Criminology, 83*(2), 338–363.

Crank, J. P., & Langworthy, R. H. (1996). Fragmented centralization and the organization of the police. *Policing and Society, 6*(3), 213–229.

Crawford, A. (1997). *The local governance of crime: Appeals to community and partnerships*. New York: Oxford University Press.

Crosby, P. B. (1979). *Quality is free: The art of making quality certain*. New York: Mentor.

Davis, A. Y. (1998). Masked racism: Reflections on the prison industrial complex. *Color-Lines Magazine*, pp. 11–17.

Delany, P. J., Fletcher, B. W., & Shields, J. J. (2003). Reorganizing care for the substance using offender: The case for collaboration. *Federal Probation, 67,* 64–68.

Department of Justice. (2015, March). *Investigation of the Ferguson Police Department*. Retrieved from https://www.courts.mo.gov/file.jsp?id=95274

Dill, W. R. (1958). Environment as an influence on managerial autonomy. *Administrative Science Quarterly, 2*(4), 409–443.

DiMaggio, P. J., & Powell, W. W. (1983). The iron cage revisited: Institutional isomorphism and collective rationality in organizational fields. *American Sociological Review, 48*(2), 147–160.

DiMaggio, P. J., & Powell, W. W. (1991). The iron cage revisited: Institutional isomorphism and collective rationality in organizational fields. In W. Powell & P. DiMaggio (Eds.). *The new institutionalism in organizational analysis* (pp. 63–82). Chicago: The University of Chicago Press.

Doerner, W. G. (2015). *Florida's criminal justice system* (2nd ed.). Durham, NC: Carolina Academic Press.

Duffee, D., & Allen, E. (2007). Criminal justice, criminology, and criminal justice theory. In D. Duffee & E. Maguire (Eds.), *Criminal justice theory: Explaining the nature and behavior of criminal justice* (pp. 1–22). New York: Routledge.

Dunworth, T. (2000). Criminal justice and the IT revolution. In Horney, J. (Ed.) *Policies, processes, and decisions of the criminal justice system* (pp. 371–426). Washington, DC: National Institute of Justice.

Dunworth, T. (2006). Information technology and the criminal justice system: An historical overview. In A. Pattavina (Ed.), *Information technology and the criminal justice system* (pp. 3–28). Thousand Oaks, CA: Sage Publications, Inc.

Eisenstein, J., & Jacob, H. (1991). *Felony justice: An organizational analysis of criminal courts*. Boston: Little, Brown.

Emerson, R. M. (1976). Social exchange theory. *Annual Review of Sociology, 2*, 335–362.

Ferguson manager is 5th out after DOJ report alleging bias. (2015, March 11). *Chicago Tribune*. Retrieved from http://www.chicagotribune.com/news/nationworld/chi-ferguson-city-manager-out-20150310-story.html

Finckenauer, J. (2005). Problems of definition: What is organized crime? *Trends in Organized Crime, 8*(3), 63–83.

Finklea, K. (2010). *Organized crime in the United States: Trends and issues for Congress*. Washington, DC: Congressional Research Service.

Fletcher, B. W., Lehman, W. E. K., Wexler, H. K., Melnick, G., Taxman, F. S., & Young, D. W. (2009). Measuring collaboration and integration activities in criminal justice and substance abuse treatment agencies. *Drug and Alcohol Dependence, 103*, S54–S64.

Frazier, B. D., Sung, H. E., Gideon, L., & Alfaro, K. (2015). The impact of prison deinstitutionalization on community services. *Health & Justice, 3*, 9.

Frazier, C., Richards, P., & Potter, R. (1983). Juvenile diversion and netwidening: Toward a clarification of assessment strategies. *Human Organization, 42*(2), 115–122.

Gaines, L. K., & Kappeler, V. E. (2011). *Policing in America* (7th ed.). New York: Routledge.

Gau, J. M. (2014). Procedural justice and police legitimacy: A test of measurement and structure. *American Journal of Criminal Justice, 39*(2), 187–205.

Gerth, H. H., & Mills, C. W. (1973 [1946]). *From Max Weber: Essays in sociology*. New York: Oxford University Press.

Gifis, S. (1996). *Law dictionary*. Hauppauge, NY: Barron's Educational Series, Inc.

Goffman, E. (1961). *Asylums: Essays on the social situation of mental patients and other inmates*. Garden City, NY: Anchor Books.

Goldsmith, S., &. Eggers, W. D. (2004). *Governing by network: The new shape of the public sector*. Washington, DC: The Brookings Institution.

Gottfredson, M. R., & Gottfreson, D. M. (1988). *Decision making in criminal justice: Toward the rational exercise of discretion* (2nd ed.). New York: Plenum Press.

Graham, D. A. (2015, March 11). Four firings won't fix Ferguson. *The Atlantic*. Retrieved from https://www.theatlantic.com/national/archive/2015/03/ferguson-firing-quitting-department-of-justice-report-bias-police-chief/387505/

Gray, B. (1989). *Collaborating: Finding common ground for multiparty problems*. San Francisco: Jossey-Bass.

Greene, J. R. (2000). *Community policing in America: Changing the nature, structure, and function of the police* (NCJ 185533). Washington, DC: National Institute of Justice. Retrieved from https://www.ncjrs.gov/criminal_justice2000/vol_3/03g.pdf.

Groch, S. (1994). Oppositional consciousness: Its manifestation and development. The Case of People With Disabilities. *Sociological Inquiry, 64*(4), 369–395.

Guo, C., & Acar, M. (2005). Understanding collaboration among nonprofit organizations: Combining resource dependency, institutional, and network perspectives. *Nonprofit and Voluntary Sector Quarterly, 34*(3), 340.

Gurin, P., Miller, A., & Gurin, G. (1980). Stratum identification and consciousness. *Social Psychology Quarterly, 43*(1), 30–47.

Hagan, F. (2006). "Organized crime" and "organized crime": Indeterminate problems of definition. *Trends in Organized Crime, 9*(4), 127–137.

Hannan, M. T., & Freeman, J. (1977). The population ecology of organizations. *American Journal of Sociology, 82*(5), 929–964.

Harding, R. (2001). Private prisons. In M. Tonry (Ed.), *Crime and justice: A review of research, Volume 28* (pp. 265–346). Chicago: University of Chicago Press.

Harrison, M. I. (2005). *Diagnosing organizations: Methods, models, and processes* (3rd ed.). Thousand Oaks, CA: Sage Publications.

Himmelman, A. T. (1996). On the theory and practice of transformational collaboration: Collaboration as a bridge from social service to social justice. In C. Huxham (Ed.), *Creating collaborative advantage* (pp. 19–43). London: Sage.

Hodge, B. J., Anthony, W. P., & Gales, L. M. (2003). *Organization theory: A strategic approach*. Upper Saddle River, NJ: Prentice-Hall.

Hudzik, J. K., & Cordner, G. W. (1983). *Planning in criminal justice organizations and systems*. New York: Macmillan.

Human, S. E., & Provan, K. G. (2000). Legitimacy building in the evolution of small–firm multilateral networks: A comparative study of success and demise. *Administrative Science Quarterly, 45*(2), 327–365.

Humiston, G. D. S. (2014). *Offender reentry: A mixed model study of interorganizational commitment to partnership.* Unpublished doctoral dissertation, University of Central Florida.

Ioimio, R. (2016). *Introduction to criminal justice information systems.* Boca Raton, FL: CRC Press.

Jannetta, J., & Lachman, P. (2011). *Promoting partnerships between police and community supervision agencies.* Washington, DC: U.S. Department of Justice.

Jary, D., & Jary, J. (1991). *Collins dictionary of sociology.* London: Harper Collins Publishers.

Jucovy, L. (2006). *Just out: Early lessons from the Ready4Work prisoner reentry initiative.* Philadelphia, PA: Public/Private Ventures.

Kamensky, J. (1999). National partnership for reinventing government: A brief history. Retrieved from http://govinfo.library.unt.edu/npr/whoweare/history2.html

Kappeler, V. (2006). *The police and society: Touchstone readings* (3rd). Long Grove, IL: Waveland Press.

Kaufman, R., & Stone, B. (1983). *Planning for organizational success: A practical guide.* New York: John Wiley and Sons.

Kelling, G. L., Pate, T., Dieckman, D., & Brown, C. E. (1974). *The Kansas City preventive patrol experiment: A technical report.* Washington, DC: Police Foundation.

Kling, R. (2000). Learning about information technologies and social change: The contribution of social informatics. *The Information Society, 16*(3), 217–232.

Kling, R. (2007). What is social informatics and why does it matter? *The Information Society, 23*(4), 205–220.

Klofas, J., Stojkovic, S., & Kalinich, D. B. (1990). *Criminal justice organizations: Administration and management.* Pacific Grove, CA: Brooks/Cole Publishing Company.

Knowlton, L. W., & Phillips, C. C. (2013). *The logic model guidebook: Better strategies for great results.* Thousand Oaks, CA: Sage Publishing.

Konrad, E. L. (1996). A multidimensional framework for conceptualizing human services integration initiatives. *New Directions for Evaluation, 69*, 5–19.

Kovener, M., & Stark, E. (2002). *Making collaboration work: The experiences of Denver Victim Services 2000 (NCJ 194177)*. Washington, DC: U.S. Department of Justice.

Lane, J., & Turner, S. (1999). Interagency collaboration in juvenile justice: Learning from experience. *Federal Probation, 63*(2), 33–39.

Langworthy, R. H. (1986). T*he structure of police organizations*. New York: Praeger.

Lauer, R. H., & Handel, W. H. (1977). *Social psychology: The theory and application of symbolic interaction*. Boston: Houghton Mifflin Company.

Lawrence, P. R., & Lorsch, J. W. (1967). Differentiation and integration in complex organizations. *Administrative Science Quarterly, 12*(1), 1–47.

Levine, S., & White, P. E. (1961). Exchange as a conceptual framework for the study of interorganizational relationships. *Administrative Science Quarterly, 5*(4), 583–601.

Lippitt, R., Watson, J., & Westley, B. (1958). *Planned change*. New York. Harcourt, Brace & World.

Lipsky, M. (1979). *Street-level bureaucracy: Dilemmas of the individual in public services*. New York: Russell Sage Foundation.

Maguire, E. R., Shin, Y., Zhao, J., & Hassell, K. D. (2003). Structural change in large police agencies during the 1990s. *Policing: An International Journal of Police Strategies & Management, 26*(2), 251–275.

March, J., & Simon, H. (1958). *Organizations*. New York: Wiley.

March, J., & Simon, H. (1993). *Organizations* (2nd ed.). Cambridge, MA: Blackwell.

McAdam, D., & Scott, W. R. (2005). Organizations and movements. In G. M. Davis, D. McAdam, W. R. Scott, & M. N. Zald (Eds.), *Social movements and organization theory* (pp. 4–40). New York: Cambridge University Press.

McCarthy, Jr., D., & Reynolds, L. (2003). *Local government law* (5th ed.). St. Paul, MN: West Academic.

McCorkle, R., & Crank, J. P. (1996). Meet the new boss: Institutional change and loose coupling in parole and probation. *American Journal of Criminal Justice, 21*(1), 1–25.

McDavid, J. C., Huse, I., & Hawthorn, L. R. L. (2013). *Program evaluation and performance measurement: An introduction to practice* (2nd ed.). Lose Angeles: Sage Publications.

McGarrell, E. F. (2010). Strategic problem solving, Project Safe Neighborhoods, and the new criminal justice. In J. Klofas, N. K. Hipple & E. McGarrell (Eds.), *The new criminal justice: American communities and the changing world of crime control* (pp. 28–38). New York: Routledge.

Mehan, H., & Wood, H. (1975). *The reality of ethnomethodology.* New York: John Wiley & Sons.

Mellow, J., Christensen, G., Warwick, K., & Willison, J. (2011). *Transition from jail to community: Implementation toolkit.* Washington, DC: Urban Institute.

Merton, R. (1967). *Social theory and social structure.* New York: The Free Press.

Meyer, J. W., & Rowan, B. (1977). Institutionalized organizations: Formal structure as myth and ceremony. *American Journal of Sociology, 83*(2), 340–363.

Meyer, J. W., & Scott, W. R. (1983). Centralization and the legitimacy problems of local government. In J. W. Meyer & W. R. Scott (Eds.), *Organizational environments: Ritual and rationality,* (pp. 199–215.). Beverly Hills, CA: Sage.

Mikhailov, A. I., Chernyl, A. I., & Gilyarevskii, R. S. (1966) Informatika—novoe nazvanie teorii naučnoj informacii. *Naučno tehničeskaja informacija, 12*, 35–39.

Miller, W. (1958). Lower class culture as a generating milieu of gang delinquency. *The Journal of Social Issues, 14*(3), 5–19.

Mills, C. (1956). *The power elite.* New York: Oxford University Press.

Mills, C. (1959). *The sociological imagination.* London: Oxford University Press.

Mintzberg, H. (1979). *The structure of organizations.* Upper Saddle River, NJ: Prentice Hall.

Molm, L. D. (1997). *Coercive power in social exchange.* Cambridge, UK: Cambridge University Press.

Moore, K. (1966). Organizing integrity: American science and the creation of public interest organizations, 1955–1975. *American Journal of Sociology, 101*(6), 1592–1627.

Morgan, G. (2006). *Images of organization* (4th ed.). Thousand Oaks, CA: Sage.

Morris, A. (1992). Political consciousness and collective action. In A. Morris & C. Mueller (Eds.), *Frontiers in social movement theory* (pp. 351–373). New Haven, CT: Yale University Press.

Murphy, D., & Lutze, F. (2009). Police-probation partnerships: Professional identity and the sharing of coercive power. *Journal of Criminal Justice, 37*(1), 65–76

O'Connell, P., & Straub, F. (2007). *Performance-based management for police organizations*. Long Grove, IL: Waveland Press.

Office of the Inspector General. (2016). *Review of the Federal Bureau of Prisons' monitoring of contract prisons*. Washington, DC: U. S. Department of Justice. Retrieved August 22, 2016, from https://oig.justice.gov/reports/2016/e1606.pdf

O'Hara, P. (2012). *Why law enforcement organizations fail: Mapping the organizational fault lines in policing*. Durham, NC: Carolina Academic Press.

Oliver, C. (1990). Determinants of interorganizational relationships: Integration and future directions. *Academy of Management Review, 15*(2), 241–265.

Orrick, W. (n.d.). *Best practices guide: Developing a police department policy-procedure manual*. Retrieved March 27, 2017, from http://www.theiacp.org/portals/0/pdfs/bp-policyprocedures.pdf

Osborne, D., & Gaebler, T. (1992). *Reinventing government: How the entrepreneurial spirit is transforming the public sector*. Reading, MA: Addison-Wesley.

Oser, C., Knudsen, H., Staton-Tindall, M., & Leukefeld, C. (2009). The adoption of wraparound services among substance abuse treatment organizations serving criminal offenders: The role of a women-specific program. *Drug and Alcohol Dependence, 103*, S82–S90.

Packer, H. L. (1964). Two models of the criminal process. *University of Pennsylvania Law Review, 113*(1), 1–68.

Parsons, T. (1956a). Suggestions for a Sociological approach to the theory of organizations—I. *Administrative Science Quarterly, 1*(1), 63–85.

Parsons, T. (1956b). Suggestions for a Sociological approach to the theory of organizations—II. *Administrative Science Quarterly, 1*(2), 225–239.

Peak, K. J. (2012). *Justice administration: Police, courts, and corrections management* (7th ed.). Boston: Pearson.

Petersilia, J. (2003). *When prisoners come home: Parole and prisoner reentry.* New York: Oxford University Press.

Pew Charitable Trusts. (2015, June 11). *Federal and state funding of higher education: A changing landscape.* Retrieved from http://www.pewtrusts.org/en/research-and-analysis/issue-briefs/2015/06/federal-and-state-funding-of-higher-education

Pfeffer, J. (1987). A resource dependence perspective on intercorporate relations. In M. S. Mizruchi & M. Schwartz (Eds.), *Intercorporate relations: The structural analysis of business* (pp. 25–55). New York: Cambridge.

Pfeffer, J., & Salancik, G. R. (2003). *The external control of organizations: A resource dependence perspective.* Stanford, CA: Stanford University Press.

Polanyi, K. (1944). *The great transformation: The political and economic origins of our time.* Boston, MA: Beacon Press.

Police Foundation. (1981). *The Newark foot patrol experiment.* Washington, DC: The Police Foundation.

Kelling, G. L., Pate, A., Ferrara, A., Utne, M., & Brown, C. E. (1981). The Newark foot patrol experiment. *Washington, DC: Police Foundation*, 94–96.

Potter, R. H. (2007). Why jails are important to community health. *American Jails Magazine, XXI*(5), 41–43.

Potter, R. H., & Krider, J. E. (2000). Teaching about violence prevention: A bridge between public health and criminal justice educators. *Journal of Criminal Justice Education, 11*(2), 339–351.

Provan, K. G., & Kenis, P. (2007). Modes of network governance: Structure, management, and effectiveness. *Journal of Public Administration Research and Theory, 18*, 229–252.

Provan, K. G., Kenis, P., & Human, S. E. (2008). Legitimacy building in organizational networks. In L. B. Bingham & R. O'Leary (Eds.), *Big ideas in collaborative public management* (pp. 121–137). Armonk, NY: M. E. Sharpe.

Quinney, R. (1970). *The social reality of crime.* New Brunswick, NJ: Transaction Publishers.

Quinney, R. (1977). *Class, state, and crime: On the theory and practice of criminal justice.* New York: David McKay Company, Inc.

Reaves, B. (2015a). *Local police departments, 2013: Equipment and technology.* Washington, DC: Bureau of Justice Statistics.

Reaves, B. (2015b). *Local police departments, 2013: Personnel, policies, and practices*. Washington, DC: Bureau of Justice Statistics.

Redlinger, L. J. (1994). Community policing and changes in the organizational structure. *Journal of Contemporary Criminal Justice, 10* (1), 36–58.

Reuters. (2016, August 21). Private prison operators shrug off U.S. policy shift. Fortune. Retrieved from http://fortune.com/2016/08/21/private-prison-operators-shift/

Roman, C. G., Moore, G. E., Jenkins, S., & Small, K. M. (2002). *Understanding community justice partnerships: Assessing the capacity to partner*. Washington, DC: Urban Institute, Justice Policy Center.

Roman, J., Brooks, L., Lagerson, E., Chalfin, A., & Tereshchenko, B. (2007). *Impact and cost-benefit analysis of the Maryland reentry partnership initiative*. Washington, DC: Urban Institute, Justice Policy Center.

Rosenbaum, D. P. (2002). Evaluating multi-agency anti-crime partnerships: Theory, design, and measurement issues. *Crime Prevention Studies, 14*, 171–225.

Rossman, S. (2003). Building partnerships to strengthen offenders, families, and communities. In J. Travis & M. Waul (Eds.), *Prisoners once removed: The impact of incarceration and reentry on children, families, and communities* (pp. 343–379). Washington, DC: The Urban Institute Press.

Roszak, T. (1969). *The making of a counter culture: Reflections on the technocratic society and its youthful opposition*. Berkeley: University of California Press.

Salamon, L. M. (2002). The new governance and the tools of public action: An introduction. In L. M. Salamon & O. V. Elliott (Eds.), *The tools of government: A guide to the new governance* (pp. 1–47). New York: Oxford University Press.

Sampson, R. J., & Groves, W. B. (1989). Community structure and crime: Testing social-disorganization theory. *American Journal of Sociology*, 94(4), 774–802.

Satzinger, J. W., Jackson, R. B., & Burd, S. D. (2002). *Systems analysis and design in a changing world* (2nd ed.). Boston, MA: Course Technology.

Savage, C. (2016, August 18). U.S. to phase out use of private prisons for federal inmates. *The New York Times*. Retrieved from https://www.nytimes.com/2016/08/19/us/us-to-phase-out-use-of-private-prisons-for-federal-inmates.html?_r=0

Sawyer, S., & Tyworth, M. (2006). Social informatics: Principles, theory, and practice. In J. Berleur, M. Nurminen, & J. Impagliazzo (Eds.), *Social informatics: An information society for all? In remembrance of Rob Kling* (pp. 49–62). Boston: Springer.

Schmidt, M., & Moynihan, C. (2012, December 24). F.B.I. counterterrorism agents monitored Occupy Movement, records show. *New York Times*, p. A18. Retrieved from http://www.nytimes.com/2012/12/25/nyregion/occupy-movement-was-investigated-by-fbi-counterterrorism-agents-records-show.html

Scott, W. R. (1991). Unpacking institutional arguments. In W. W. Powell & P. J. DiMaggio (Eds.), *The new institutionalism in organizational analysis* (pp. 164–182). Chicago: University of Chicago Press.

Scott, W. R. (2008). *Institutions and organizations: Ideas and interests* (3rd ed.). Thousand Oaks, CA: Sage Publications, Inc.

Scott, W. R., &. Davis, G. F. (2007). *Organizations and organizing: Rational, natural, and open system perspectives.* Upper Saddle River, NJ: Pearson- Prentice Hall.

Shade, J. (2010). *Business associations in a nutshell* (3rd ed.). St. Paul, MN: West Academic.

Shaw, C. R., & McKay, H. D. (1942). *Juvenile delinquency and urban areas.* Chicago, IL: University of Chicago Press.

Shoar, D., & Dunagan, M. (2015). The 21st century Florida sheriff. *The Sheriff's Star, 59*(3), 6–8, 17.

Silberman, C. E. (1978). *Criminal violence, criminal justice.* New York: Random House.

Simon, D. (1996). *Elite deviance* (5th ed.). Boston: Allyn and Bacon.

Skogan, W. G. (1990). *Disorder and decline: Crime and the spiral of decay in American neighborhoods.* Berkley, CA: University of California Press.

Smelser, N. (1962). *Theory of collective behavior.* New York: The Free Press.

Solansky, S. T., & Beck, T. E. (2009). Enhancing community safety and security through understanding interagency collaboration in cyber-terrorism exercises. *Administration & Society, 40*(8), 852–875.

Spector, M., & Kitsuse, J. I. (1987). *Constructing social problems.* Hawthorne, NY: Walter de Gruyter.

Stojkovic, S., Kalinich, D., & Klofas, J. (2015). *Criminal justice organizations: Administration and management* (6th ed.). Stamford, CT: Cengage Learning.

Stojkovic, S., Klofas, J., & Kalinich, D., & (2010). *The administration and management of criminal justice organizations: A book of readings*. Long Grove, IL: Waveland Press, Inc.

Suchman, M. C. (1995). Managing legitimacy: Strategic and institutional approaches. *The Academy of Management Review, 20*(3), 571–610.

Sudnow, D. (1965). Normal crimes: Sociological features of the penal code in a public defender office. *Social Problems, 12*(3), 255–276.

Surette, R. (2013). Cause or catalyst: The interaction of real world and media crime models. *American Journal of Criminal Justice, 38*(3), 392–409.

Surette, R. (2015). *Media, crime, and criminal justice: Images, realities and policies*. Belmont, CA: Cengage.

Sutherland, E. (1947). *Principles of Criminology* (4th ed.). Philadelphia: Lippincott.

Sylvia, R., & Sylvia, K. (2012). *Program planning and evaluation for the public manager* (4th ed.). Long Grove, IL: Waveland Press.

Taxman, F. S., & Belenko, S. (2012). *Implementing evidence-based practices in community corrections and addiction treatment*. New York: Springer.

Taylor, S. A. (2011). *The law of tax-exempt organizations in a nutshell*. St. Paul, MN: West Academic.

Terrill, W., Paoline, E., & Gau, J. (2016). Three pillars of police legitimacy: Procedural justice, use of force, and occupational culture. In M. Deflem (Ed.), *The politics of policing: Between force and legitimacy (Sociology of crime, law and ceviance)* (pp. 59–76). Bingley, UK: Emerald Group Publishing, Limited.

Thomas, W. I., & Thomas, D. S. (1928). *The child in America: Behavior problems and programs*. New York: Knopf.

Thompson, J. D. (2008). *Organizations in action: Social science bases of administrative theory*. New Brunswick, NJ: Transaction Publishers.

Townshend, P. (1971). *Won't get fooled again*. Retrieved from http://www.marc-antoine-rey.fr/IMG/pdf/van_halen_-_fooled_again_live.pdf

Travis, J. (2002). Invisible punishment: An instrument of social exclusion. In M. Mauer & M. Chesney-Lind (Eds.), *Invisible punishment: The collateral consequences of mass imprisonment* (pp. 15–36). New York: The New Press.

Tyler, T. (2003). Procedural justice, legitimacy, and the effective rule of law. In M. Tonry (Ed.), *Crime and justice: A review of research, volume 30* (pp. 283–357). Chicago: University of Chicago Press.

U.S. Department of Education (2009). *Partnerships between community colleges and prisons*. Washington, DC: Author.

U.S. Geological Survey. (n.d.). USGS FAQs. Retrieved from https://www2.usgs.gov/faq/categories/9799/2971

Van de Ven, A. H. (1976). On the nature, formation, and maintenance of relations among organizations. *Academy of Management Review, 1*(4), 24–36.

Van de Ven, A. H., & Ferry, D. L. (1980). *Measuring and assessing organizations*. New York: John Wiley & Sons, Inc.

Van de Ven, A. H., & Walker, G. (1984). The dynamics of interorganizational coordination. *Administrative Science Quarterly, 29*(4), 598–621.

Visher, C. A. (2007). Returning home: Emerging findings and policy lessons about prisoner reentry. *Federal Sentencing Reporter, 20*(1), 93–102.

von Lampe, K. (2008). Organized crime in Europe: Conceptions and realities. *Policing: A Journal of Policy and Practice, 2*(1), 7–17.

von Lampe, K. (2011a). Re-conceptualizing transnational organized crime: Offenders as problem solvers. *International Journal of Security and Terrorism, 2*(1), 1–23.

von Lampe, K. (2011b). The application of the framework of situational crime prevention to 'organized crime'. *Criminology & Crimnal Justice, 11*(2), 145–163.

Wakefield, W., & Webb, V. (1979). An application of the interorganizational perspective to community based corrections in an urban area. *Criminal Justice Review, 4*, 41–50.

Walker, S. (1984). "Broken windows" and fractured history: The use and misuse of history in recent police patrol analysis. In V. E. Kappeler (Ed.), *The police and society: Touchstone readings* (3rd ed., pp. 51–65). Long Grove, IL: Waveland Press.

Walker, S. (2011). *Sense and non-sense about crime, drugs, and communities*. Belmont, CA: Wadsworth Cengage.

Wan, T. T. H. (2006). Introduction: Public affairs informatics research. *International Journal of Public Policy, 1*(4), 333–342.

Weber, M. (1954). *Max Weber on law in economy and society* (E. Shils & M. Rheinstein, Trans.). New York: Simon and Schuster. (Original work published 1925).

Weick, K. E. (1976). Educational organizations as loosely coupled systems. *Administrative Science Quarterly, 21*, 1–19.

Weisheit, R. A., Falcone, D. N., & Wells L. E. (2006). *Crime and policing in rural and small–town America* (3rd ed.) Long Grove, IL: Waveland Press.

White, M. (2016). *The end of protest: A new playbook for revolution.* Toronto: Knopf Canada.

Wilkinson, R. A., Bucholtz, G. A., & Siegfried, G. M. (2004). Prison reform through offender reentry: A partnership between courts and corrections. *Pace Law Review, 24*, 609–847.

Williams, I. (2009). Offender health and social care: A review of the evidence on inter agency collaboration. *Health & Social Care in the Community, 17*(6), 573–580

Williamson, O. E. (1981). The economics of organization: The transaction cost approach. *American Journal of Sociology, 87*(3), 548–577.

Williamson, O. E. (1985). *The economic institutions of capitalism.* New York: Free Press.

Wilson, J. Q., & Kelling, G. L. (1982). Broken windows. In V. E. Kappeler (Ed.), *The police and society: Touchstone readings* (3rd ed., pp. 154–167). Long Grove, IL: Waveland Press.

Wirth, L. (1931). Clinical sociology. *American Journal of Sociology, 37*, 49–66.

Wright, K. (2010). Strange bedfellows? Reaffirming rehabilitation and prison privatization. *Journal of Offender Rehabilitation, 49*, 74–90.

Yoon, J., & Nickel, J. (2008). *Reentry partnerships: A guide for states and faith-based and community organizations.* New York: Council of State Governments.

Young, D. W., Taxman, F. S., & Byrne, J. (2002). *Engaging the community in offender reentry.* College Park, MD: University of Maryland, Bureau of Governmental Research.

Websites

A Second Look at Alleviating Jail Crowding: A Systems Perspective
https://www.ncjrs.gov/pdffiles1/bja/182507.pdf

Abt Associates
http://www.abtassociates.com/Practice-Areas/U-S-Health/Criminal-Justice.aspx

American Civil Liberties Union National Prison Project
https://www.aclu.org/issues/prisoners-rights

American Judges Association
http://aja.ncsc.dni.us/

American Legislative Exchange Councils
https://www.alec.org/

American Probation and Parole Association
http://www.appa-net.org/eweb/

ASIS
https://www.asisonline.org/Pages/default.aspx

Association of Prosecuting Attorneys
http://www.apainc.org/

Census of Law Enforcement Training Academies
http://www.bjs.gov/index.cfm?ty=dcdetail&iid=280

Census of Medical Examiner and Coroner Offices
http://www.bjs.gov/index.cfm?ty=dcdetail&iid=281

Census of Public Defender Offices
http://www.bjs.gov/index.cfm?ty=dcdetail&iid=401

Census of Publicly Funded Forensic Crime Laboratories
http://www.bjs.gov/index.cfm?ty=dcdetail&iid=244

Census of State and Federal Adult Correctional Facilities
http://www.bjs.gov/content/pub/pdf/csfcf05.pdf

Census of State and Local Law Enforcement Agencies
http://www.bjs.gov/index.cfm?ty=dcdetail&iid=249

Census of State Court Organization
http://www.bjs.gov/index.cfm?ty=dcdetail&iid=284

Census of State Parole Supervising Agencies
http://www.bjs.gov/content/pub/pdf/cspsa06.pdf

Center for State Governments' Justice Center
https://csgjusticecenter.org/jr

Chicago Crime Lab—University of Chicago
http://crimelab.uchicago.edu/page/about-us

Communal Experiments
http://www.ushistory.org/us/26b.asp;

Council of State Governments,
http://www.csg.org/

Criminal Justice Data Improvement Program
http://www.bjs.gov/index.cfm?ty=tp&tid=4#data_collections

Department of Justice Press Releases:
https://www.justice.gov/sites/default/files/opa/press-releases/attachments/2015/03/04/ferguson_police_department_report.pdf

Drug Policy Alliance
http://www.drugpolicy.org/

Eckholm, E. (2016). Pfizer blocks the use of its drugs in executions.
http://www.nytimes.com/2016/05/14/us/pfizer-execution-drugs-lethal-injection.html?_r=0,

Families Against Mandatory Minimums
http://famm.org/about/

Federal Bureau of Investigation (FBI)
https://www.fbi.gov/investigate/organized-crime

Washington Post on Ferguson, MO
http://www.chicagotribune.com/news/nationworld/chi-ferguson-city-manager-out-20150310-story.html

Florida County Charters
http://www.fl-counties.com/about-floridas-counties/charter-county-information

Florida Department of State Division of Corporations
http://www.sunbiz.org/search.html

Florida Government Information
http://dos.myflorida.com/library-archives/research/florida-information/government/

Florida State University Center for Criminology and Public Policy Research
http://criminology.fsu.edu/center-for-criminology-public-policy-research/

Florida Statutes
http://www.leg.state.fl.us/statutes/

Florida Taxwatch
http://old.floridataxwatch.org/Research/centers/csj.aspx

Foundation Center
http://foundationcenter.org/find-funding/990-finder

Office of the Inspector General. (2016). *Review of the Federal Bureau of Prisons' Monitoring of Contract Prisons.* **United States Department of Justice. Washington: United States Department of Justice**
https://oig.justice.gov/reports/2016/e1606.pdf

Georgia Board of Community Supervision
http://dcs.georgia.gov/adult-misdemeanor-probation-oversight

Grants.gov
www.grants.gov

Health Resources Services Administration on Quality Approaches
http://www.hrsa.aquilentprojects.com/healthit/toolbox/HealthITAdoptiontoolbox/QualityImprovement/whatarediffbtwqinqa.html

Implementation Science
http://implementationscience.biomedcentral.com

Inventory of State and Federal Corrections Information Systems
http://www.bjs.gov/content/pub/pdf/sfcisq.pdf

Justice Expenditure and Employment Data
http://www.bjs.gov/index.cfm?ty=tp&tid=5#data_collections

Law Enforcement Management and Administration Statistics—LEMAS
http://www.bjs.gov/index.cfm?ty=dcdetail&iid=248

Moore's Law,
http://www.mooreslaw.org/

National Association of Counties (NACo)
www.naco.org/resources/programs-and-initiatives/smart-justice

National Association of Public Defenders
http://www.publicdefenders.us/

National Census of State Court Prosecutors
http://www.bjs.gov/index.cfm?ty=dcdetail&iid=265

National Center for Education Statistics
http://nces.ed.gov/programs/coe/indicator_csa.asp

National Center for State Courts
http://www.ncsc.org/, http://aja.ncsc.dni.us/

National Conference of State Legislatures,
http://www.ncsl.org/

National Council on Crime & Delinquency
http://www.nccdglobal.org/about-us/mission-values

National Partnership for Reinventing Government 1999; accessed at:
http://govinfo.library.unt.edu/npr/whoweare/history2.html

National Crime Victims Survey
http://www.bjs.gov/index.cfm?ty=dca

National Survey of DNA Crime Laboratories
http://www.bjs.gov/index.cfm?ty=dcdetail&iid=279

National Survey of Indigent Defense Systems
http://www.bjs.gov/index.cfm?ty=dcdetail&iid=285

Occupy Wall Street
http://occupywallst.org/

Orange County (FL) Government information
http://www.orangecountyfl.net/OpenGovernment/Budgets.aspx#.V9WkNfkrJpg

Partnership for Civil Justice Fund
http://www.justiceonline.org/

Police Executive Research Forum
http://www.policeforum.org/

The President's Commission on Law Enforcement and Administration of Justice
https://www.ncjrs.gov/pdffiles1/Digitization/174NCJRS.pdf

Prison Rape Elimination Act (PREA)
http://www.ncja.org/issues-and-legislation/prea#sthash.FwoiXlPg.dpuf

Pretrial Justice Institute
http://www.pretrial.org/about/

Rand, Inc.
http://www.rand.org/about.html

Reuters. (2016, August 21). *Private Prison Operators Shrug Off U.S. Policy Shift*. Retrieved from Fortune.com:
http://fortune.com/2016/08/21/private-prison-operators-shift/

Right on Crime
http://rightoncrime.com/about/

Savage, C. (2016, August 18). U.S. to Phase Out Use of Private Prisons for Federal Inmates. *New York Times*, p. A11. Retrieved from
http://www.nytimes.com/2016/08/19/us/us-to-phase-out-use-of-private-prisons-for-federal-inmates.html?_r=0

Smart Justice Canada
http://smartjustice.ca/

Southern Center for Human Rights
www.schr.org

Stanford University "Mapping Militant Organizations"
http://web.stanford.edu/group/mappingmilitants/cgi-bin/

Survey of Campus Law Enforcement Agencies
http://www.bjs.gov/index.cfm?ty=dcdetail&iid=247

United Nations Convention against Transnational Organized Crime
https://www.unodc.org/documents/treaties/UNTOC/Publications/TOC%20Convention/TOCebook-e.pdf

United State Congress
https://www.congress.gov/content/conan/pdf/GPO-CONAN-REV-2016-10-6.pdf at https://www.congress.gov/constitution-annotated

United States Department of Justice on Transnational Crime
http://www.justice.gov/criminal/ocgs/org-crime/docs/08-30-11-toc-strategy.pdf

United States Office of Personnel Management
https://www.opm.gov/services-for-agencies/performance-management/organizational-performance-management

United States tax codes (Title 26)
https://www.gpo.gov/fdsys/browse/collectionUScode.action?collectionCode=USCODE

University of Chicago's Center for Studies in Criminal Justice
http://www.uchicago.edu/research/center/center_for_studies_in_criminal_justice/

University of Cincinnati Center for Criminal Justice Research
https://www.uc.edu/ccjr/about.html

University of Wisconsin's Extension Service
http://fyi.uwex.edu/programdevelopment/logic-models/bibliography/

Urban Institute
http://www.urban.org/about

Urban Institute Justice Policy Center
http://www.urban.org/policy-centers/justice-policy-center/sound-strategies-combating-crime-and-promoting-public-safety

Vera Institute of Justice
https://www.vera.org/about

World Socialist Web Site
https://www.wsws.org/en/articles/2015/01/22/ferg-j22.html

Index

501(c)(3) organization, 20–23, 25, 170
Accreditation, 110, 139, 149, 158–166
Accreditation teams, 160
Advocacy research, 180–182, 187
Annual Report, 26, 170, 254
Anomie theory, 136
Appointed officials, 33
Articles of Incorporation, 19, 26
Assumptions, 44, 46, 55, 71–72,
  83–84, 231, 233–235, 237
Asymmetry, 92–97, 100–102
Authority, 1, 4, 11, 13, 15, 17–22,
  25–26, 29, 32, 34–39, 42, 45, 55,
  63, 73, 91, 98, 114–115, 121,
  123, 131–132, 156, 212, 215,
  218, 266, 268
Authority of reputation, 212
Automation boundary, 246

Boards of directors, 19, 170, 184–185
Bounded rationality, 46, 60
Bureaucracy, 45
Business association, 16–17, 19, 24
By-Laws, 19

Capable guardianship, 141, 216, 218
Career service employees, 33
Cause-effect associations, 9–10, 65–66,
  77–78, 82, 104–106, 108–109
Census of State and Local Law
  Enforcement Agencies, 130
Certification, 51, 148–149, 156–157,
  161–164
Change, 55, 61, 70, 73–77, 83, 85,
  87–88, 92, 109, 111, 114–115,
  124, 126, 128, 137, 139, 143,
  147, 156, 158, 163–164, 173–175,
  181, 191–194, 197, 199–200, 205,
  215, 221–223, 226–227, 229–233,
  235–239, 244–245, 251–252, 257,
  263–264, 268–270
Chicago School, 124, 271
Claims-making (groups), 191–192,
  195–197
Closed boundaries, 140
Closed systems, 47, 60, 63, 75
Code of secrecy, 211
Collaboration, 83, 85–86, 89–90, 94,
  99, 101, 124, 163, 229
Collective behavior, 190
Collective identity, 198, 203, 212, 273
Community-based organization, 22,
  84, 115, 136
Compromise strategy, 10, 66, 78, 104
Computational strategy, 9–10, 66,
  104
Conferences, 107, 149, 151–152,
  154
Conflict, 13–15, 44, 95, 104, 108, 124,
  131, 135, 137, 164–165, 192, 194,
  200, 202, 214–215, 229
Congruence of interests, 217
Consensus, 5, 14, 68, 97, 157, 235
Consent decree, 33, 67, 269
Constitution, 1, 10, 21, 26, 31–32, 34,
  36, 55, 77, 96, 125, 268
Constraints, 33–34, 49, 58, 60, 64–69,
  77, 131, 224, 226, 269–270
Contingencies, 33, 58, 60, 63–67, 92,
  99
Continuing Criminal Enterprises, 208
Continuing education, 157
Continuous quality improvement, 238
Contracting-out, 140–141, 143, 271

Control, 4–6, 11, 15, 22, 24, 35–36, 45–47, 50, 58, 62–63, 65–68, 71, 73–75, 77, 82, 95–97, 104, 120–121, 131, 133, 140–141, 144–145, 148, 150, 152, 162, 165–166, 179–180, 185–186, 192–193, 199, 208, 219, 222, 224–226, 246, 269, 271–273
Controlling strategies, 66–68
Conventional, 3, 135–140, 143, 145, 147, 152, 167, 187, 192, 197, 199, 201, 204, 212–214, 216–217, 219
Cooperation, 54, 65–66, 83, 85–86, 88–90, 94, 95, 97, 101, 124, 130, 164, 186, 200
Cooperative strategies, 68–69, 82
Coordination, 69–71, 77, 82, 86–90, 93, 95–96, 99, 101, 121, 160, 223, 249
Corporation, 14–20, 24, 26, 50, 52, 68, 115, 118, 143–145, 170, 182, 184, 268
Corruption, 32, 67, 141–143, 200, 208–209, 211–212, 216–218, 265, 267
Counter-culture, 200
Crime prevention, 100, 117, 166, 172, 218
Criminal enterprise, 3, 205, 208
Criminal justice organizations, 4, 8, 13–15, 22, 32, 34–37, 43, 45, 52, 58, 76, 78, 103, 108, 110, 131, 135, 138–139, 145, 147, 180, 185, 187, 203, 205, 208–209, 215, 217–218, 222, 242–245, 248–249, 256, 264, 268, 272
Criminal organizations, 1, 5, 14, 118, 122, 124, 136, 199–200, 203, 207–219
Criminal sophistication, 212
Crisis intervention teams (CIT), 271
Culture, 5, 53–54, 63, 91, 200–202, 214–215, 236, 270, 272–273

Data analysis, 186, 244, 250
Data collation, 250
Data collection, 44, 76, 178, 186, 205, 231, 244, 249–250, 252–253, 256
Data mining, 244–245
Data sharing, 249
Decision points, 1, 3, 6, 44, 115, 118, 226, 236
Decision support systems, 247–248
Decision-making, 1–3, 6, 9–11, 46, 55, 59, 66, 70, 74–75, 77–78, 86, 90, 92, 95, 100–101, 104, 115–116, 121, 141, 180, 223, 228, 241–242, 245, 249, 252, 255, 263, 266–267, 273
Defining problems, 225, 238
Departmentalization, 46, 71
Differential Association, 124, 214
Dissemination, 171, 184–185, 250
Domain, 37, 49, 60, 66, 70–71, 97–98, 129, 142, 156, 160, 164, 184
Domain similarity, 97
Due process, 6, 30–32, 66, 160
Dues, 148–151, 154, 185

Economic rationality, 60, 105–108
Educational organization, 22–23
Efficiency, 45–46, 60, 74, 78, 92–94, 96, 99, 100–102, 108–109, 142–143
Efficiency tests, 108–109
Elected officials, 33, 45, 176
Eminent domain, 30
Employee unions, 33
Environment, 3, 5, 8, 10–11, 35, 37, 39, 42, 47–50, 52, 54–55, 58–60, 63–65, 67–70, 73, 75–78, 82, 85, 91–92, 94, 97, 99, 101, 111, 113–114, 116, 122–125, 128, 131–133, 135–139, 142–143, 145, 147, 151–152, 154–156, 161, 163, 167, 169, 187, 190, 192–194, 196, 197–198, 202, 204–205, 218–219, 232, 235–236, 242, 246, 264–265, 268–270, 273
Equal protection, 31–32
Executive information systems, 246

External challenges, 32
External elements, 48–50, 59
External factors, 47, 228, 233–235
External structure, 59, 69, 76–77, 82, 84, 92, 108

Facilitators, 23, 236, 239, 248, 267, 270
Faith-based organization, 20, 25, 115, 117, 229
Feedback, 61, 109, 179, 250, 253, 255, 274
Fifth (5th) Amendment, 30, 32
Flattened organization, 73, 75, 211
Focal/Index agency, 114–116, 123, 125, 127–130, 272
Formal organization, 10, 15, 24, 35, 38, 43, 49, 51–52, 54–55, 115–116, 136, 174, 191, 198–199, 213, 215–216, 264
For-profit corporation, 1, 14–19, 22–25, 49–50, 62, 65, 77, 94, 110, 115, 139–140, 143–144, 170–171, 229, 239, 264
Fourteenth (14th) Amendment, 31–32, 67
Future-orientation, 223, 225

GAP analysis, 227–228
General partnerships, 16–18, 24
GIGO, 252
Goal displacement, 269
Goals, 4, 9–11, 13–15, 25, 44–51, 54–55, 58, 60, 65–66, 70, 77, 82, 85–87, 92, 94, 97, 99, 101, 104, 136–138, 155, 164, 166, 192, 197–201, 213–216, 222–225, 227, 230–231, 269
Governance structure, 87, 95
Governance units, 192–193
Government, 1, 4–6, 8, 14–15, 17, 19–23, 25–27, 29–33, 35–37, 46, 49, 58, 64–65, 67–68, 70, 73, 91, 93–94, 96, 99, 104–106, 113, 115, 117, 122, 125, 128–129, 131–133, 136, 140–142, 144–145, 152, 155, 157, 160, 162, 166, 170–181, 183, 185–186, 192–193, 195–196, 200, 208–209, 212–213, 216–217, 227, 229, 231, 256, 264–265, 267, 269
Government-unique standards, 160
Great transformation, 34

Harm, 212, 217–218
Hierarchy, 13, 26, 42, 45, 52, 71, 73, 75, 78, 208, 211
Human resources, 51, 55, 89, 100

If-then statements, 232, 235, 239
Implementation, 5, 84, 95–96, 98, 145, 156, 172, 195, 236–239, 265
Informal organization, 49, 52–54
Informatics, 11, 51, 241–242, 244–245, 267
Information, 1–3, 6, 8, 22–24, 26–27, 43, 46–48, 50, 53, 58–60, 64, 68–70, 72, 74–75, 77, 82, 86–91, 94–95, 97, 99, 101, 117, 130, 132, 142, 154–155, 170–171, 183–186, 222–223, 242–255, 266–268, 273
Information systems, 2–3, 245–247, 249, 253, 267–268, 273
Innovation, 34, 137–138, 179, 213–214, 246
Inputs, 10, 51, 59, 61, 63–66, 68–70, 77–78, 82, 85, 109, 210, 232–233
Inspirational strategy, 10, 66
Institutional, 9–11, 34–36, 43, 60, 63, 69–70, 77–78, 82, 92, 98, 100, 124, 131–133, 137, 145, 165, 187, 190, 192, 195–196, 265, 269, 273
Institutional actors, 192
Institutional logics, 192–193, 195
Institutional theory, 43, 92, 98, 131, 133, 145, 187, 192, 273
Institutional/Administrative level, 9–11, 63, 69–70, 82, 90, 100, 265, 269
Instrument rationality, 60, 105–108
Instrumental, 60, 62, 102, 105–111, 224–225

Instrumental tests, 109–110
Integrated justice information systems, 249
Intensive technology, 61–62, 70
Interest, 5, 14–15, 30, 46–47, 63, 66, 95, 98, 106, 122–123, 135, 148, 152–153, 155, 160, 163–164, 167, 169–174, 180–181, 183–185, 187, 198, 217–218
Internal challenges, 33
Internal elements, 50, 54
Internal structure, 52, 59, 60, 70, 73, 75–77, 242
Interorganizational relationship (IOR), 9, 11, 14, 17, 26, 59, 77, 81–83, 85–89, 92–101, 103, 108, 116, 133, 152, 266, 269, 274
Intimidation, 211–212, 216
IRS form 990, 26
Isomorphism, 106, 151, 165, 175, 228, 265
Issues, 3, 10–11, 14, 23, 30, 33, 36–37, 85, 90, 98, 102, 106–107, 110, 133, 141, 144, 148, 152, 154–156, 161, 163, 171, 174, 176, 177, 181, 187, 190, 194, 196, 210, 213, 218, 223, 226, 228, 236, 245, 248–249, 252, 255–256, 258–259, 264–265, 267, 269

Job design, 51, 55
Judgmental strategy, 66, 104

Law Enforcement Management and Administration Survey (LEMAS), 129–130, 250–251, 259
Legacy systems, 244, 267
Legitimacy, 10–11, 15, 35–38, 49, 63, 91–93, 96, 98, 100–102, 110, 131, 156, 218
Levels of analysis, 8–10, 41–42, 47, 71, 91, 113, 138, 270
Levels of commitment, 82, 84–86, 88–90, 102, 111
Licensure, 156–157, 160

Limited liability corporation/company, 16–17, 19–20, 24, 26
Limited liability partnerships, 17–18, 24
Limited partnerships, 16–18, 24
Logic model, 109, 231–236, 239
Longevity, 196, 211
Long-linked technology, 61–62, 71

Macro, 41–43, 47, 91
Magazines, 151, 154–155
Mainframe computers, 243, 253
Management information systems, 246, 248–249
Management level, 62–63
Mandatory IOR, 93
Mandatory standards, 159–160, 175
Marxist, 14–15
Meaningful, 222
Means-ends statements, 137, 193, 214
Measurable, 2, 65, 105, 161, 222, 230, 232–233
Mediating technology, 61–62, 71
Membership dues, 151, 185
Membership organizations, 148–150, 162
Meso, 41–43, 91
Micro, 42–43, 46
Military-industrial complex, 183–184
Misdemeanor probation, 117
Mission creep, 269
Mission statements, 62, 122–123, 181–182, 229–230
Mobilizing mechanisms, 193
Modes of adaptation, 136–137, 213–214, 216
Monopoly use of force, 35, 265
Moore's Law, 252
Motivation, 42, 81–82, 91–94, 97, 99–103, 111, 115, 199, 237

Natural systems, 3, 46, 75, 83, 162, 272
Necessity, 11, 92–93, 102
Net-widening, 140, 271–272

Networked governance, 135–136, 140–141, 143, 145, 213
Networking, 86–87, 89–90, 101, 217, 269
Newsletters, 151, 154–155
Non-criminal justice organizations, 21–22, 85
Non–faith-based organization, 20–21
Non-governmental organizations, 1, 5, 14, 20–22, 25–27, 96, 115, 124, 129, 133, 136, 139, 144–145, 162, 175, 180, 183–184, 186, 192, 213, 228
Non-profit organizations, 1, 14–15, 20–26, 49–50, 65, 68, 77, 94, 96, 106, 115, 139–140, 148, 163, 165, 175, 178–179, 214
Normative, 43–46, 55, 75, 131, 155–156, 165, 175–176, 180, 187, 224–225

Objective, 3, 12, 15, 24, 31, 45, 50, 73, 77, 131, 158, 161, 166, 172–173, 203, 208, 210, 223, 225, 227, 229–232, 236–238
Observable, 143, 222, 230
Occupation, 21, 25, 73, 75, 148, 152, 212
Offenders as problem-solvers, 216
Office support systems, 247
Open systems, 44, 47–50, 59, 63, 75–76, 84, 91, 104, 162
Oppositional Consciousness, 198, 204, 273
Organization, 3–4
Organizational accountability, 222
Organizational change, 92, 109, 111, 158, 222–223, 232–233, 235, 238
Organizational demography, 125
Organizational planning, 62, 65, 102, 136, 210, 213, 216, 222–227, 229–231, 233, 239
Organizational problem-solving, 224–225
Organizational set, 48, 127

Organizational structure, 5, 10–11, 43, 52, 58–59, 65, 73, 76, 109, 159, 191, 194, 203, 209, 211–212, 222, 232–233
Organized crime, 27, 207–211, 216–217
Outcome evaluation, 84, 102, 109
Outcomes, 2, 5, 9–10, 46, 50–51, 59–62, 65–66, 70, 77–78, 82–84, 90–91, 99, 102, 103–105, 107–111, 119, 136–137, 156, 159, 175, 182, 190–191, 194, 196–197, 201, 204, 214, 222, 225–228, 230–232, 235, 237–238, 248, 252, 265
Outputs, 50–51, 59, 61–63, 65–66, 68–70, 74, 77, 82, 85, 109, 232–233

Paradigm, 41, 43–44, 46, 91
Partnerships, 16–26, 42, 68, 73, 76–77, 83–86, 88–90, 93, 95–102, 105, 107, 111, 117, 122, 127, 129, 135–136, 150, 166, 179, 181, 208, 213, 228–229, 231
Peer-review, 155, 161, 171, 203
People, 16, 49, 51, 53–54, 60
Permeable boundaries, 140, 149
Planned change, 222–223, 237
Pluralist, 14
Police powers, 30–32, 35, 49, 96, 131
Policy analysis, 41, 226
Political opportunity structures, 194
Positional organizations, 148–149
Power to convene, 152
Prediction, 224–225, 264
Prison Rape Elimination Act, 108, 132, 151, 156, 160, 175, 181
Prison-industrial complex, 183
Privatization, 33, 65, 78, 117, 142–143
Privatizing, 116
Procedural due process, 31
Proceeds of crime, 210
Process evaluation, 102, 109, 111

Processes, 5–6, 19, 33, 37, 42, 45–47, 51, 53–54, 59–62, 64, 70–71, 86, 109–110, 131, 152, 158, 160, 162, 165, 193–194, 197, 214, 237–238, 255
Profession, 148
Professional associations, 1, 21, 145, 147–148, 150–152, 154–159, 162–165, 167, 174–175, 187, 267
Professional education, 156, 158
Professionalization, 148, 155, 157
Program evaluation, 84, 87, 90
Program fidelity, 236
Psychological perspective, 42
Public interest, 30, 63, 148, 167, 169–174, 180–181, 183–185, 187

Quality assurance, 237
Quality improvement, 237–238, 253
Quality management, 238
Quality movement, 158–159, 237

Racketeer Influenced Criminal Organization (RICO), 208
Rational, 36, 43–47, 54–55, 59–60, 62, 75, 78, 91, 94, 99–100, 105–108, 222, 228, 232
Rational systems, 44
Readiness for change, 235–236
Rebellious groups, 137–138, 192, 197, 214–215, 218
Reciprocity, 92–93, 97, 100–102
Records management systems, 248, 251
Regulation, 16–17, 30–31, 65, 70, 93, 131, 182, 195
Regulative, 131, 165, 176, 180, 187
Regulative function, 180
Research institute, 24, 173, 178, 180
Ressentiment, 137–138, 187, 191, 194, 196–198, 200, 205, 214–215
Ressentiment groups, 137, 187, 191, 196, 204, 218, 268
Restrictive membership, 149–150, 162, 211
Routine activities, 216, 218

Self-identification, 212
Slack, 70, 78
SMART objectives, 230, 232
Social Ecology, 124, 128
Social harm, 217
Social Learning, 124, 214
Social media, 153–155, 183, 199, 242, 247
Social networks, 53–54
Social problems theory, 190, 196
Social reality, 166, 272–273
Social tests, 108, 110
Social world, 200, 205, 226, 272–273
Sociological perspective, 41–43, 136, 213
Sole proprietorship, 16–17, 24, 26
Sovereigns, 132–133
Stability, 69, 92–94, 96–97, 100–102, 151, 193, 195
Standard of practice, 142, 222
Standards, 51, 62–63, 105, 119, 132, 154, 156, 158–167, 175, 181, 237, 248, 250, 267
Strategic planning, 9, 66, 70, 78, 82, 226–227, 246
Strategy, 10, 48–50, 58, 65, 67–69, 71–75, 83, 87, 89, 97–99, 106, 135–136, 156, 162, 194, 203–205, 227, 236
Structural strain, 136, 138, 193, 213
Structure, 4–5, 10–11, 14–15, 17, 21, 23, 26, 35, 42–46, 48, 51–53, 55, 58–60, 63, 65, 69–77, 82–87, 90, 92–93, 95–96, 99, 108–109, 114, 125, 130, 135, 137–138, 156, 159, 190–191, 194, 203, 208–212, 214, 222, 228, 232–233, 244, 266
Structured group, 209–210
Substantive due process, 31
Subsystems, 44, 246, 248
Supersystem, 245–246
SWOT analysis, 193, 227–228, 231, 235
Symbolic research, 110

System, 1–3, 6, 8, 10, 15, 36–37, 42–44, 46–50, 53–54, 59–60, 63–64, 75–76, 78, 83–84, 87–88, 91, 96, 104, 114, 122–124, 137, 140, 162, 212, 214, 229
Systems analysts, 245

Tactical planning, 226
Taking (appropriation), 30, 32
Task environment, 49–50, 60, 64, 77
Tax-exempt organizations, 20, 23
Technical level/core, 60–61, 63, 70, 77–78
Technology, 16, 43, 48–51, 54, 59–63, 69–70, 73, 77, 85, 99, 105, 141, 154, 156, 219, 233, 242–245, 247–249, 265
Tenth (10th) Amendment, 30
Theory of change, 231–232, 237
Time perspective, 224
Tools, 69–70, 77, 86
Total institution, 70–71
Total quality management, 238
Transaction processing systems, 246, 248
Transcarceration, 269

Transnational organized crime, 207, 209, 216–217
Troubles, 190
Typologies, 15, 54, 138, 145, 147, 169–170, 180, 185, 187, 217

Uncertainty, 9–10, 46, 59–64, 66, 68, 94, 97, 101, 248
Unit character, 130
University-affiliated research institute, 170, 177, 185
Utopian groups, 199, 201–202

Values statements, 229, 231
Violence, 4, 35, 117, 165, 179, 181, 198, 200–202, 209, 211, 216, 219, 265
Vision statements, 122, 229
Voluntary consensus standards, 159–160
Voluntary IOR, 94, 97–98, 100
Vulnerable populations, 265–266, 268

Widen the net (net-widening), 140, 271–272
Willie Sutton hypothesis, 215
Work, 49–52, 54, 60, 70